The 8th Garfield Treasury

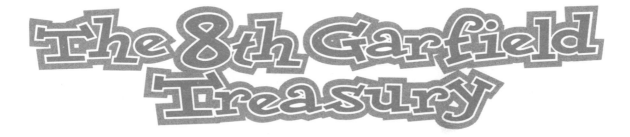

The 8th Garfield Treasury

BY: JIM DAVIS

BALLANTINE BOOKS • NEW YORK

The Sunday strips appearing here in color were previously in black and white in
GARFIELD HITS THE BIG TIME #25, GARFIELD PULLS HIS WEIGHT #26,
GARFIELD DISHES IT OUT #27, and GARFIELD LIFE IN THE FAT LANE #28.

 Published in the United States by Ballantine Books,
a division of Random House, Inc., New York, and simultaneously in
Canada by Random House of Canada Limited, Toronto.

http://www.randomhouse.com

Library of Congress Catalog Card Number: 95-94224

ISBN: 0-345-39778-9

First Edition: November 1995

10 9 8 7 6

The 8th Garfield Treasury

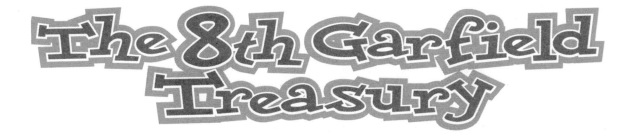

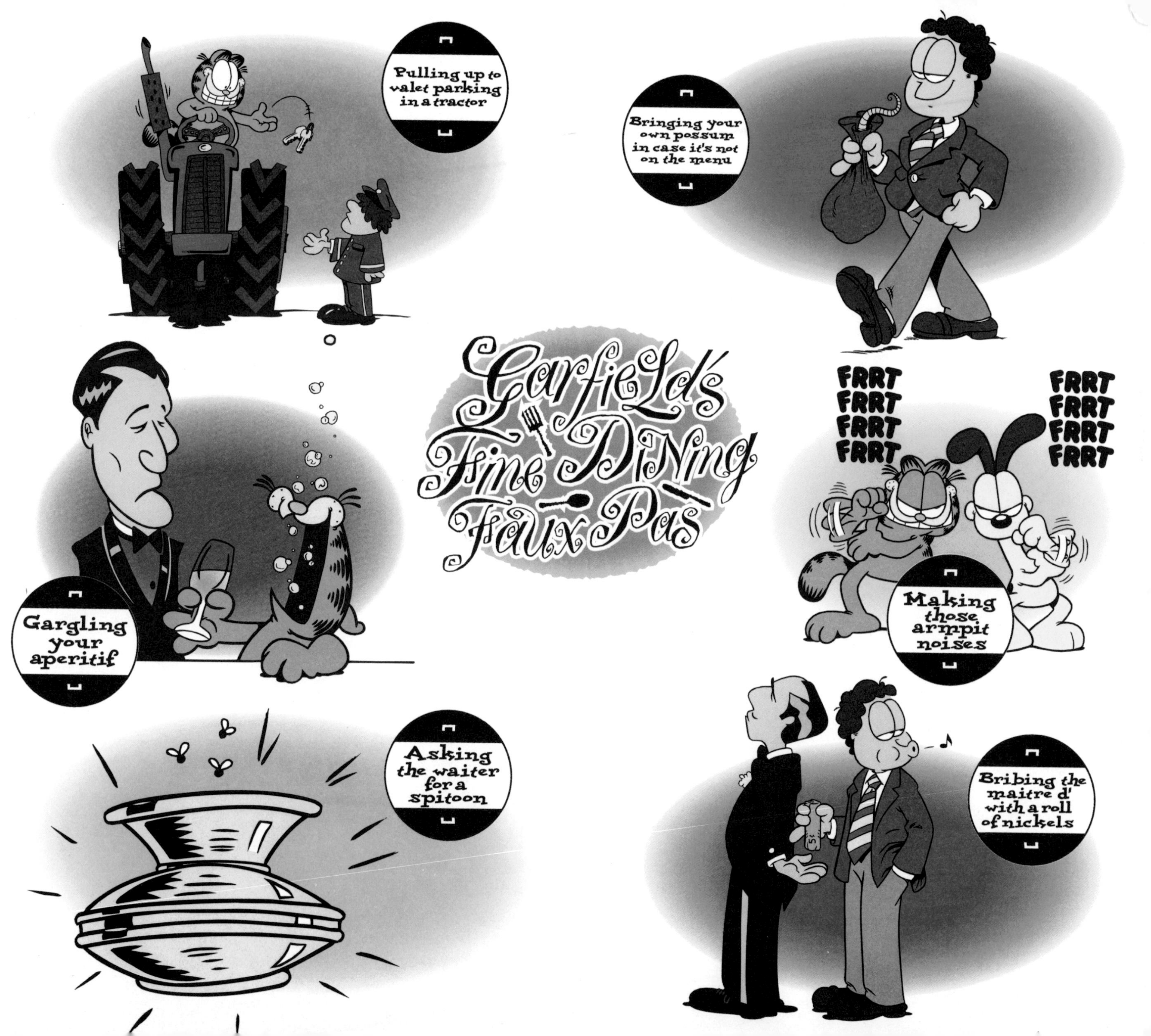
Garfield's Fine Dining Faux Pas
Pulling up to valet parking in a tractor
Bringing your own possum in case it's not on the menu
Gargling your aperitif
FRRT FRRT FRRT FRRT
FRRT FRRT FRRT FRRT
Making those armpit noises
Asking the waiter for a spitoon
Bribing the maitre d' with a roll of nickels

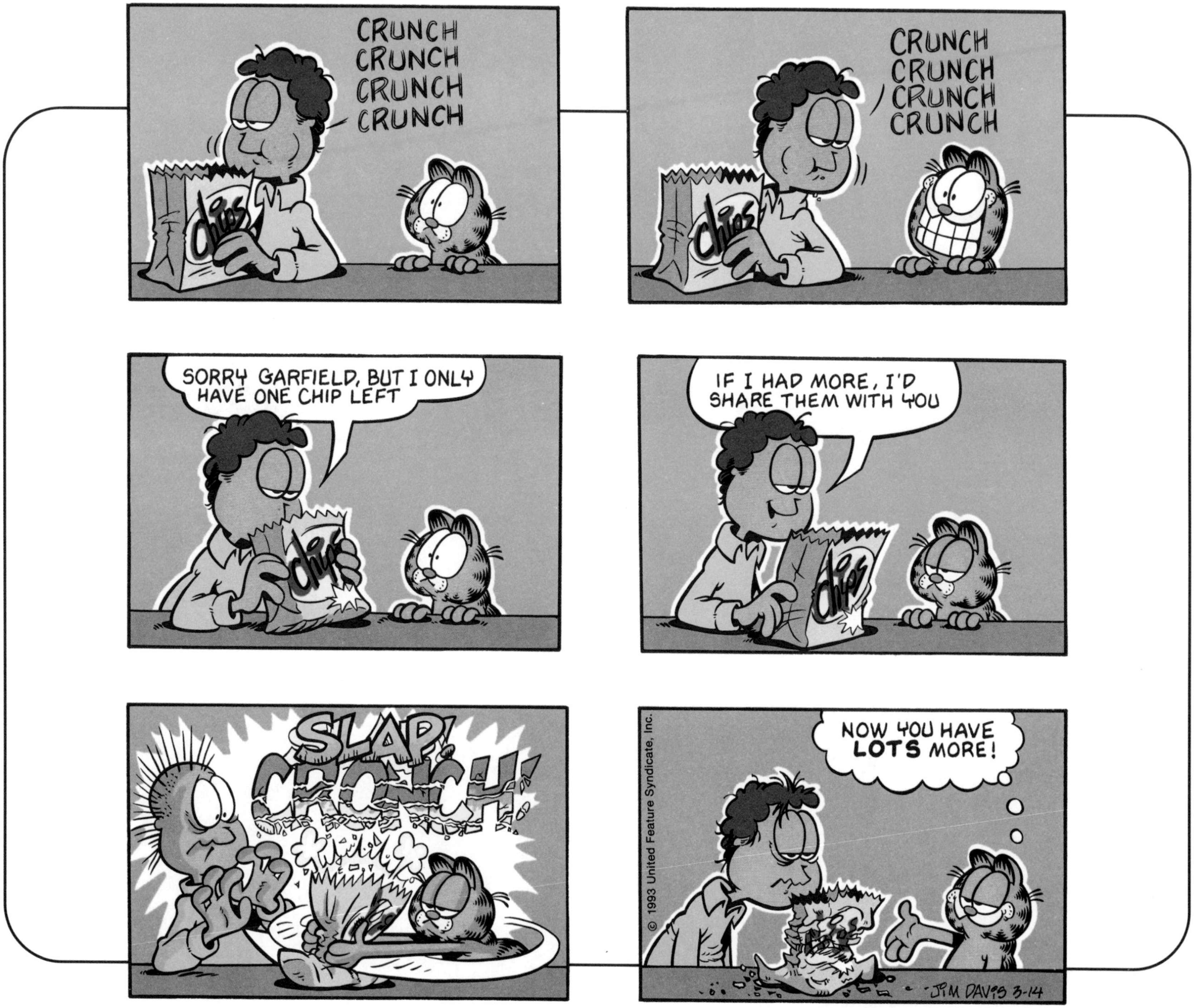

CRUNCH
CRUNCH
CRUNCH
CRUNCH
CRUNCH
CRUNCH
CRUNCH
CRUNCH
SORRY GARFIELD, BUT I ONLY HAVE ONE CHIP LEFT
IF I HAD MORE, I'D SHARE THEM WITH YOU
SLAP!
NOW YOU HAVE LOTS MORE!
© 1993 United Feature Syndicate, Inc.
JIM DAVIS 3-14

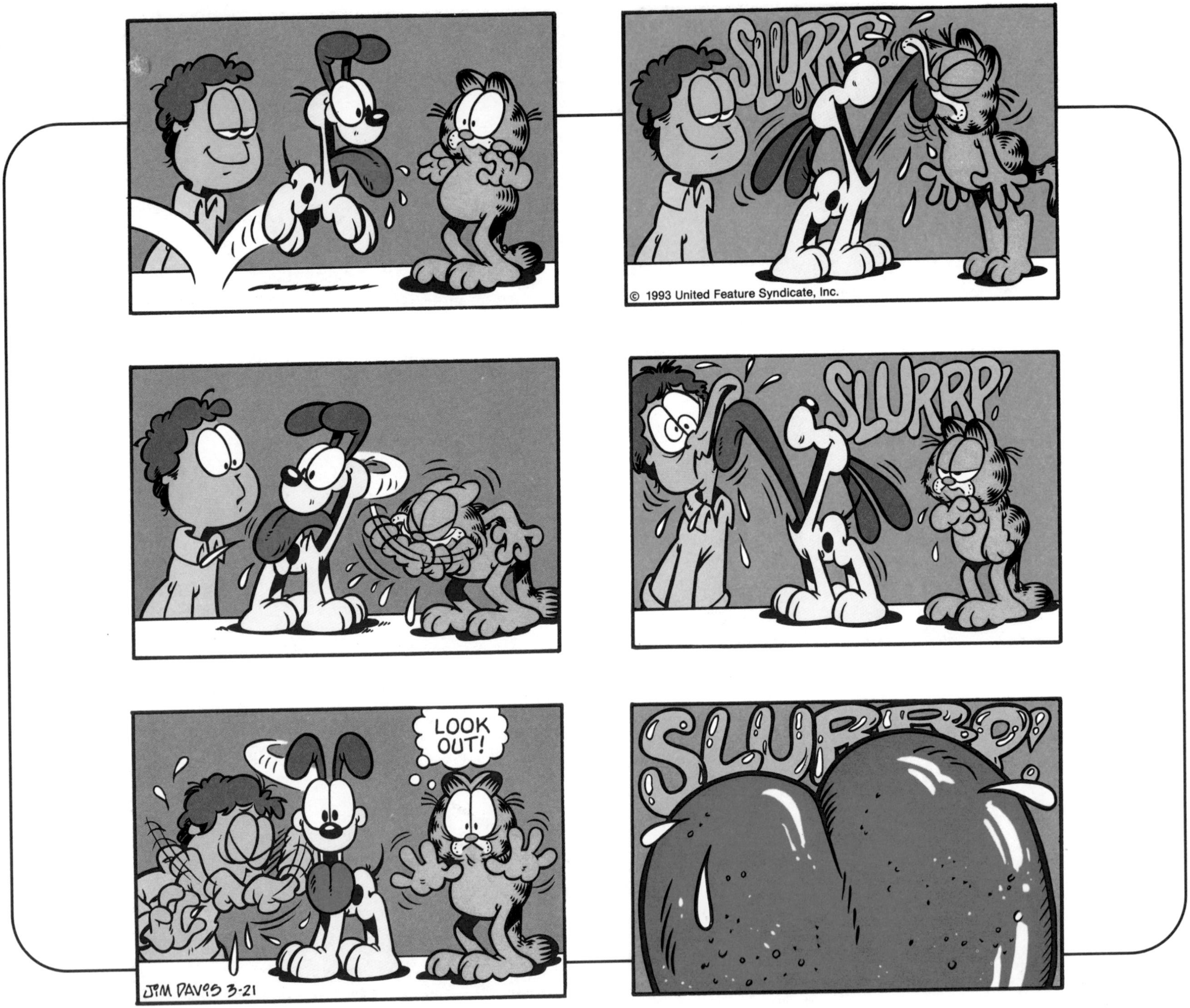
LOOK OUT!
JIM DAVIS 3-21
SLURRP!

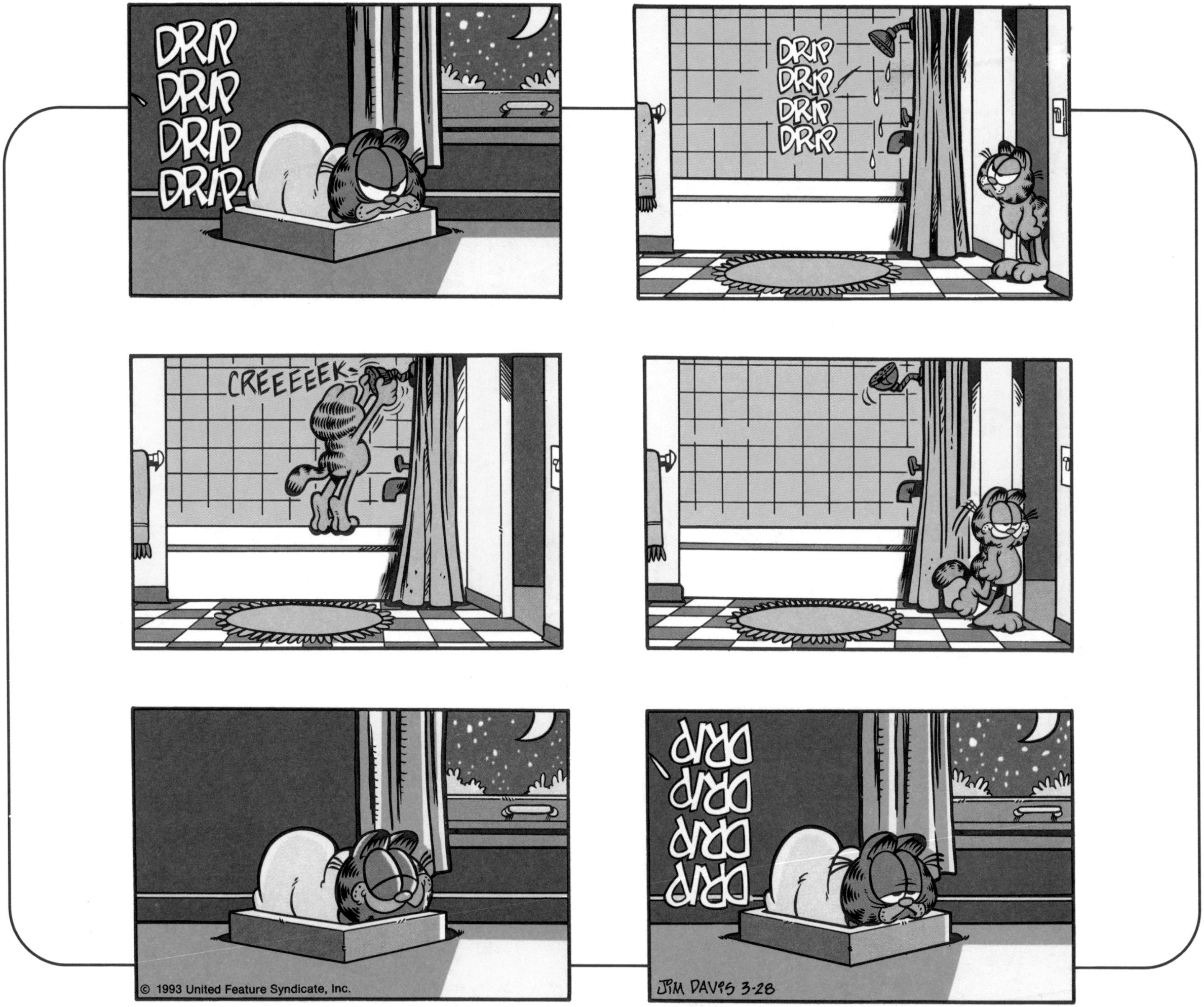
DRIP
DRIP
DRIP
DRIP
DRIP
DRIP
DRIP
DRIP
CREEEEEK
DRIP
DRIP
DRIP
DRIP
JIM DAVIS 3-28

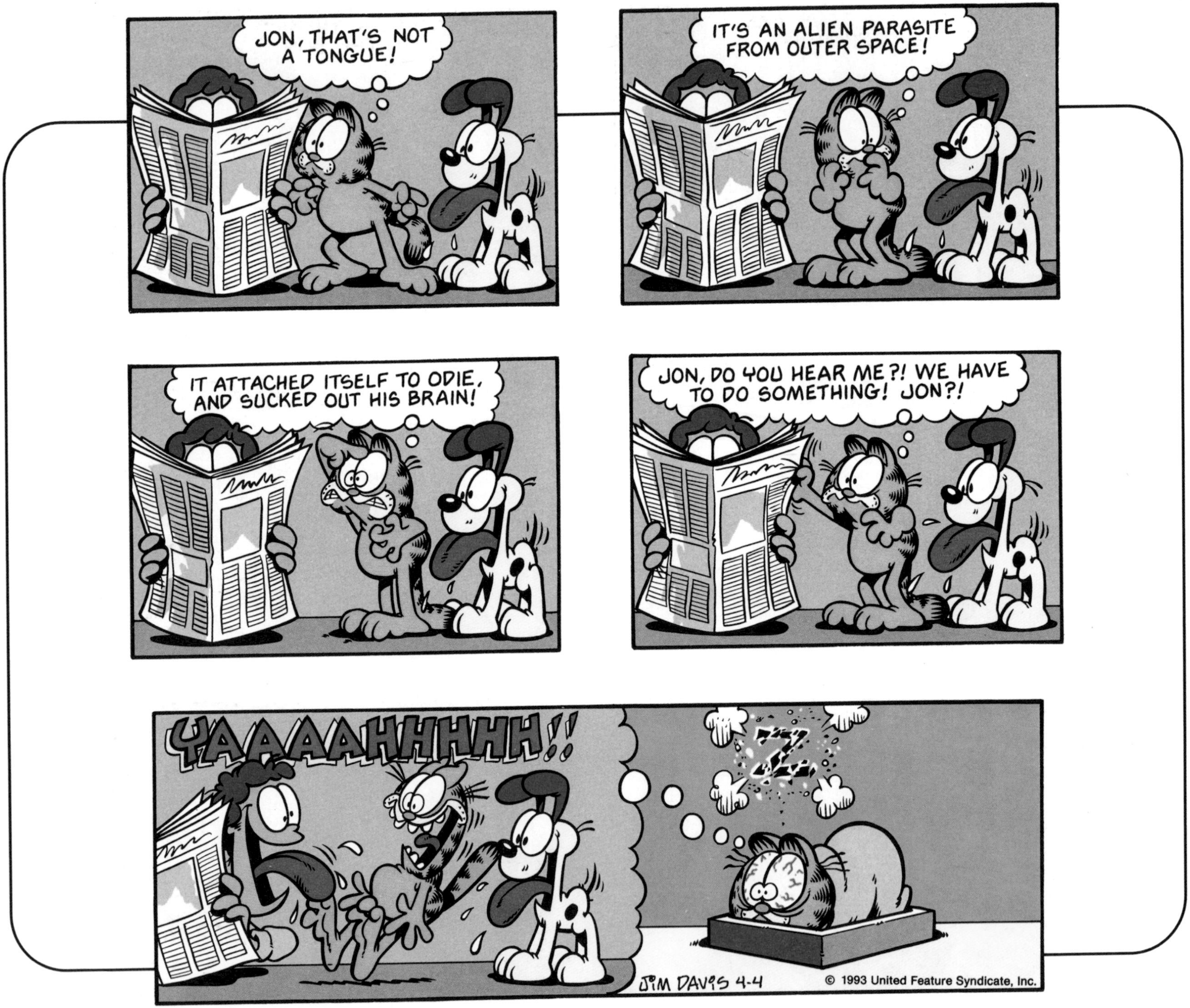
JON, THAT'S NOT A TONGUE!
IT'S AN ALIEN PARASITE FROM OUTER SPACE!
IT ATTACHED ITSELF TO ODIE, AND SUCKED OUT HIS BRAIN!
JON, DO YOU HEAR ME?! WE HAVE TO DO SOMETHING! JON?!
YAAAAHHHHH!!
Z
JIM DAVIS 4-4
© 1993 United Feature Syndicate, Inc.

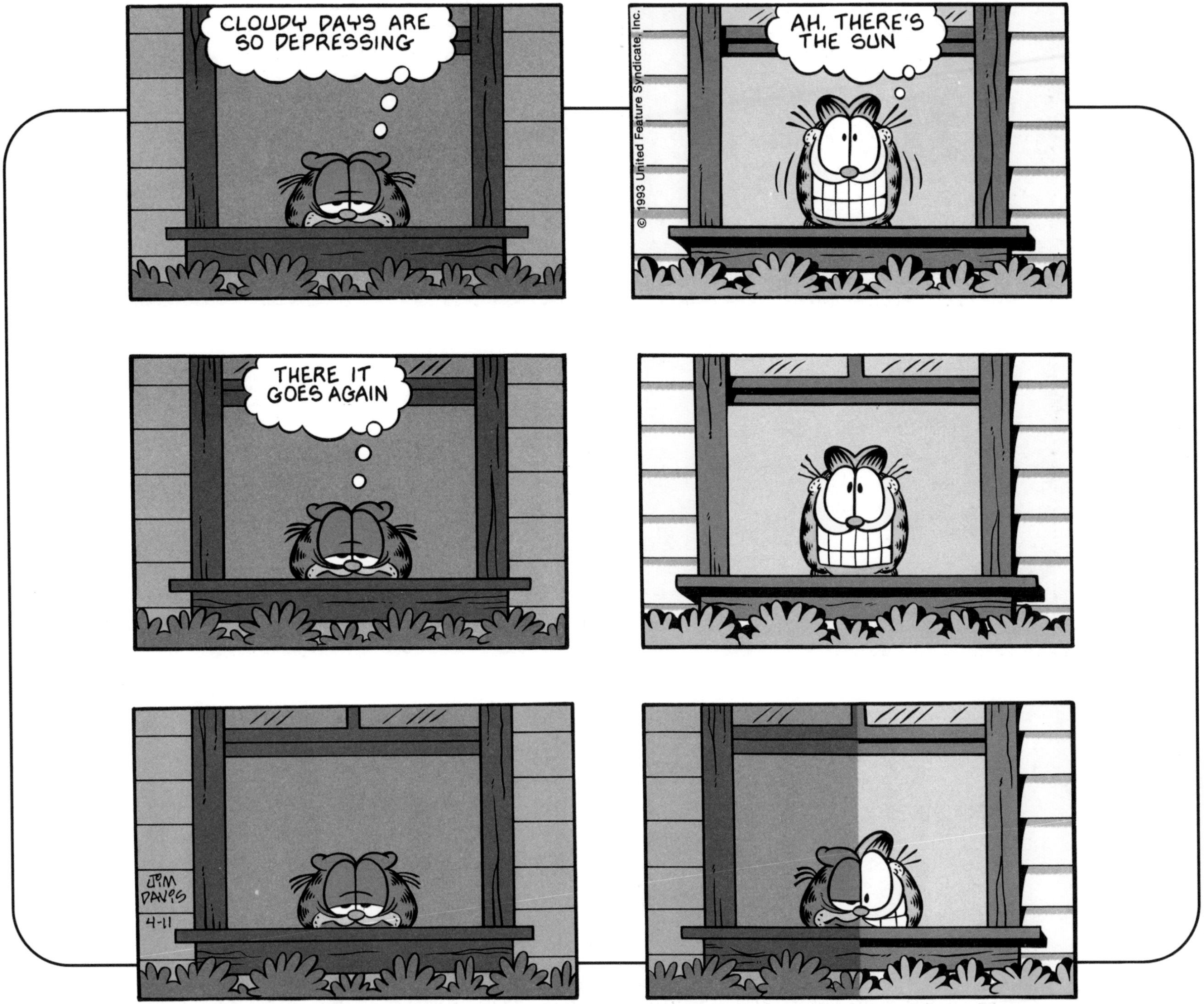
CLOUDY DAYS ARE SO DEPRESSING
THERE IT GOES AGAIN
JIM DAVIS 4-11
AH, THERE'S THE SUN
© 1993 United Feature Syndicate, Inc.

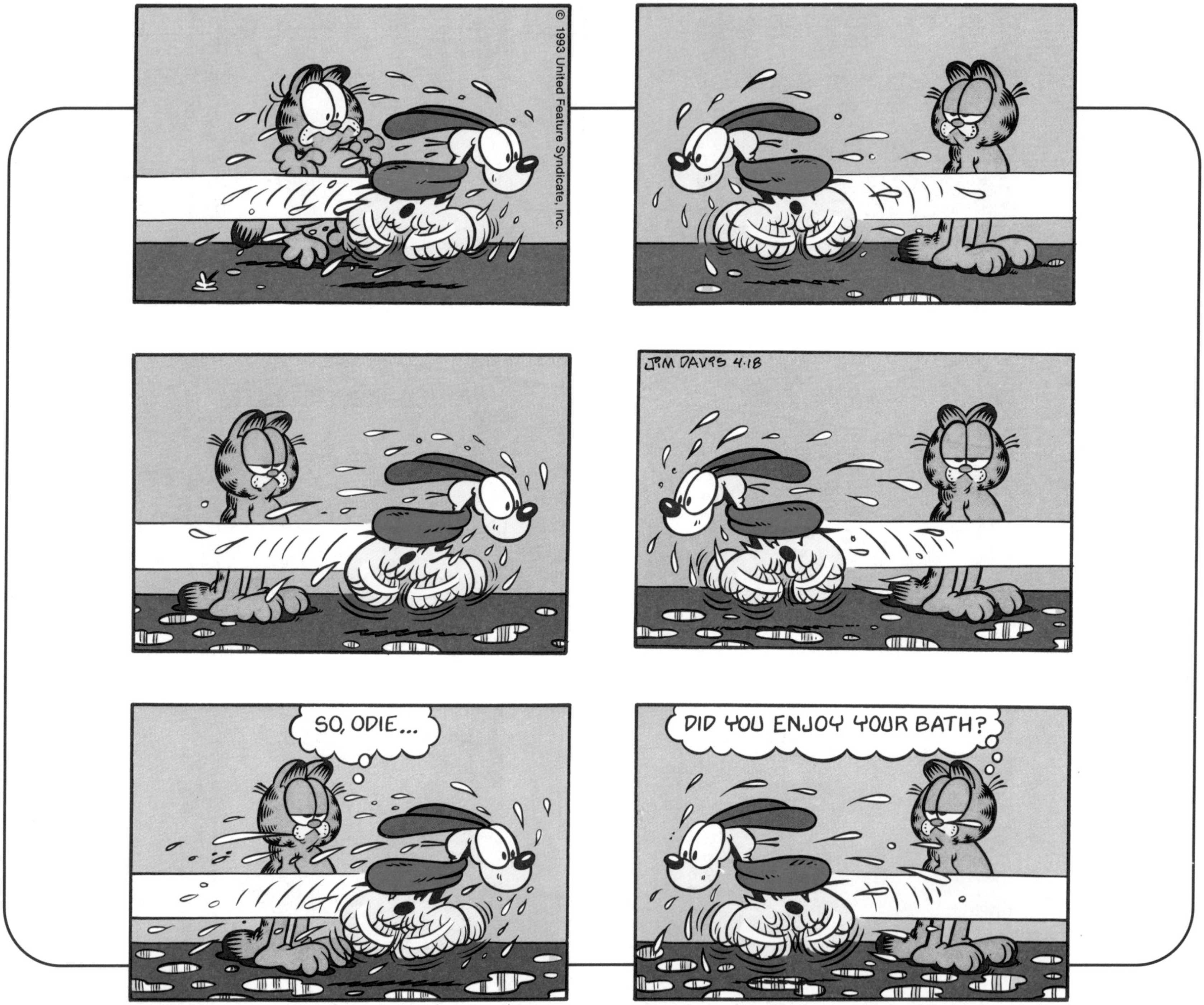
© 1993 United Feature Syndicate, Inc.
JIM DAVIS 4.18
SO, ODIE...
DID YOU ENJOY YOUR BATH?

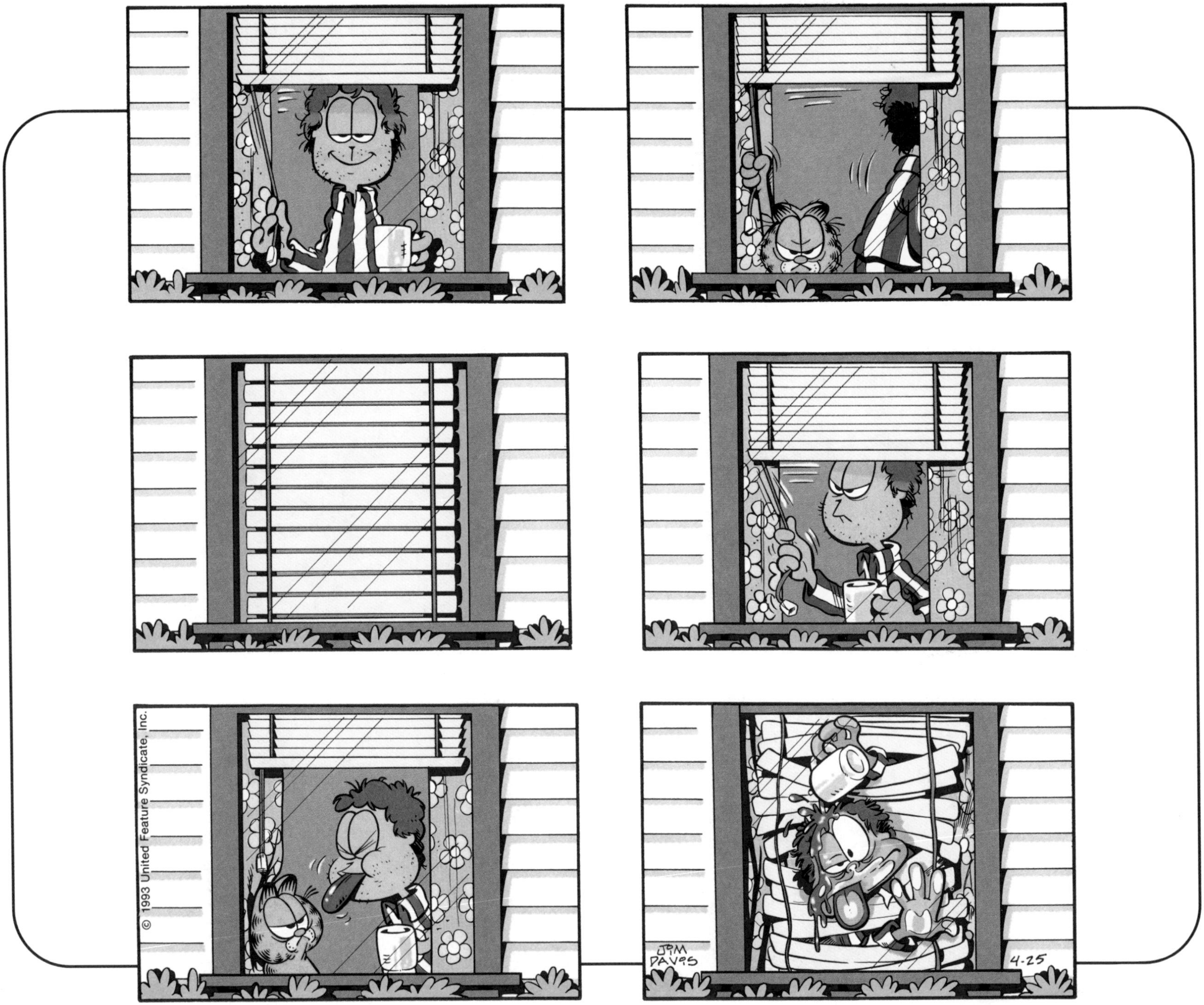
© 1993 United Feature Syndicate, Inc.
JIM DAVIS
4-25

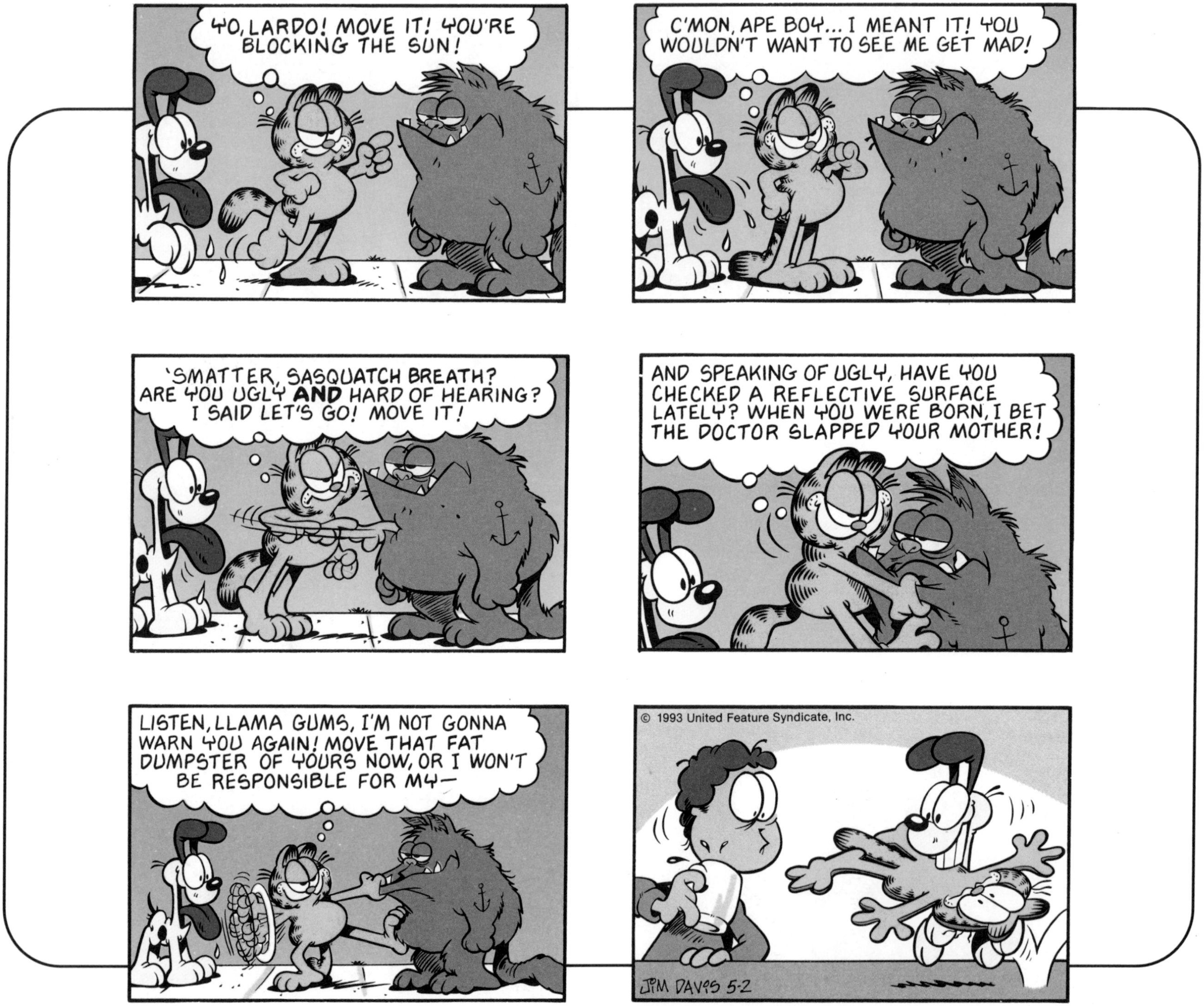
YO, LARDO! MOVE IT! YOU'RE BLOCKING THE SUN!
C'MON, APE BOY... I MEANT IT! YOU WOULDN'T WANT TO SEE ME GET MAD!
'SMATTER, SASQUATCH BREATH? ARE YOU UGLY **AND** HARD OF HEARING? I SAID LET'S GO! MOVE IT!
AND SPEAKING OF UGLY, HAVE YOU CHECKED A REFLECTIVE SURFACE LATELY? WHEN YOU WERE BORN, I BET THE DOCTOR SLAPPED YOUR MOTHER!
LISTEN, LLAMA GUMS, I'M NOT GONNA WARN YOU AGAIN! MOVE THAT FAT DUMPSTER OF YOURS NOW, OR I WON'T BE RESPONSIBLE FOR MY—
© 1993 United Feature Syndicate, Inc.
JIM DAVIS 5-2

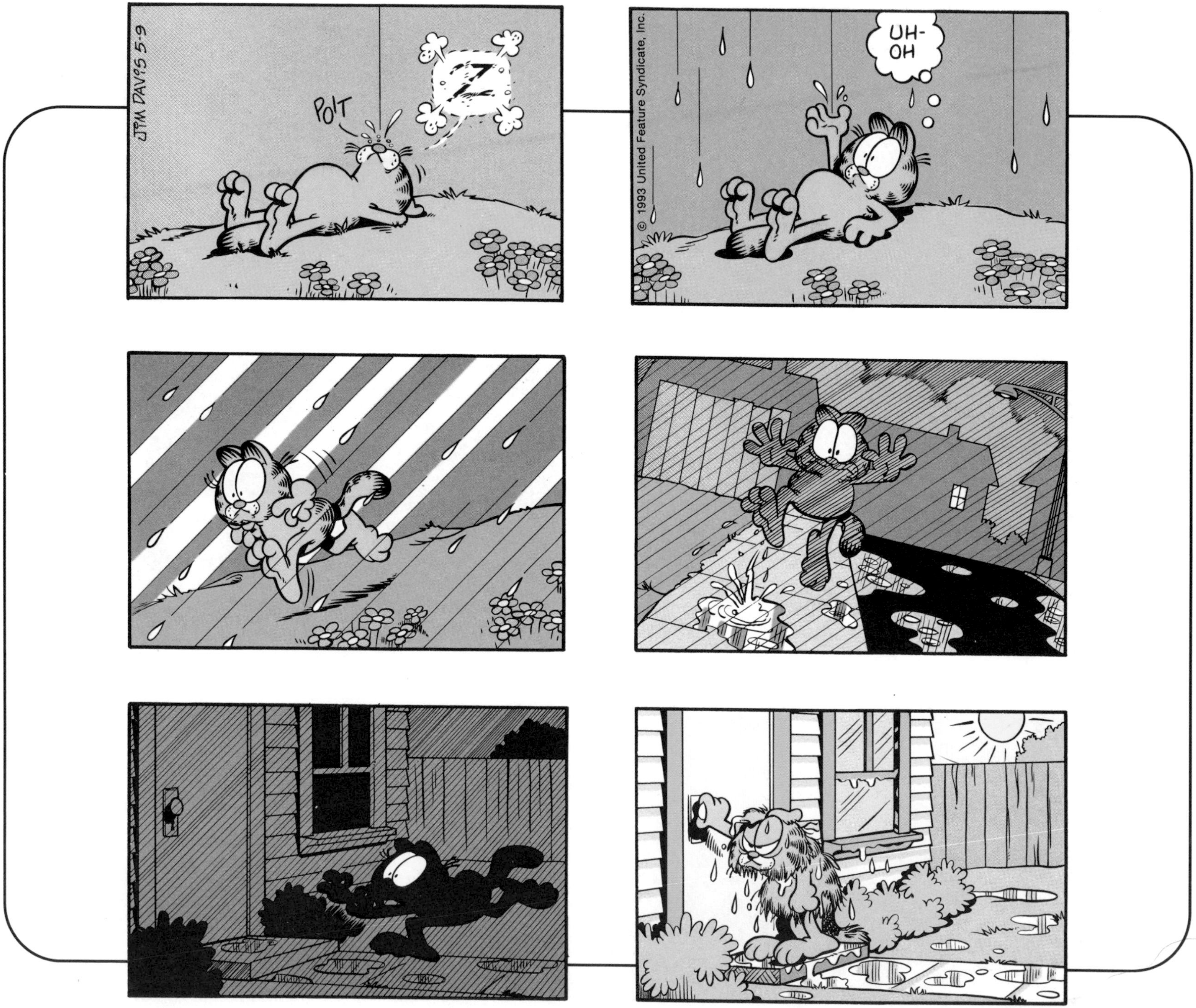
JIM DAVIS 5-9
POIT
Z
© 1993 United Feature Syndicate, Inc.
UH-OH

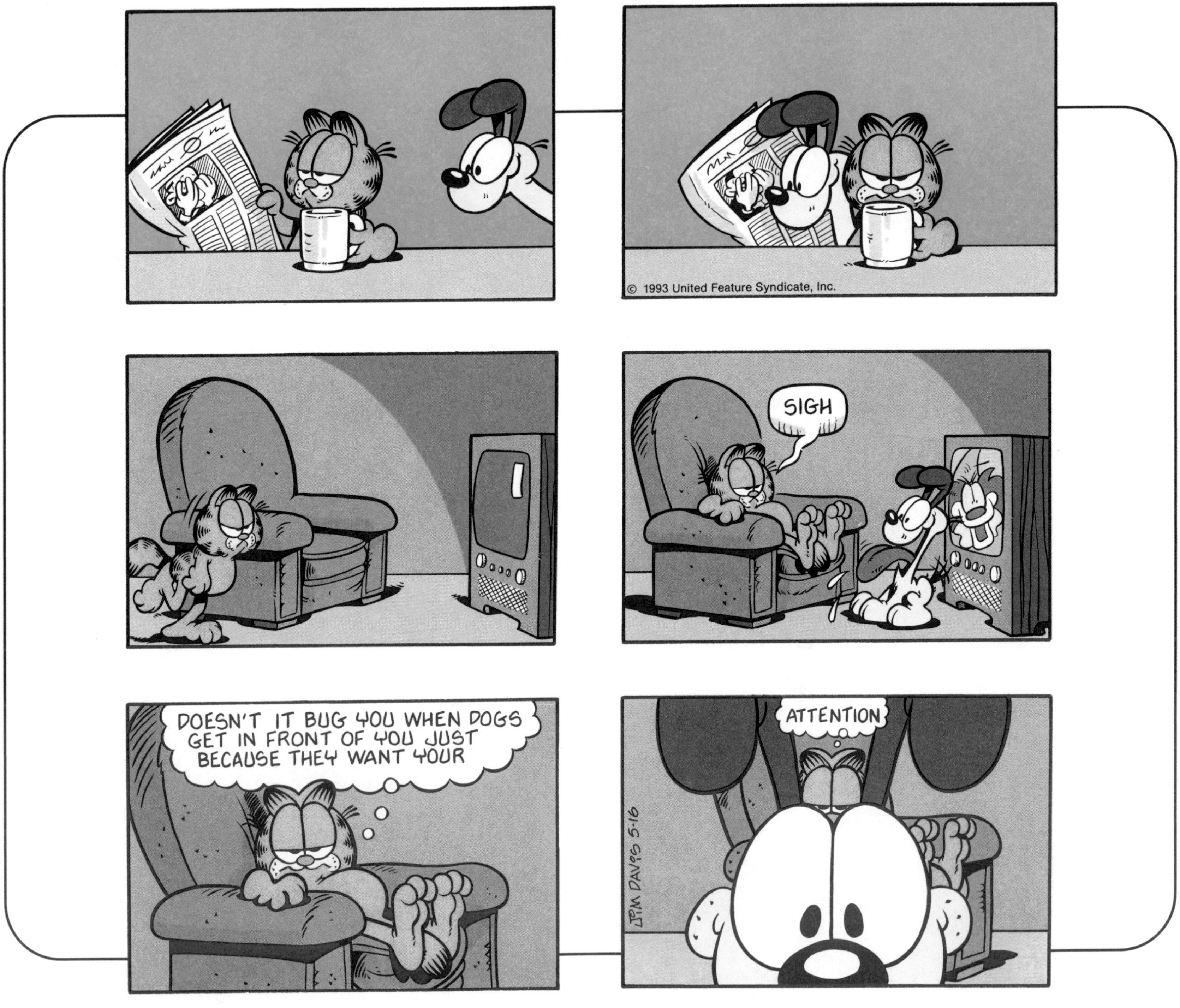
SIGH
DOESN'T IT BUG YOU WHEN DOGS GET IN FRONT OF YOU JUST BECAUSE THEY WANT YOUR
JIM DAVIS 5-16
ATTENTION

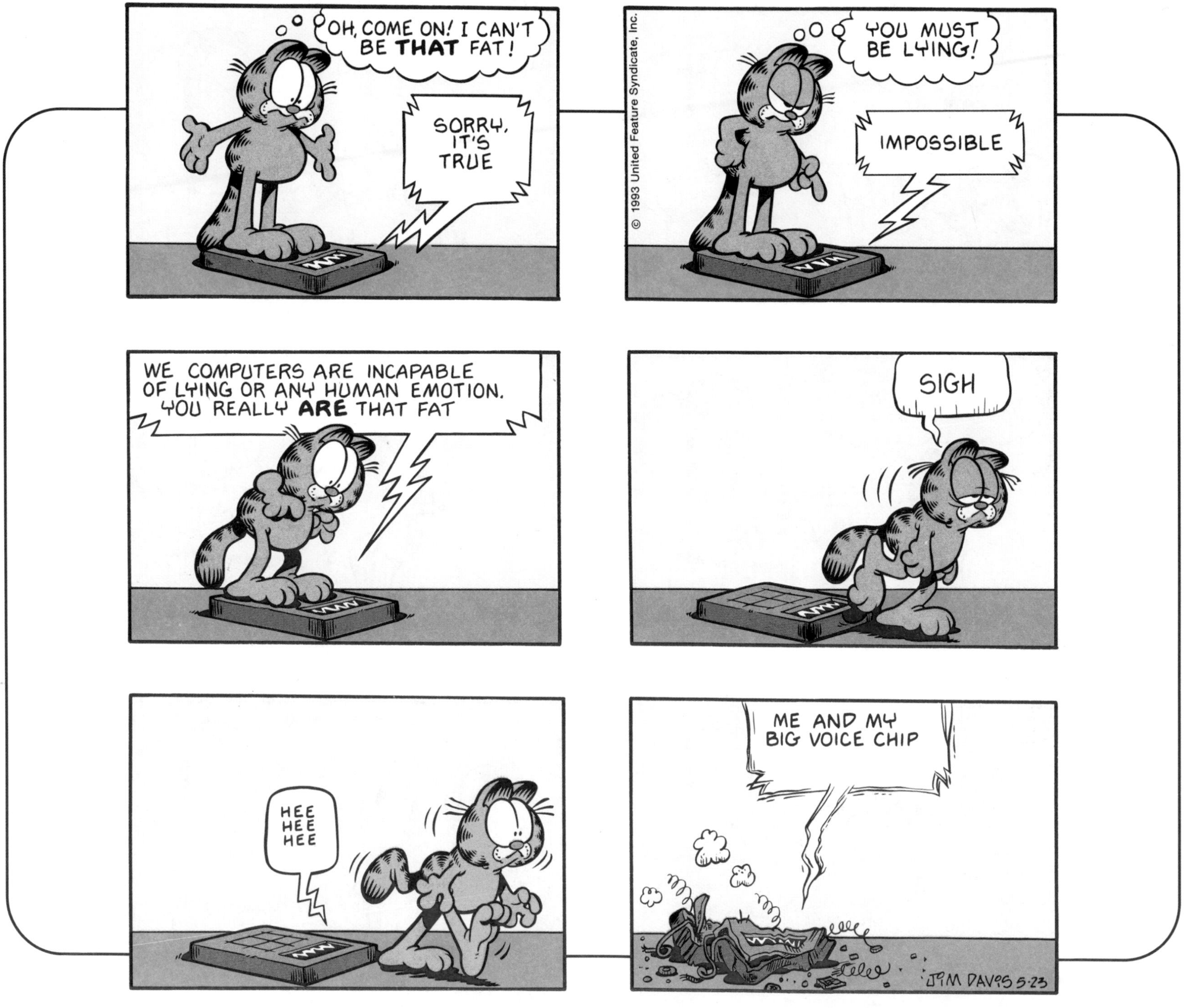
OH, COME ON! I CAN'T BE **THAT** FAT!
SORRY, IT'S TRUE
YOU MUST BE LYING!
IMPOSSIBLE
WE COMPUTERS ARE INCAPABLE OF LYING OR ANY HUMAN EMOTION. YOU REALLY **ARE** THAT FAT
SIGH
HEE HEE HEE
ME AND MY BIG VOICE CHIP
JIM DAVIS 5-23

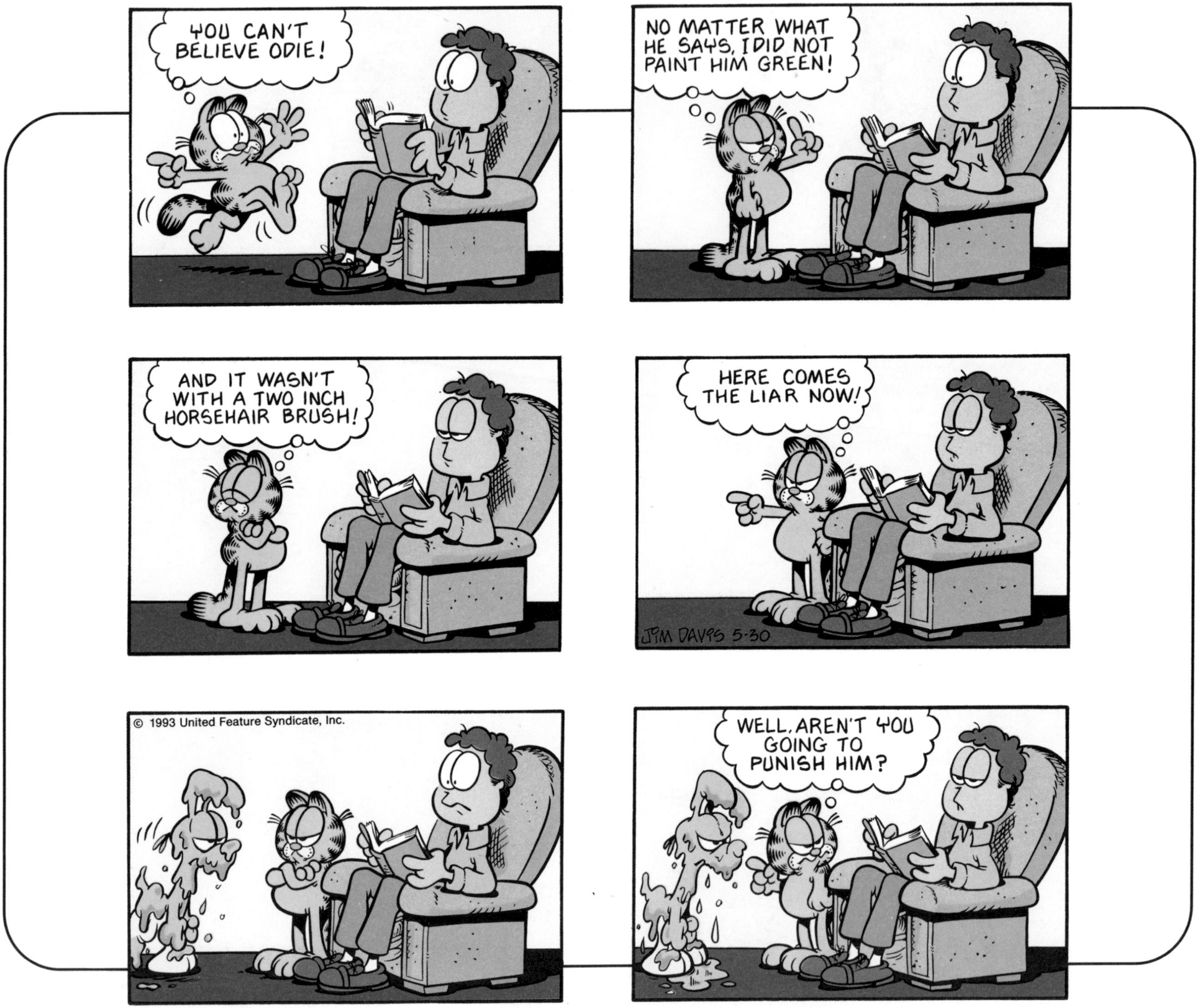
YOU CAN'T BELIEVE ODIE!
NO MATTER WHAT HE SAYS, I DID NOT PAINT HIM GREEN!
AND IT WASN'T WITH A TWO INCH HORSEHAIR BRUSH!
HERE COMES THE LIAR NOW!
JIM DAVIS 5-30
© 1993 United Feature Syndicate, Inc.
WELL, AREN'T YOU GOING TO PUNISH HIM?

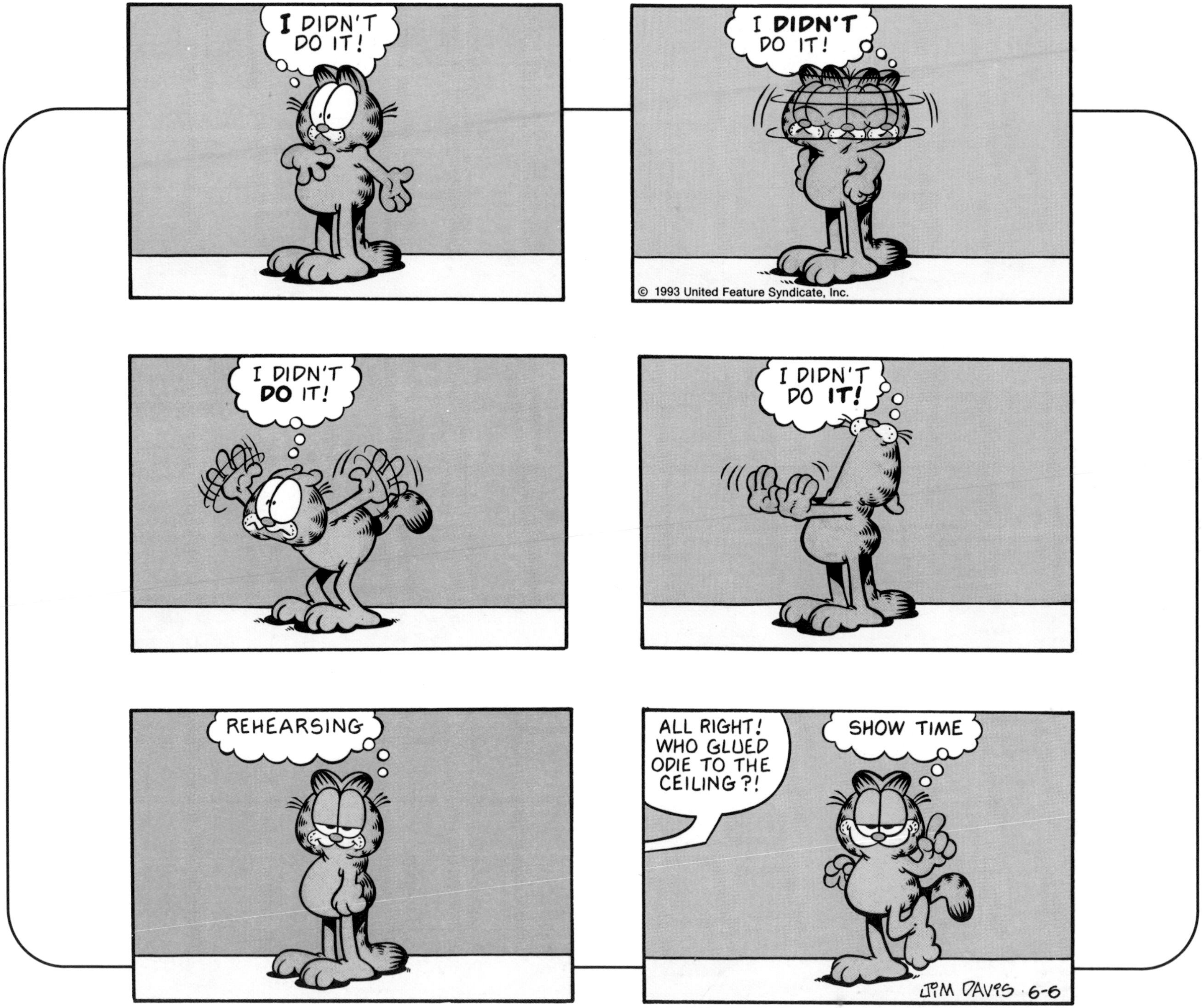

I DIDN'T DO IT!
I DIDN'T DO IT!
© 1993 United Feature Syndicate, Inc.
I DIDN'T DO IT!
I DIDN'T DO IT!
REHEARSING
ALL RIGHT! WHO GLUED ODIE TO THE CEILING?!
SHOW TIME
JIM DAVIS 6-6

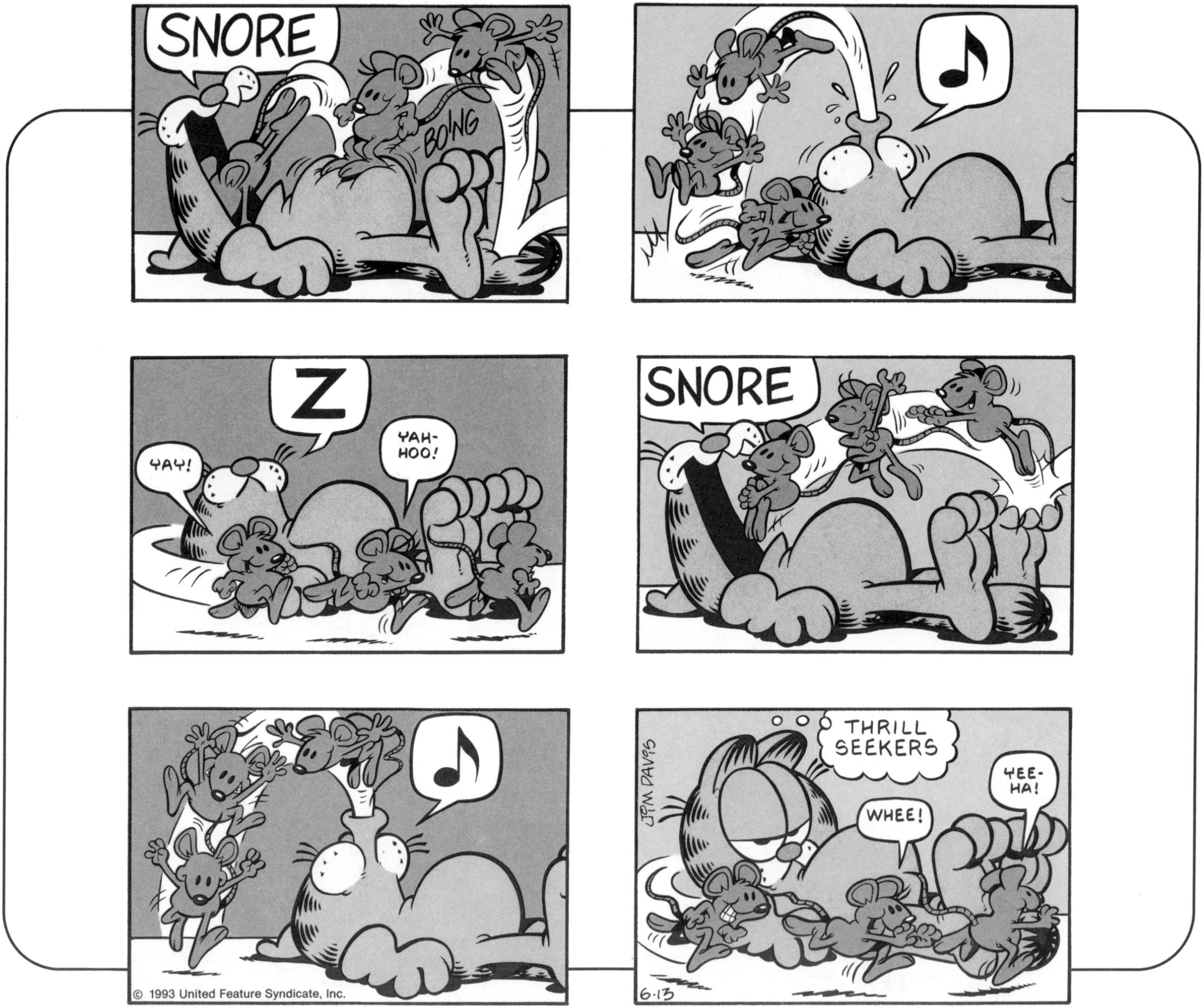
SNORE
BOING
♪
Z
YAY!
YAH-HOO!
SNORE
♪
THRILL SEEKERS
JIM DAVIS
WHEE!
YEE-HA!
6-13

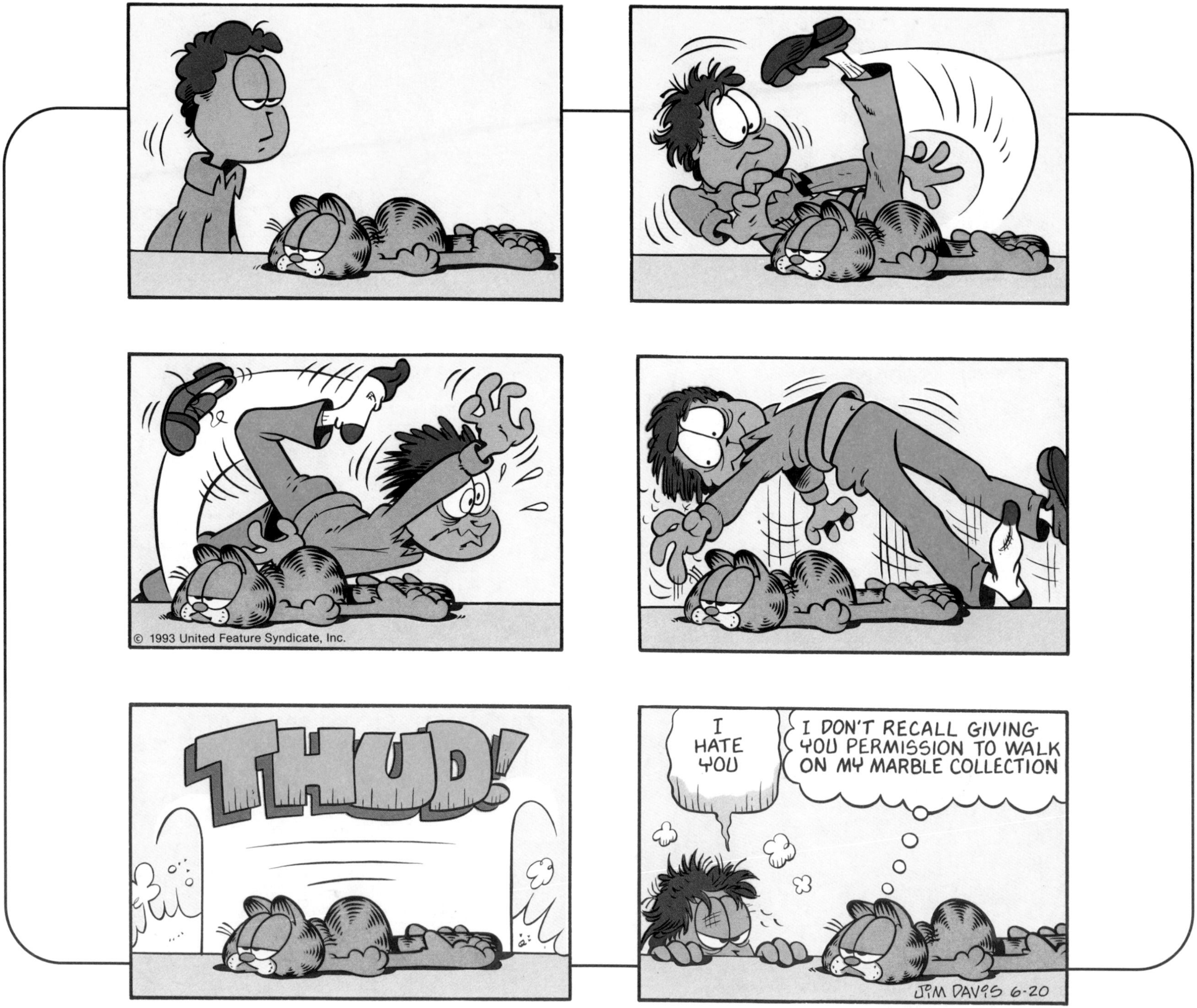
© 1993 United Feature Syndicate, Inc.
THUD!
I HATE YOU
I DON'T RECALL GIVING YOU PERMISSION TO WALK ON MY MARBLE COLLECTION
JIM DAVIS 6-20

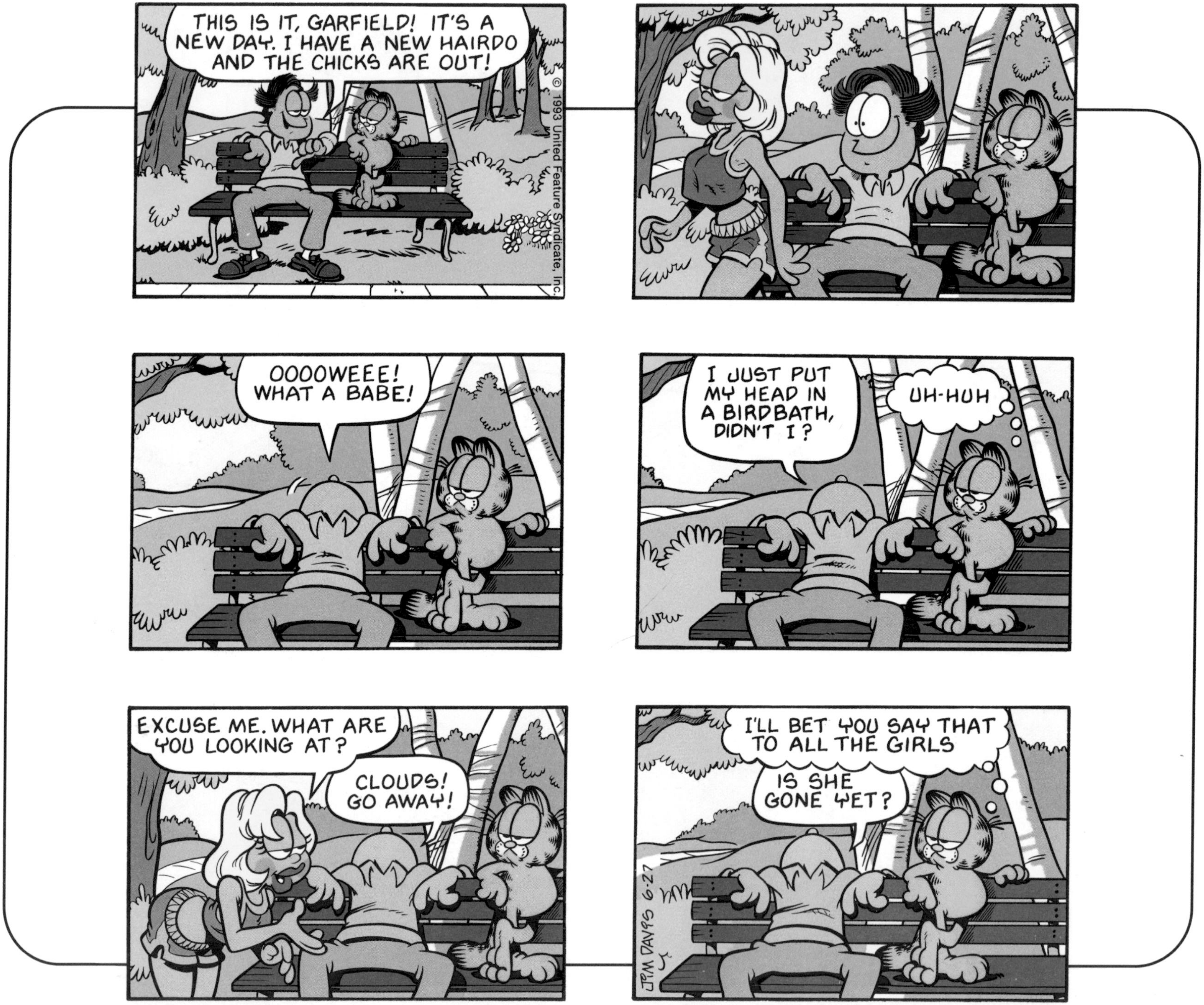
THIS IS IT, GARFIELD! IT'S A NEW DAY. I HAVE A NEW HAIRDO AND THE CHICKS ARE OUT!
© 1993 United Feature Syndicate, Inc.
OOOOWEEE! WHAT A BABE!
I JUST PUT MY HEAD IN A BIRDBATH, DIDN'T I?
UH-HUH
EXCUSE ME. WHAT ARE YOU LOOKING AT?
CLOUDS! GO AWAY!
I'LL BET YOU SAY THAT TO ALL THE GIRLS
IS SHE GONE YET?
JPM DAVPS 6-27

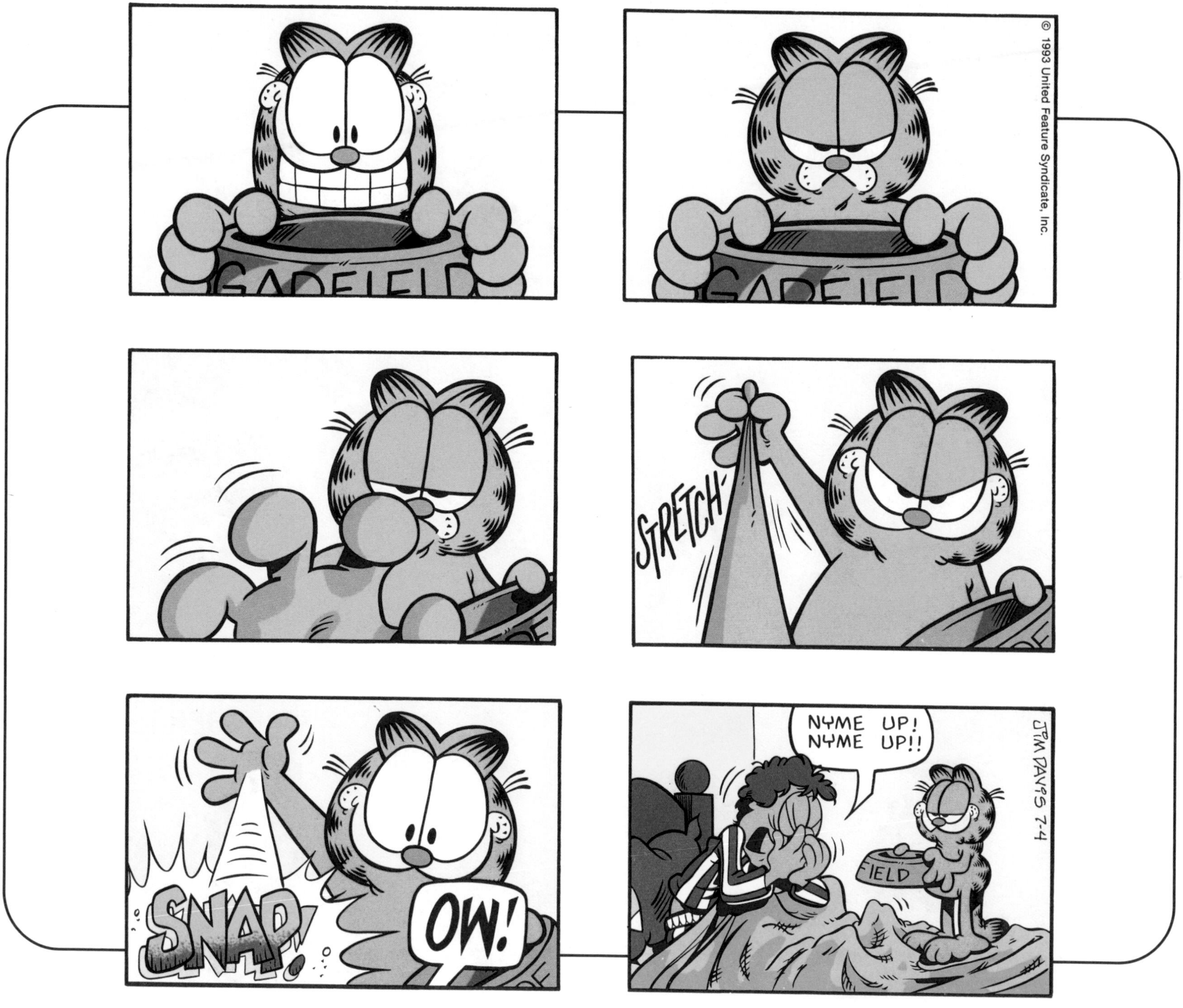
© 1993 United Feature Syndicate, Inc.
STRETCH
SNAP
OW!
NYME UP! NYME UP!!
JPM DAVPS 7-4

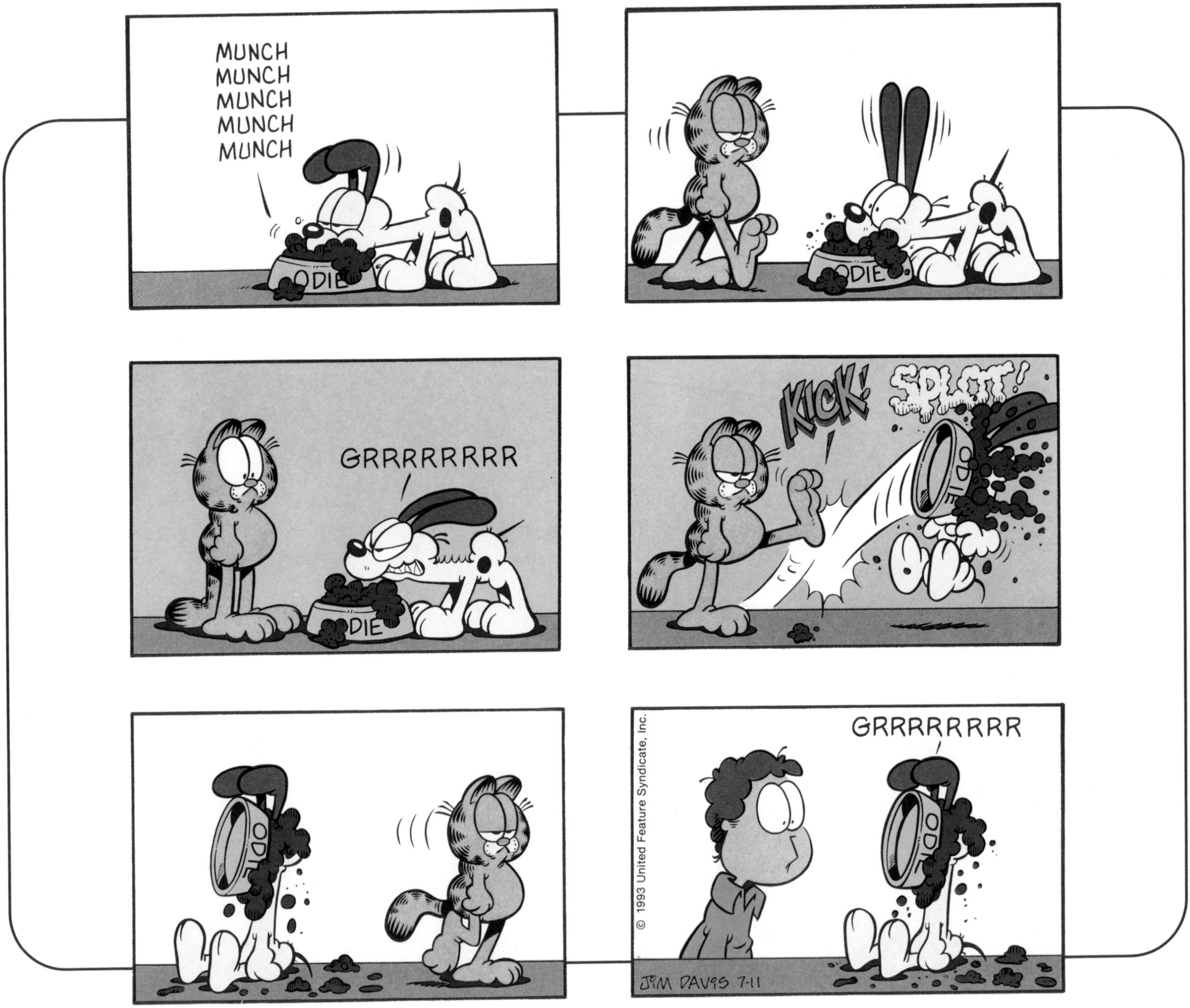
MUNCH MUNCH MUNCH MUNCH MUNCH
ODIE
ODIE
GRRRRRRRR
ODIE
KICK!
SPLOT!
GRRRRRRRR
© 1993 United Feature Syndicate, Inc.
JIM DAVIS 7-11

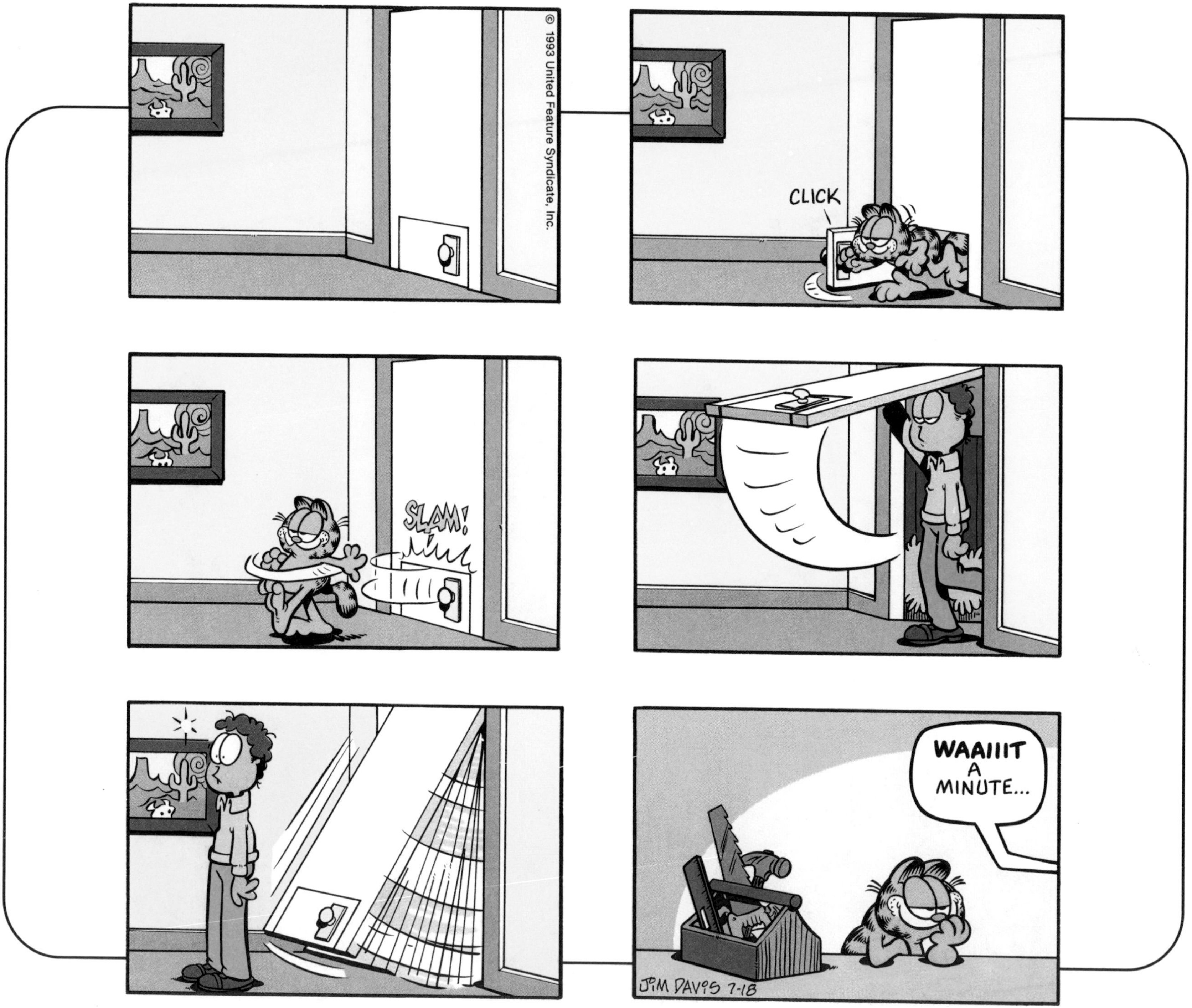
© 1993 United Feature Syndicate, Inc.
CLICK
SLAM!
WAAIIIT A MINUTE...
JIM DAVIS 7-18

RATS!
© 1993 United Feature Syndicate, Inc.
I JUST CAN'T GET COMFORTABLE
JIM DAVIS 7-25
Z

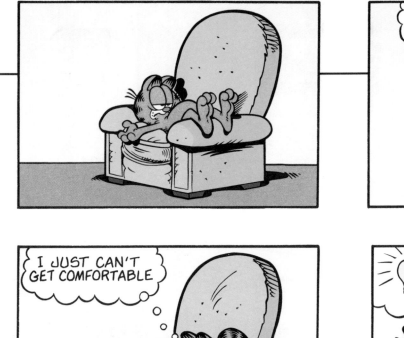

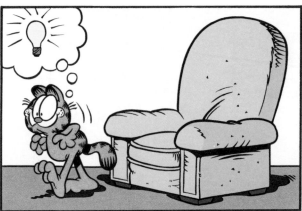

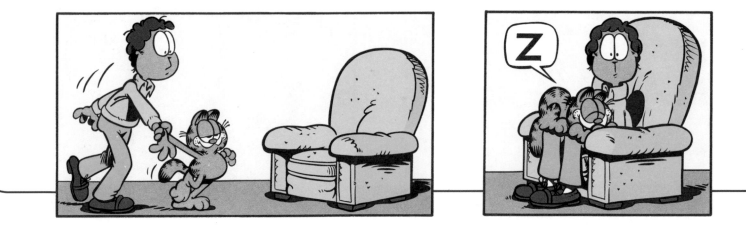

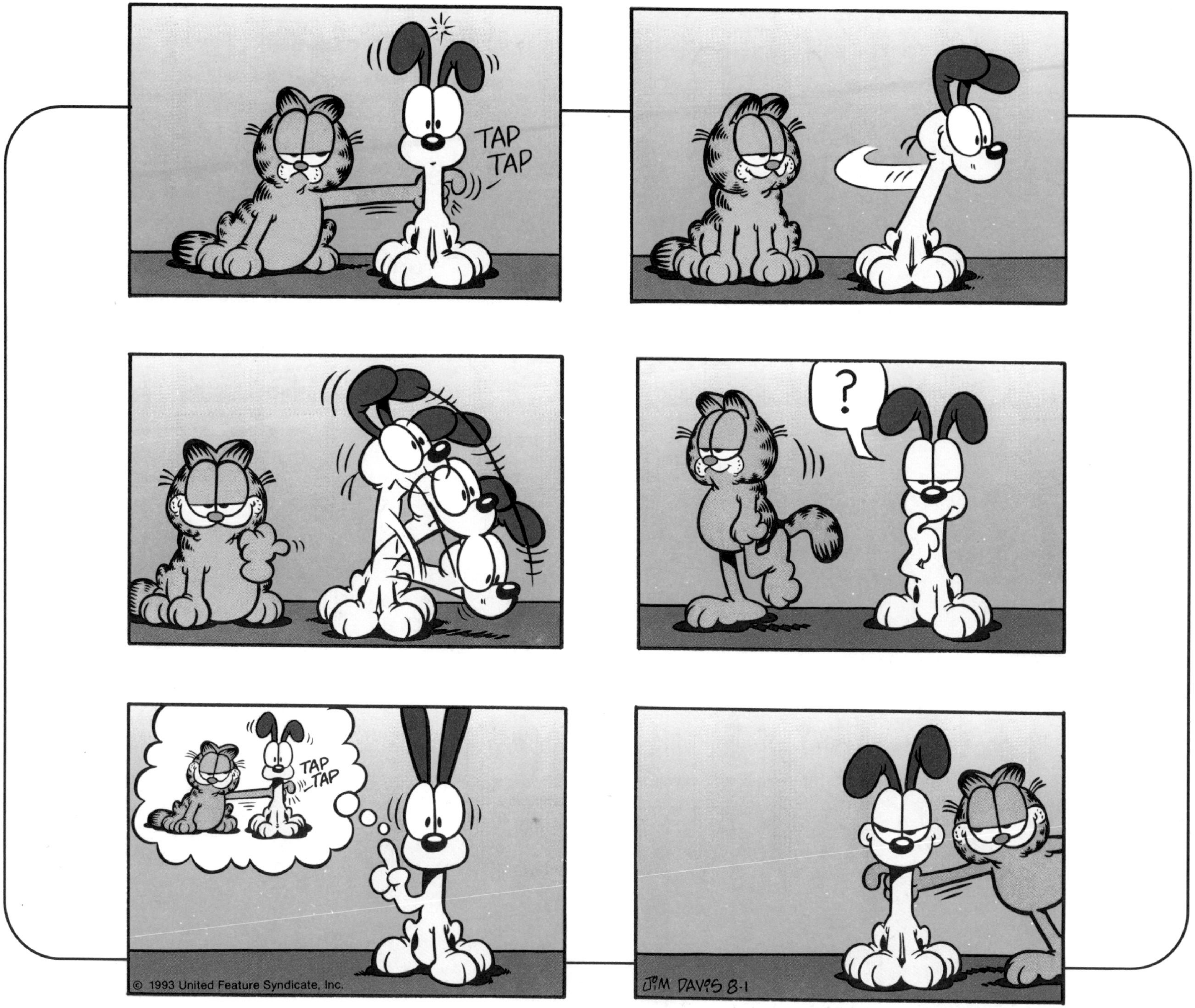
TAP TAP
?
TAP TAP
© 1993 United Feature Syndicate, Inc.
JIM DAVIS 8-1

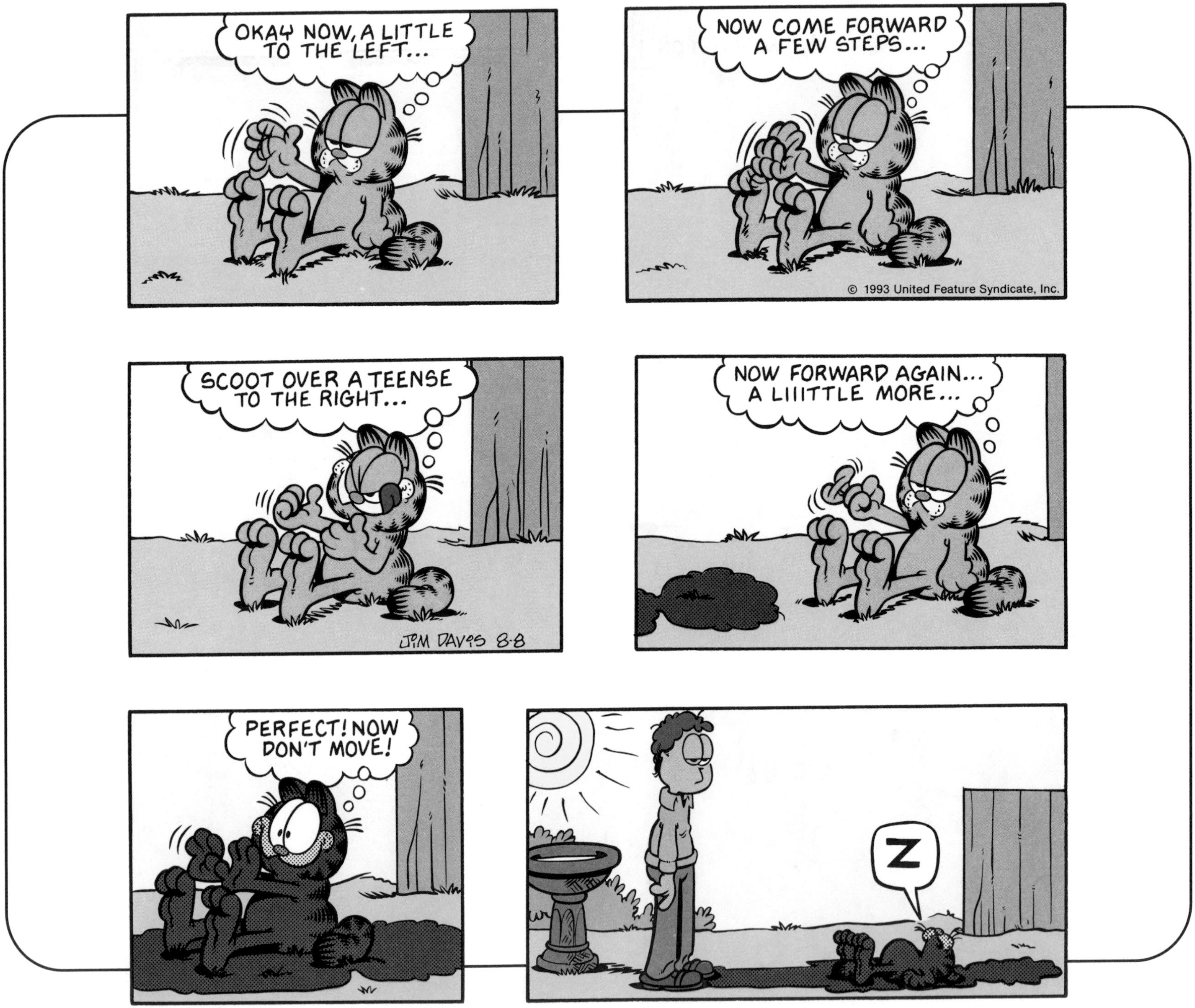
OKAY NOW, A LITTLE TO THE LEFT...
NOW COME FORWARD A FEW STEPS...
© 1993 United Feature Syndicate, Inc.
SCOOT OVER A TEENSE TO THE RIGHT...
JIM DAVIS 8-8
NOW FORWARD AGAIN... A LIIITTLE MORE...
PERFECT! NOW DON'T MOVE!
Z

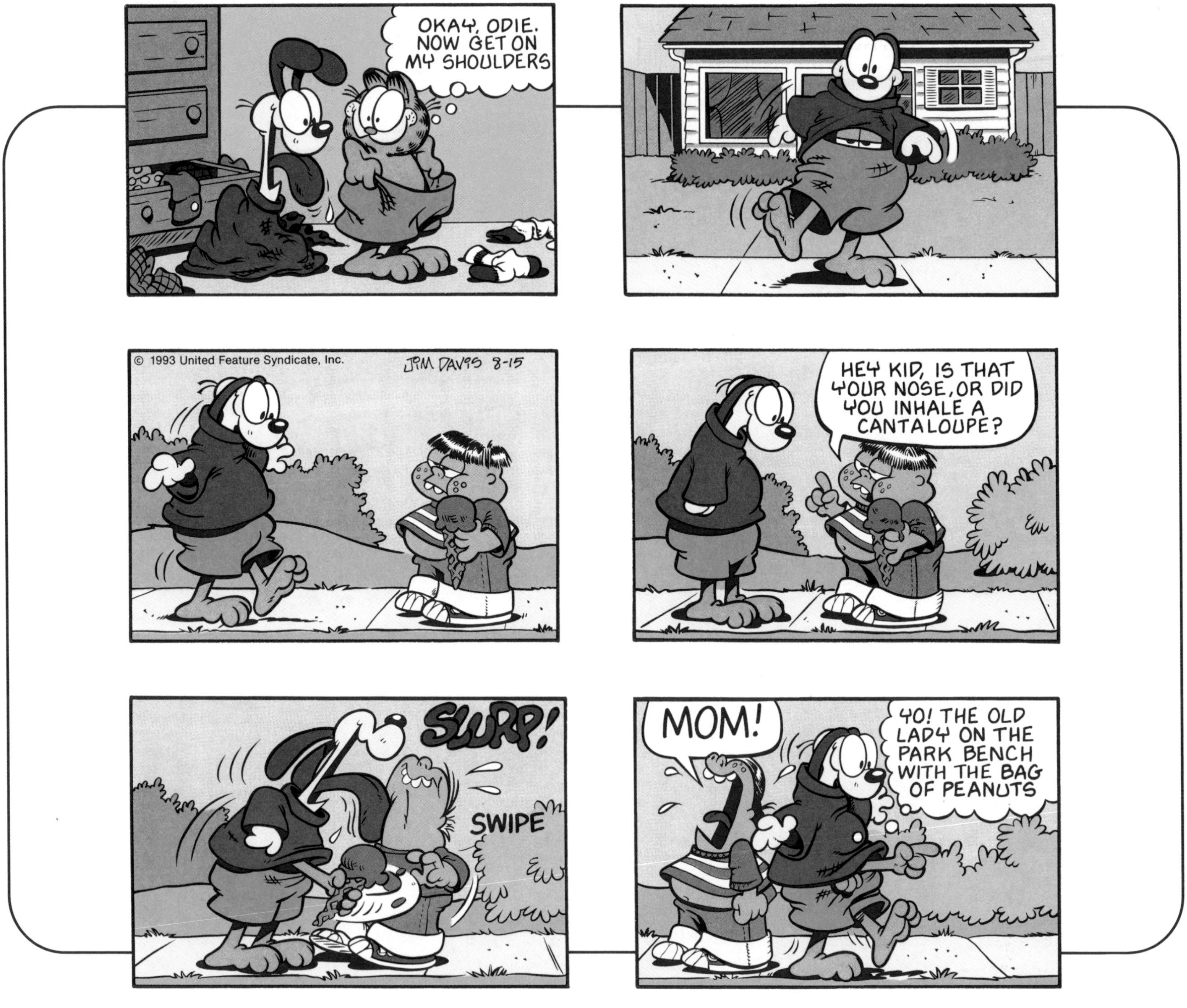

OKAY, ODIE. NOW GET ON MY SHOULDERS
© 1993 United Feature Syndicate, Inc.
JIM DAVIS 8-15
HEY KID, IS THAT YOUR NOSE, OR DID YOU INHALE A CANTALOUPE?
SLURP!
SWIPE
MOM!
YO! THE OLD LADY ON THE PARK BENCH WITH THE BAG OF PEANUTS

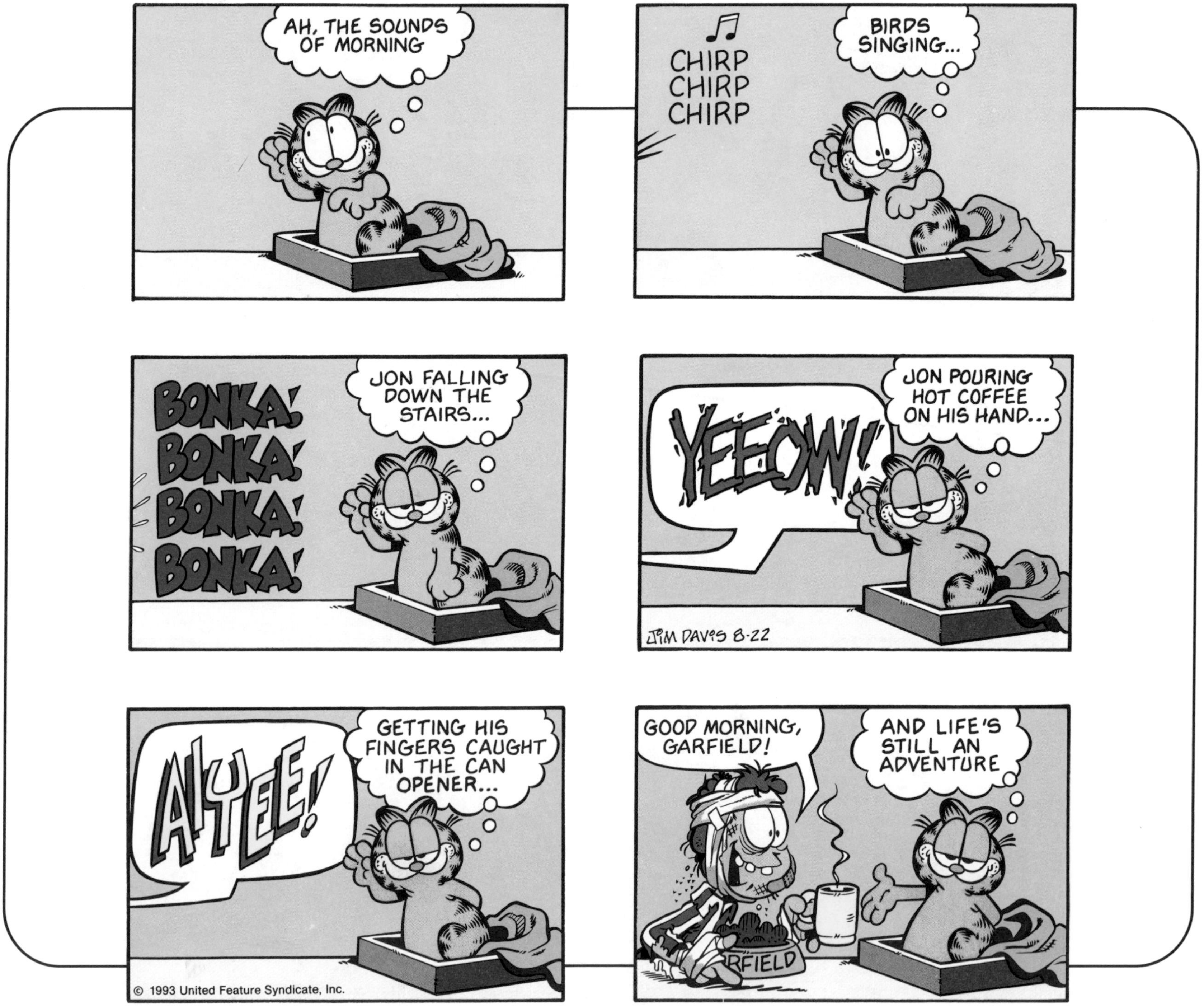
AH, THE SOUNDS OF MORNING
CHIRP CHIRP CHIRP
BIRDS SINGING...
BONKA! BONKA! BONKA! BONKA!
JON FALLING DOWN THE STAIRS...
YEEOW!
JON POURING HOT COFFEE ON HIS HAND...
JIM DAVIS 8-22
AIYEE!
GETTING HIS FINGERS CAUGHT IN THE CAN OPENER...
© 1993 United Feature Syndicate, Inc.
GOOD MORNING, GARFIELD!
AND LIFE'S STILL AN ADVENTURE
RFIELD

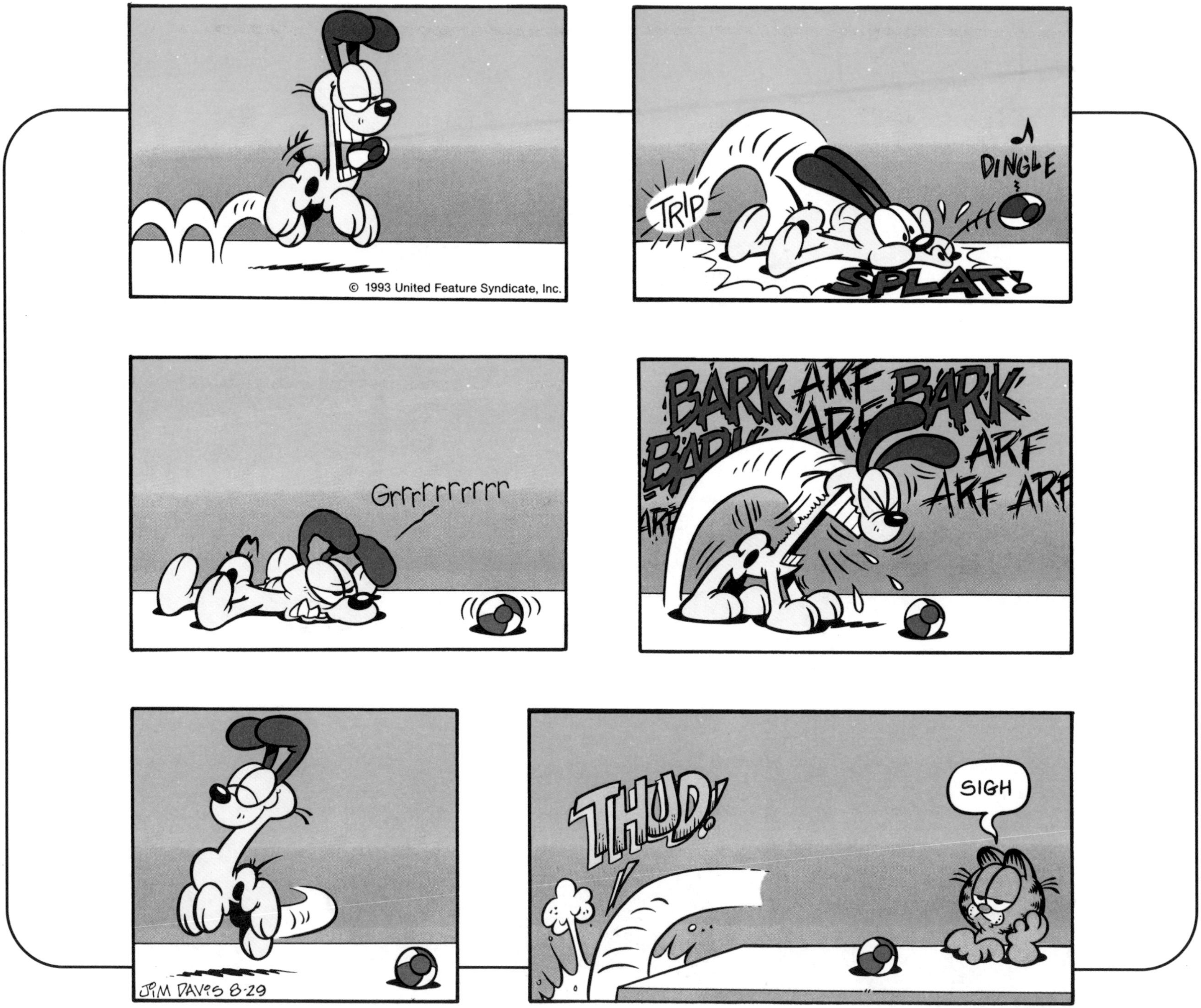
© 1993 United Feature Syndicate, Inc.
TRIP
DINGLE
SPLAT!
Grrrrrrrrr
BARK
ARF
BARK
ARF
ARF ARF
JIM DAVIS 8-29
THUD!
SIGH

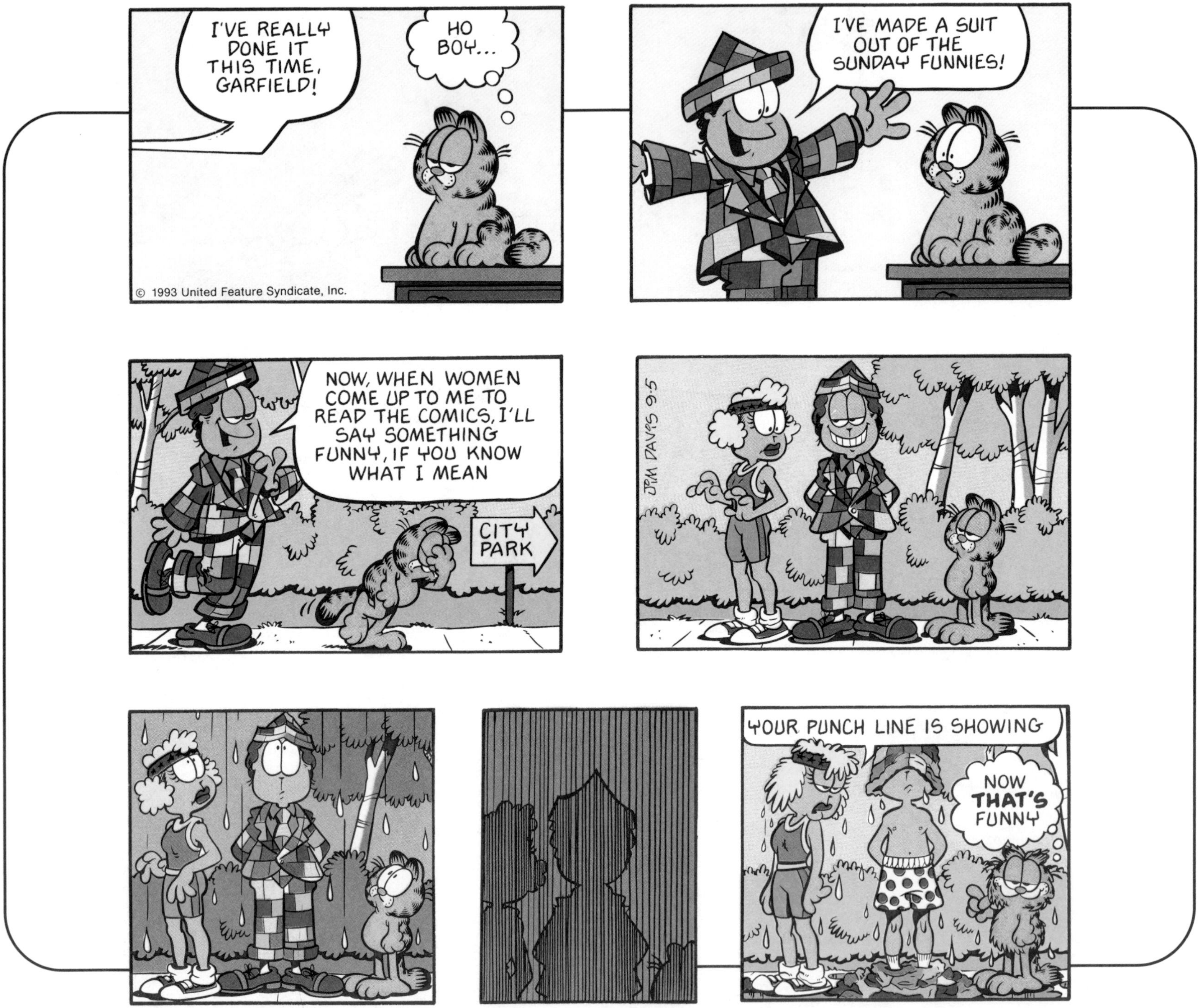
I'VE REALLY DONE IT THIS TIME, GARFIELD!
HO BOY...
© 1993 United Feature Syndicate, Inc.
I'VE MADE A SUIT OUT OF THE SUNDAY FUNNIES!
NOW, WHEN WOMEN COME UP TO ME TO READ THE COMICS, I'LL SAY SOMETHING FUNNY, IF YOU KNOW WHAT I MEAN
CITY PARK
JPM DAVPS 9-5
YOUR PUNCH LINE IS SHOWING
NOW THAT'S FUNNY

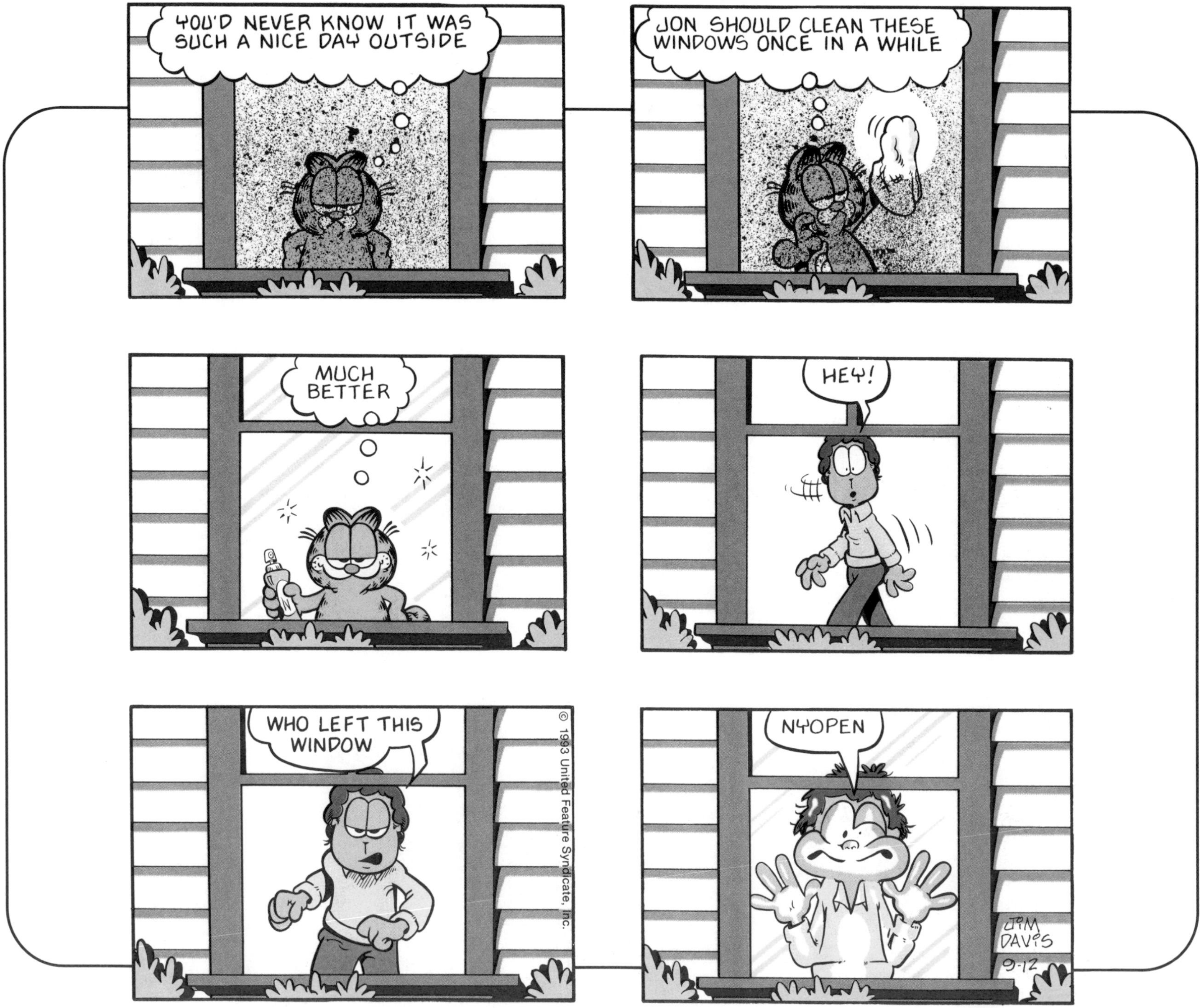
YOU'D NEVER KNOW IT WAS SUCH A NICE DAY OUTSIDE
JON SHOULD CLEAN THESE WINDOWS ONCE IN A WHILE
MUCH BETTER
HEY!
WHO LEFT THIS WINDOW
NYOPEN
© 1993 United Feature Syndicate, Inc.
JIM DAVIS 9-12

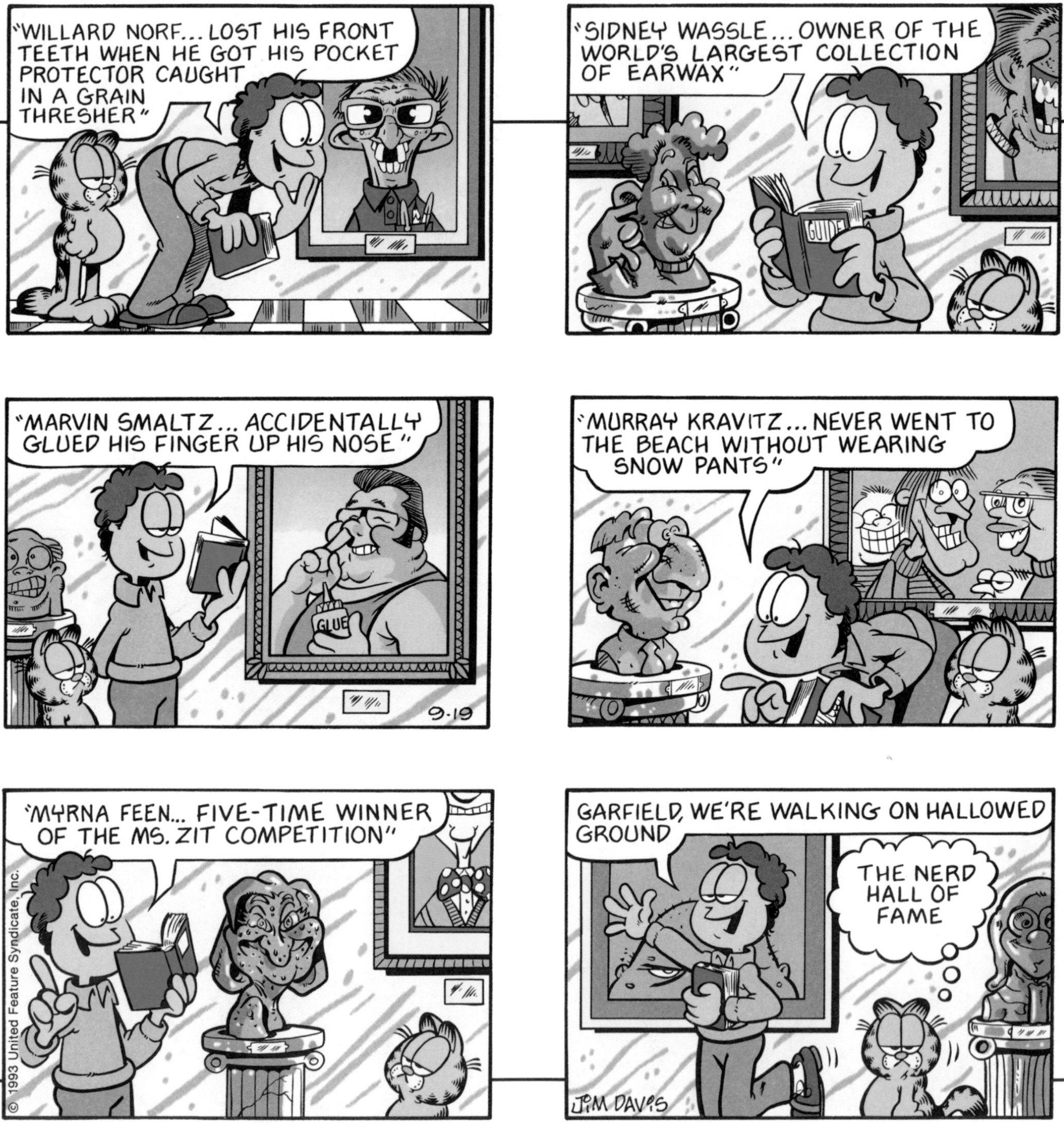
"WILLARD NORF... LOST HIS FRONT TEETH WHEN HE GOT HIS POCKET PROTECTOR CAUGHT IN A GRAIN THRESHER"
"SIDNEY WASSLE... OWNER OF THE WORLD'S LARGEST COLLECTION OF EARWAX"
GUIDE
"MARVIN SMALTZ... ACCIDENTALLY GLUED HIS FINGER UP HIS NOSE"
GLUE
9-19
"MURRAY KRAVITZ... NEVER WENT TO THE BEACH WITHOUT WEARING SNOW PANTS"
"MYRNA FEEN... FIVE-TIME WINNER OF THE MS. ZIT COMPETITION"
GARFIELD, WE'RE WALKING ON HALLOWED GROUND
THE NERD HALL OF FAME
JIM DAVIS

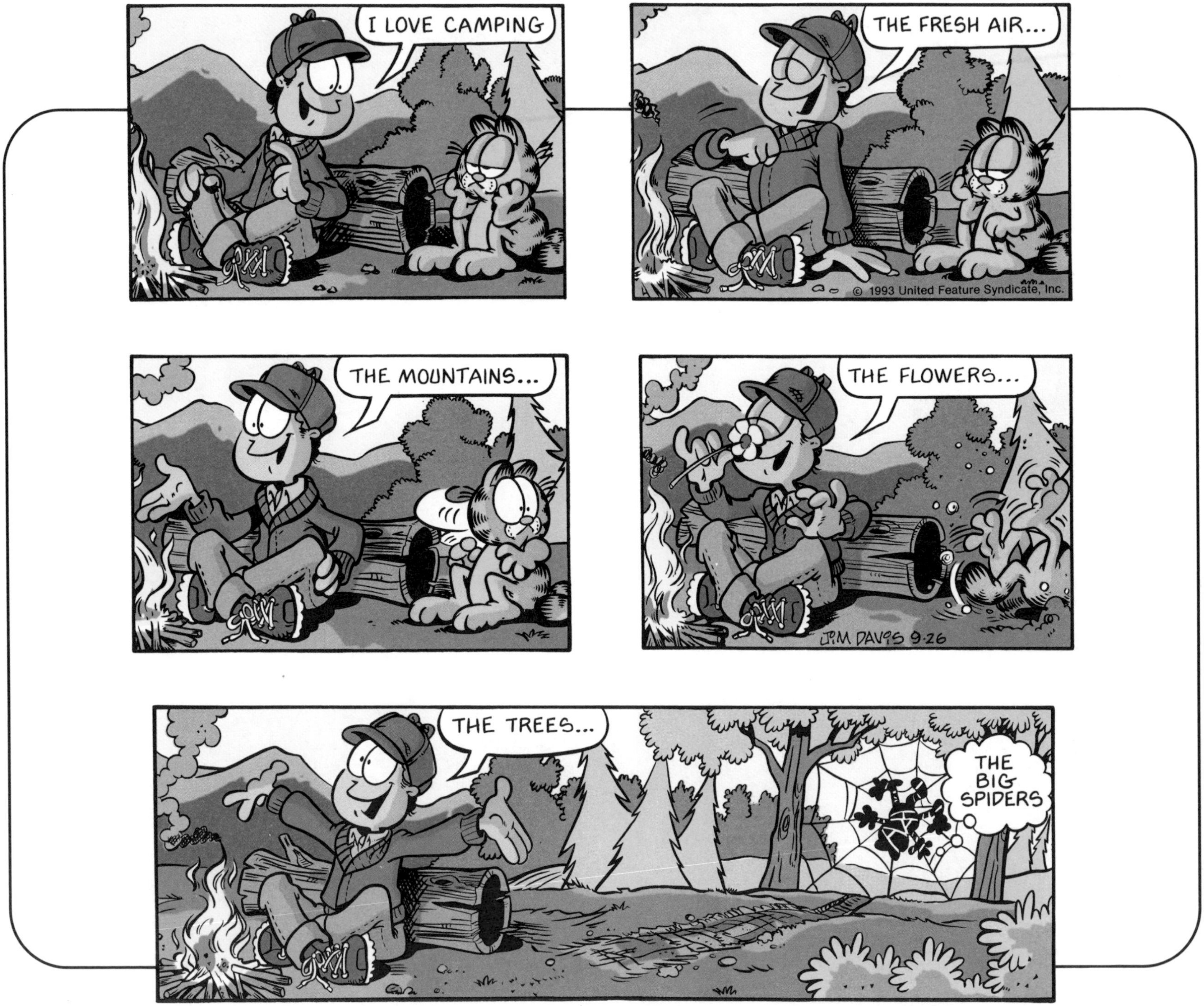
I LOVE CAMPING
THE FRESH AIR...
© 1993 United Feature Syndicate, Inc.
THE MOUNTAINS...
THE FLOWERS...
JIM DAVIS 9·26
THE TREES...
THE BIG SPIDERS

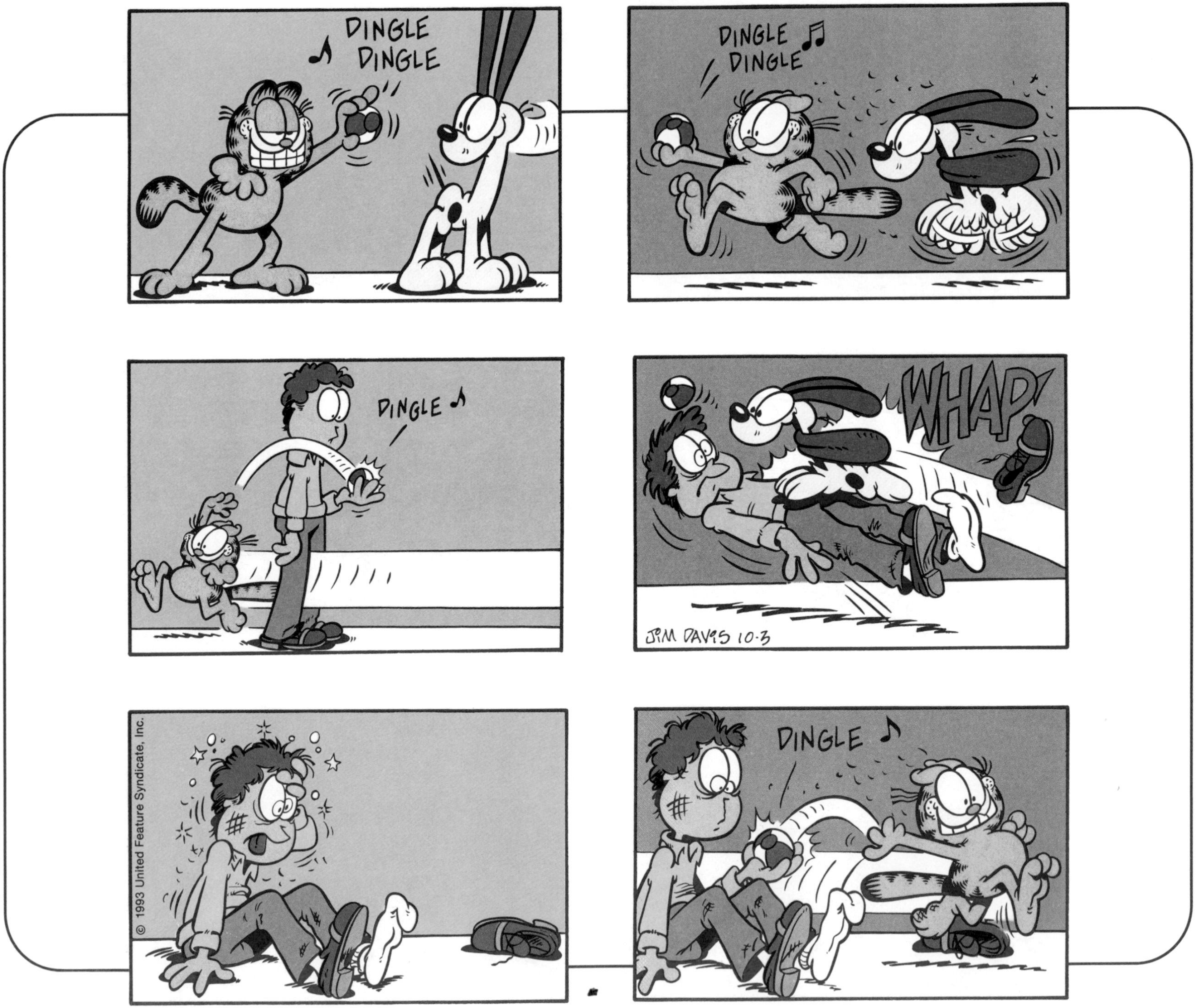
DINGLE DINGLE
DINGLE DINGLE
DINGLE
WHAP!
JIM DAVIS 10-3
© 1993 United Feature Syndicate, Inc.
DINGLE

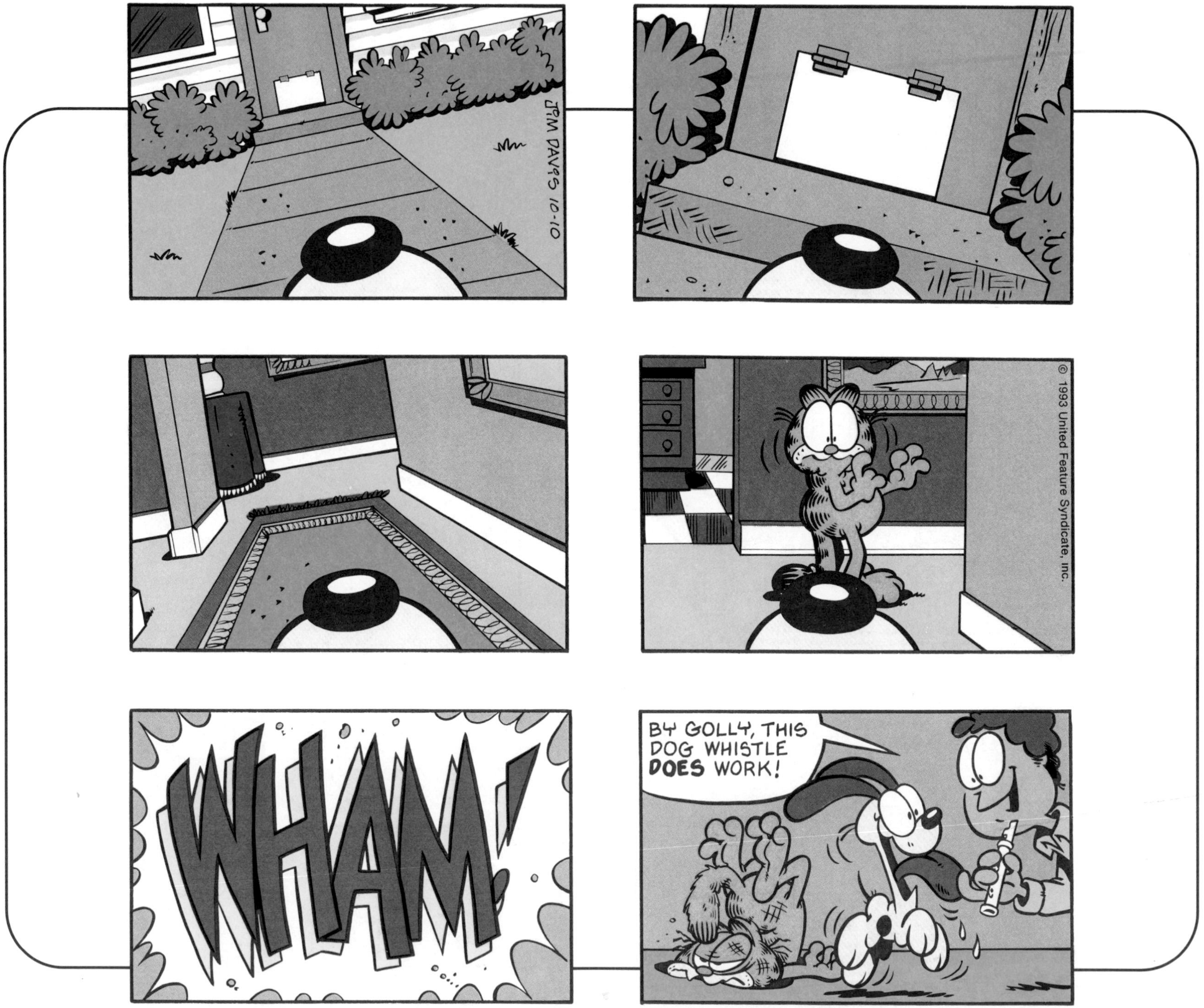
JIM DAVIS 10-10
© 1993 United Feature Syndicate, Inc.
WHAM!
BY GOLLY, THIS DOG WHISTLE DOES WORK!

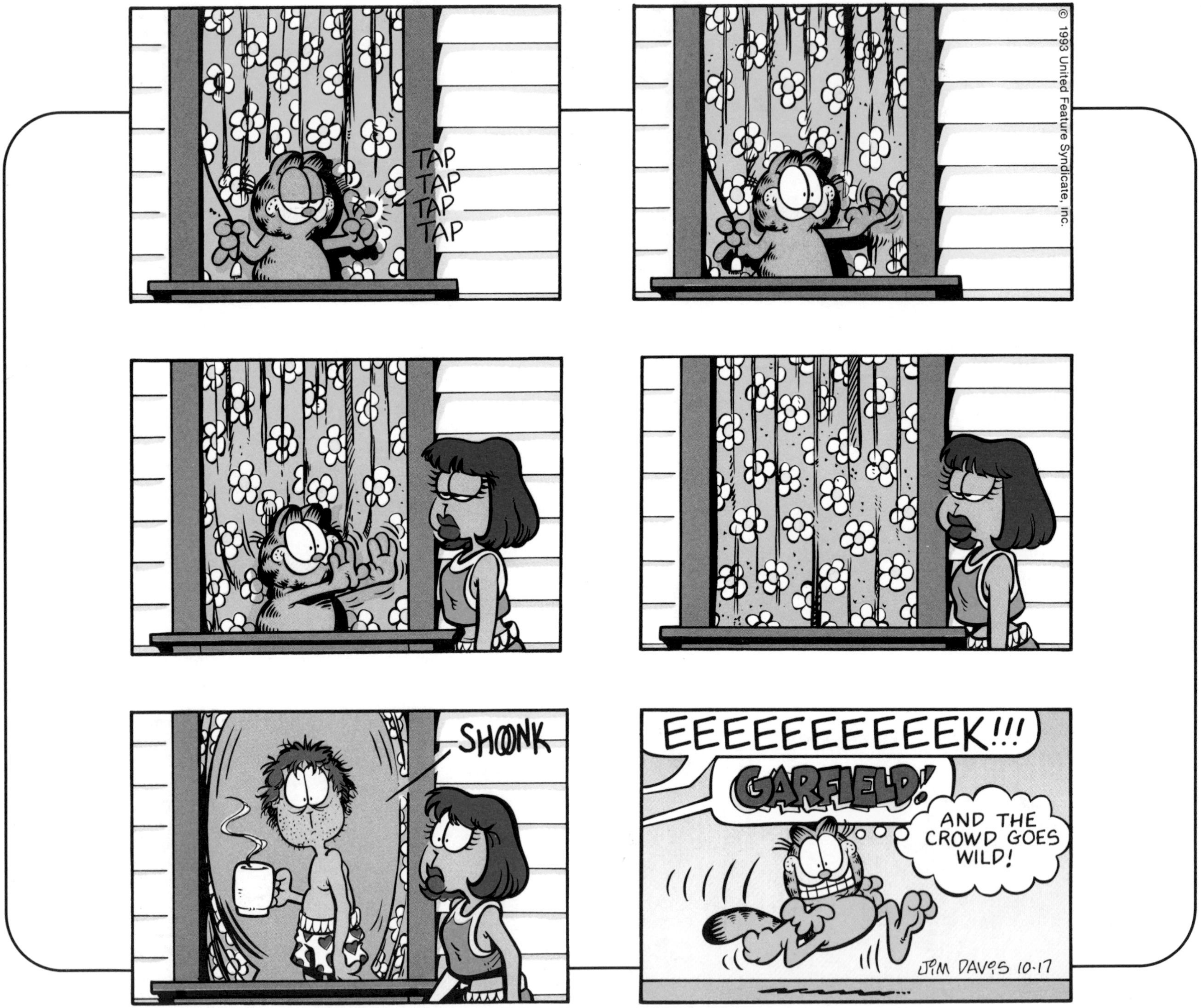
TAP
TAP
TAP
TAP
© 1993 United Feature Syndicate, Inc.
SHOONK
EEEEEEEEEEEK!!!
GARFIELD!
AND THE CROWD GOES WILD!
JIM DAVIS 10-17

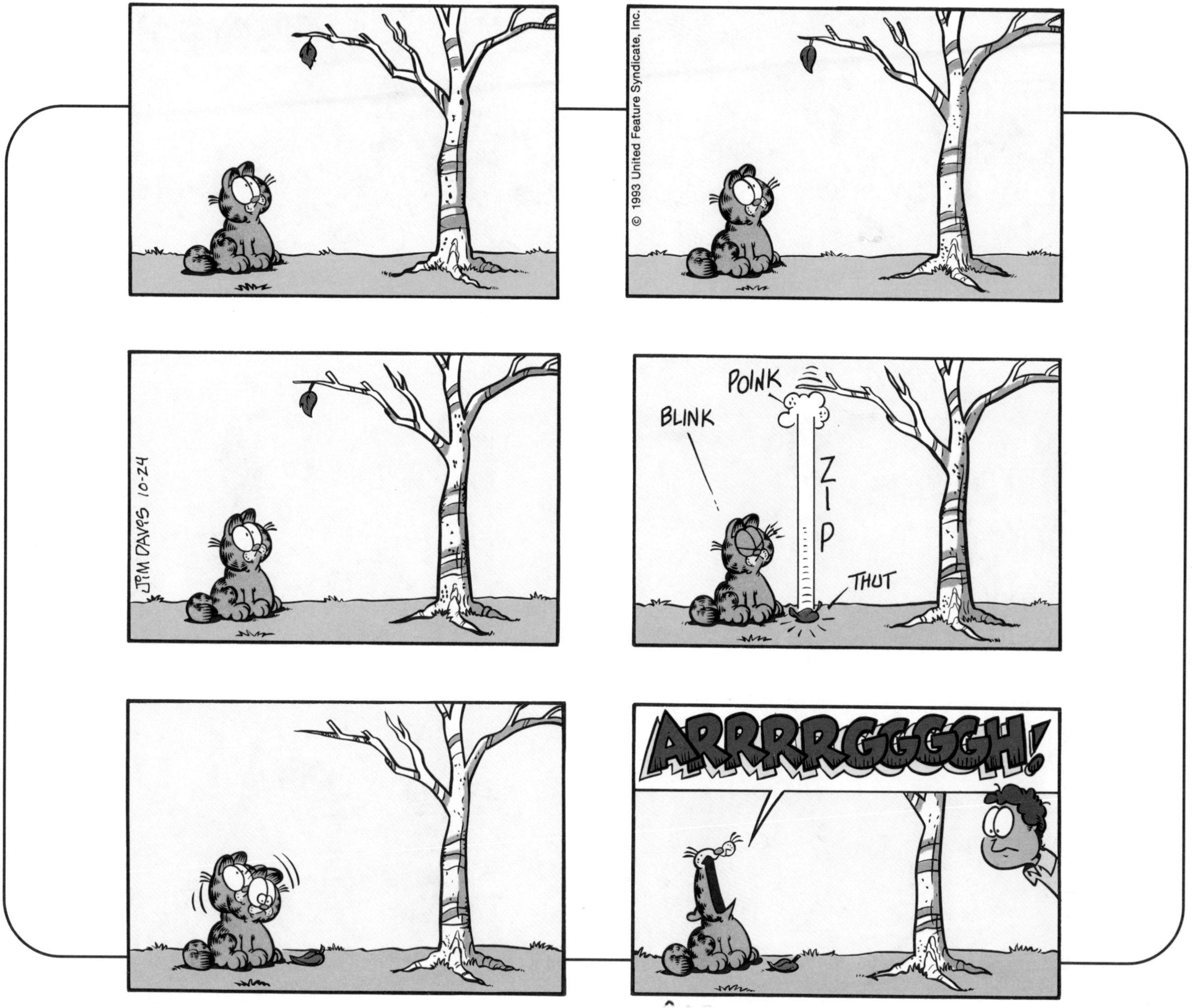
© 1993 United Feature Syndicate, Inc.
JPM DAVPS 10-24
BLINK
POINK
ZIP
THUT
ARRRRGGGGH!

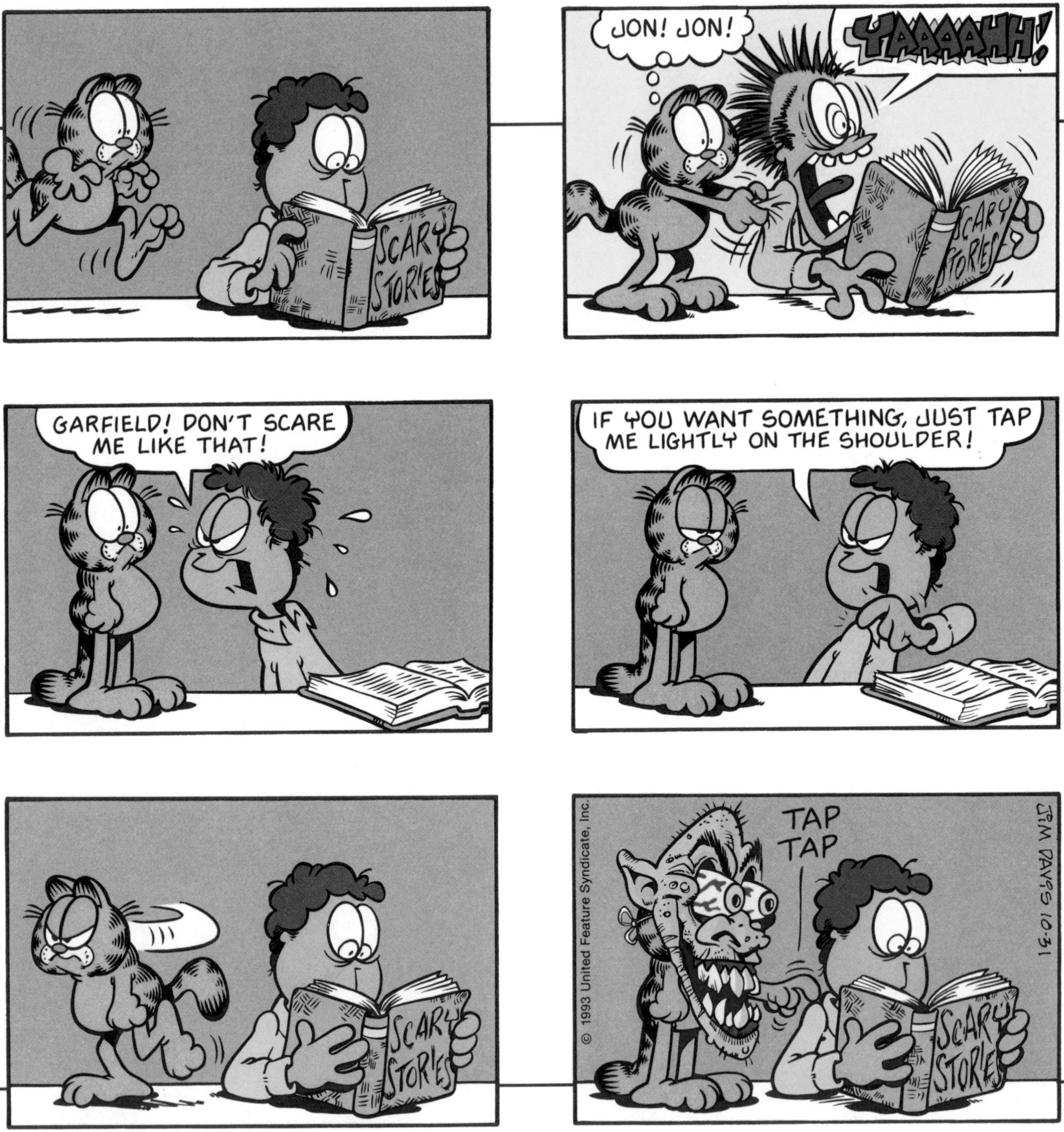
JON! JON!
YAAAAHH!
GARFIELD! DON'T SCARE ME LIKE THAT!
IF YOU WANT SOMETHING, JUST TAP ME LIGHTLY ON THE SHOULDER!
TAP TAP
SCARY STORIES
JIM DAVIS 10-31
© 1993 United Feature Syndicate, Inc.

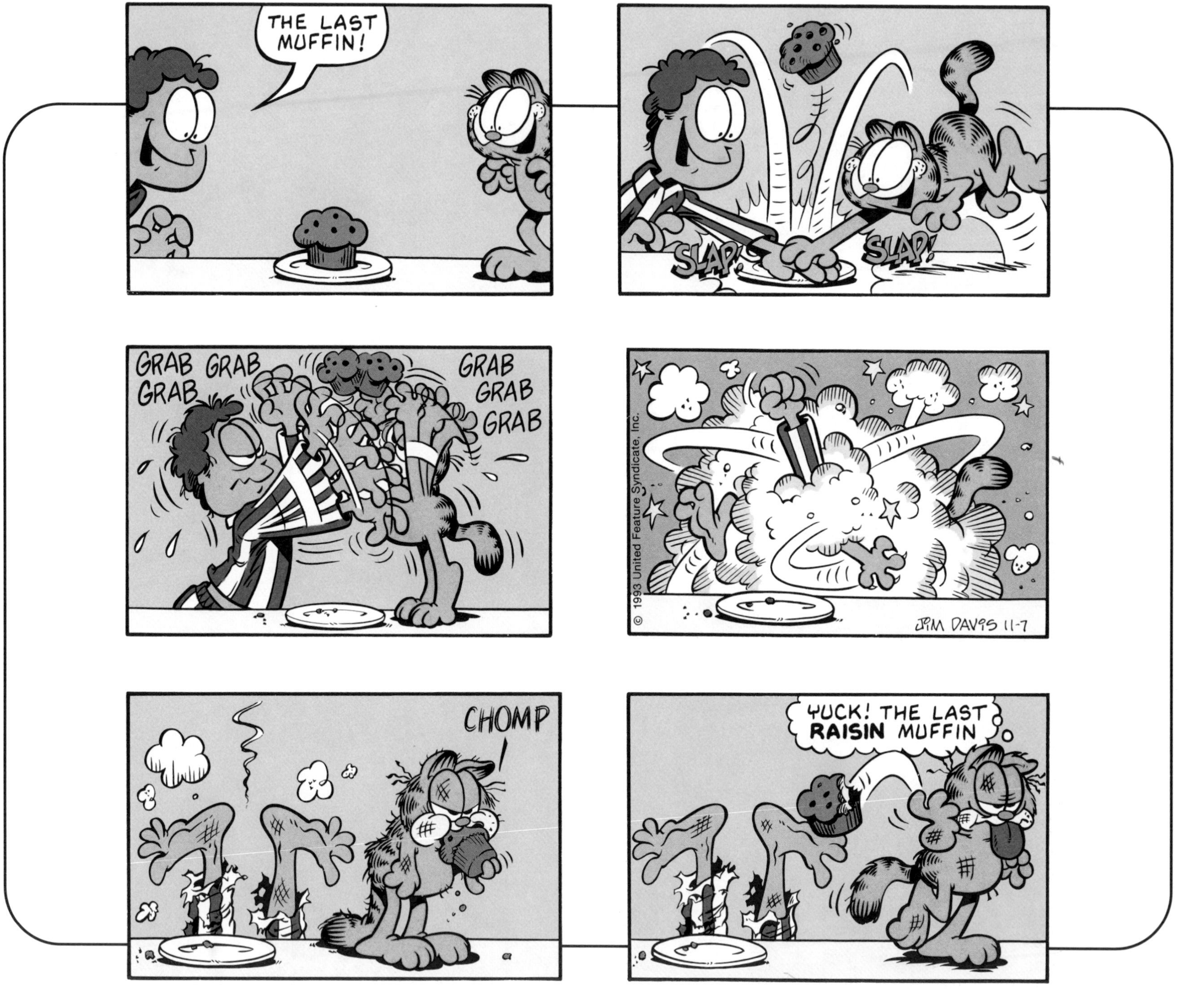
THE LAST MUFFIN!
SLAP!
SLAP!
GRAB GRAB GRAB
GRAB GRAB GRAB
© 1993 United Feature Syndicate, Inc.
JIM DAVIS 11-7
CHOMP
YUCK! THE LAST RAISIN MUFFIN

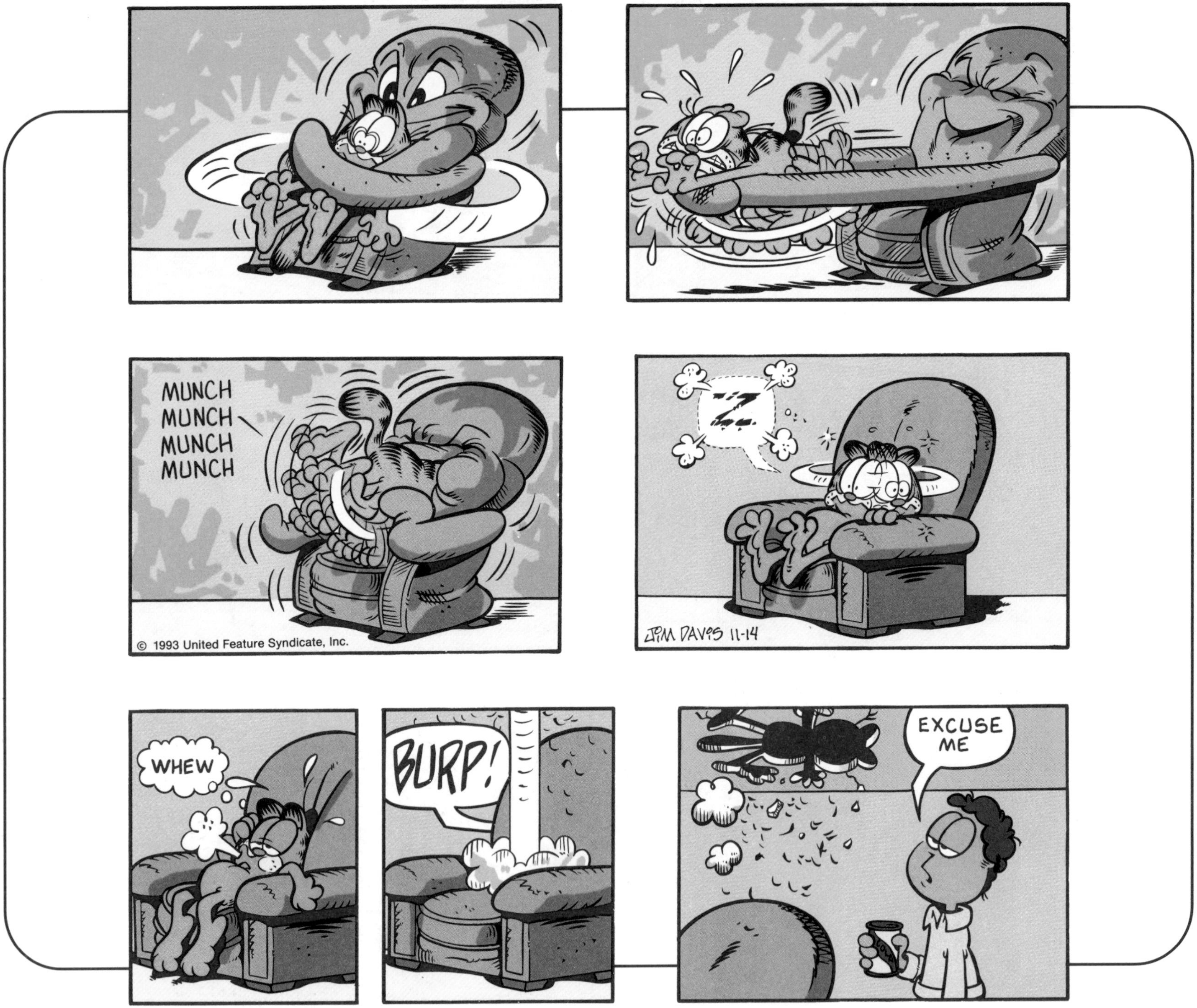
MUNCH
MUNCH
MUNCH
MUNCH
© 1993 United Feature Syndicate, Inc.
Z
JIM DAVIS 11-14
WHEW
BURP!
EXCUSE ME

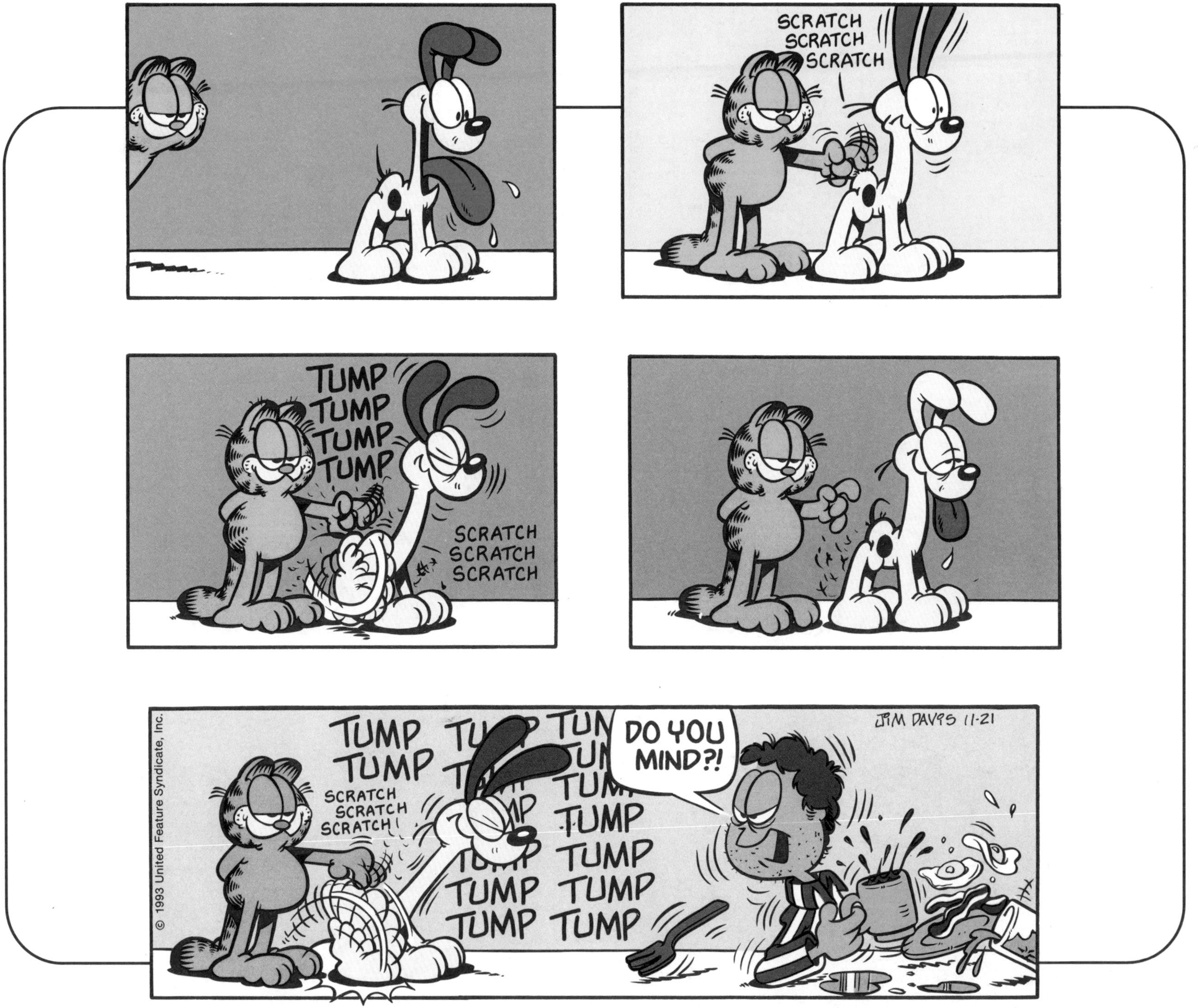
SCRATCH
SCRATCH
SCRATCH
TUMP
TUMP
TUMP
TUMP
SCRATCH
SCRATCH
SCRATCH
TUMP
TUMP
SCRATCH
SCRATCH
SCRATCH
TUMP
TUMP
TUMP
TUMP
TUMP
TUMP
TUMP
DO YOU MIND?!
JIM DAVIS 11-21
© 1993 United Feature Syndicate, Inc.

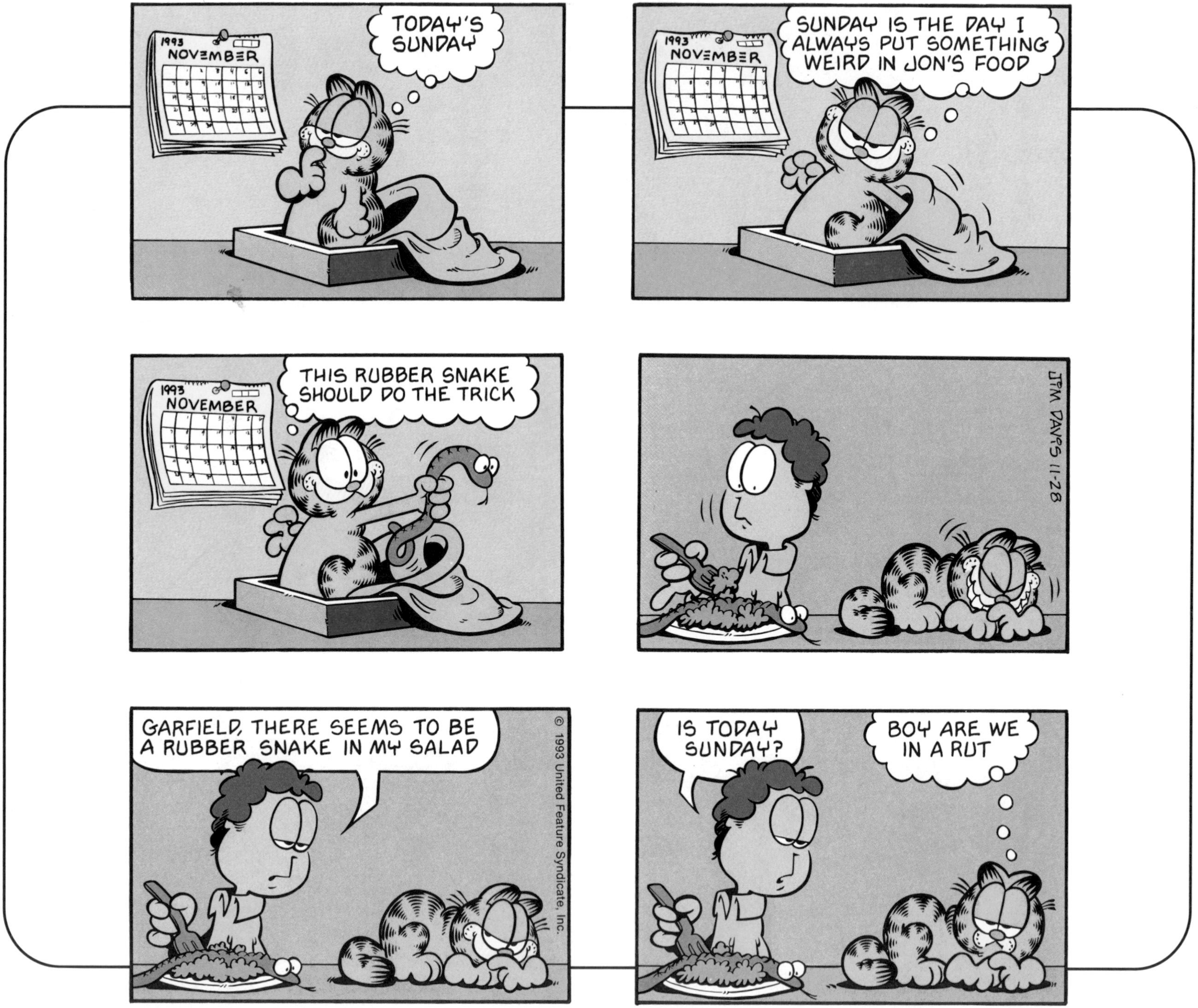
TODAY'S SUNDAY
1993
NOVEMBER
SUNDAY IS THE DAY I ALWAYS PUT SOMETHING WEIRD IN JON'S FOOD
THIS RUBBER SNAKE SHOULD DO THE TRICK
JIM DAVIS 11-28
GARFIELD, THERE SEEMS TO BE A RUBBER SNAKE IN MY SALAD
© 1993 United Feature Syndicate, Inc.
IS TODAY SUNDAY?
BOY ARE WE IN A RUT

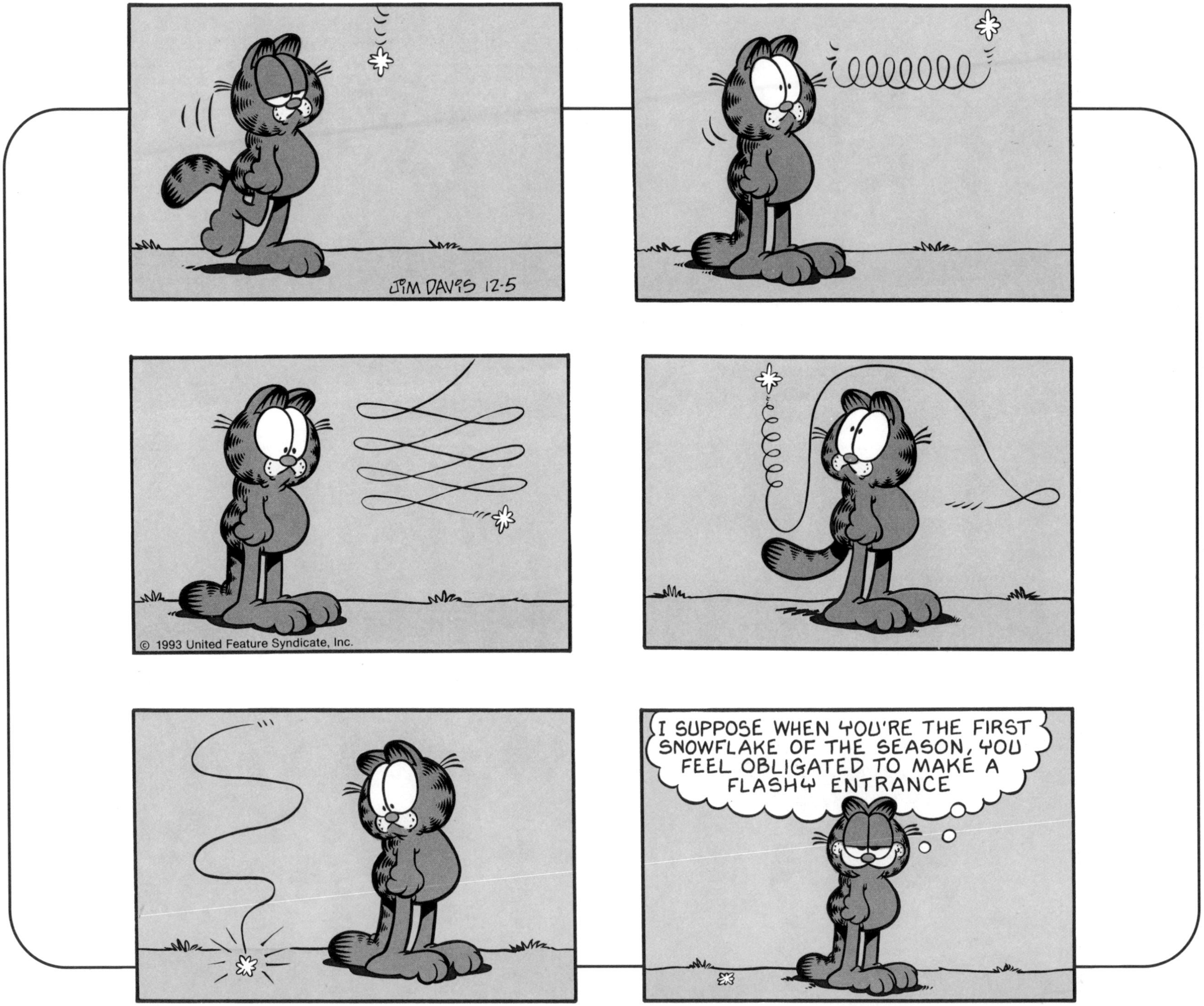
JIM DAVIS 12-5
© 1993 United Feature Syndicate, Inc.
I SUPPOSE WHEN YOU'RE THE FIRST SNOWFLAKE OF THE SEASON, YOU FEEL OBLIGATED TO MAKE A FLASHY ENTRANCE

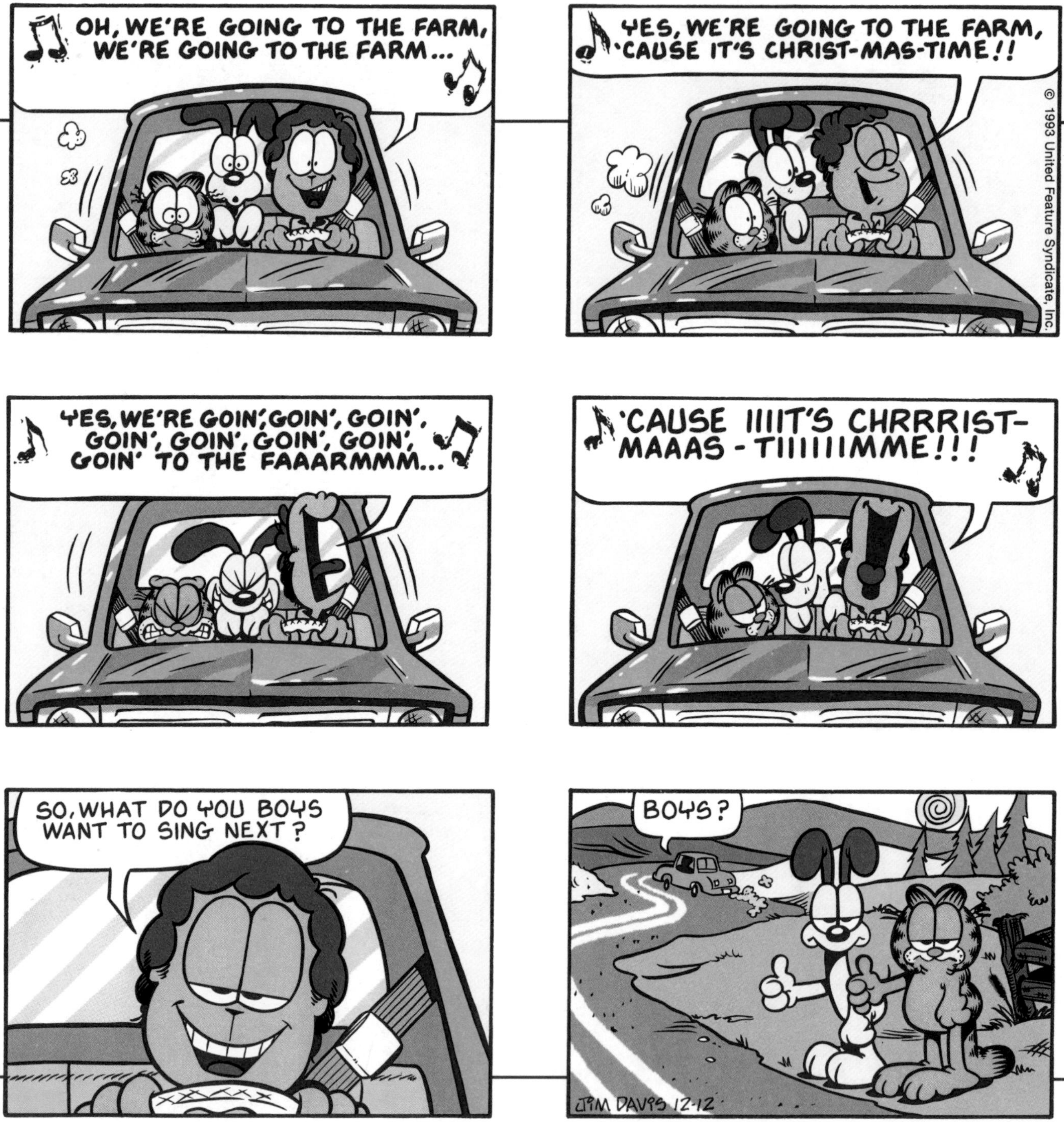
OH, WE'RE GOING TO THE FARM, WE'RE GOING TO THE FARM...
YES, WE'RE GOING TO THE FARM, 'CAUSE IT'S CHRIST-MAS-TIME!!
© 1993 United Feature Syndicate, Inc.
YES, WE'RE GOIN', GOIN', GOIN', GOIN', GOIN', GOIN', GOIN', GOIN' TO THE FAAARMMM...
'CAUSE IIIIT'S CHRRRIST-MAAAS-TIIIIIIIMME!!!
SO, WHAT DO YOU BOYS WANT TO SING NEXT?
BOYS?
JIM DAVIS 12-12

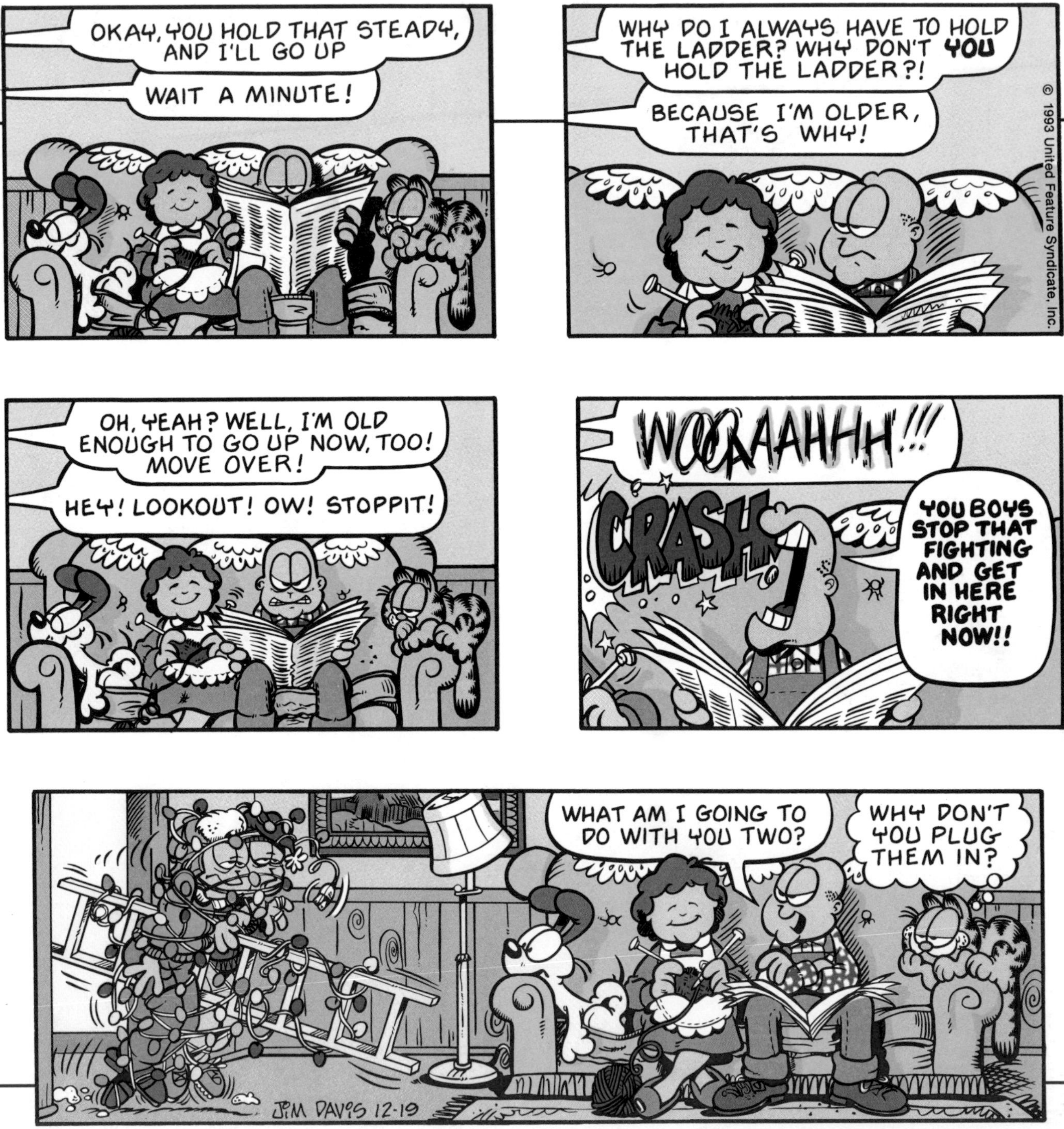
OKAY, YOU HOLD THAT STEADY, AND I'LL GO UP
WAIT A MINUTE!
WHY DO I ALWAYS HAVE TO HOLD THE LADDER? WHY DON'T YOU HOLD THE LADDER?!
BECAUSE I'M OLDER, THAT'S WHY!
© 1993 United Feature Syndicate, Inc.
OH, YEAH? WELL, I'M OLD ENOUGH TO GO UP NOW, TOO! MOVE OVER!
HEY! LOOKOUT! OW! STOPPIT!
WOOAAAHHH!!!
CRASH
YOU BOYS STOP THAT FIGHTING AND GET IN HERE RIGHT NOW!!
WHAT AM I GOING TO DO WITH YOU TWO?
WHY DON'T YOU PLUG THEM IN?
JIM DAVIS 12-19

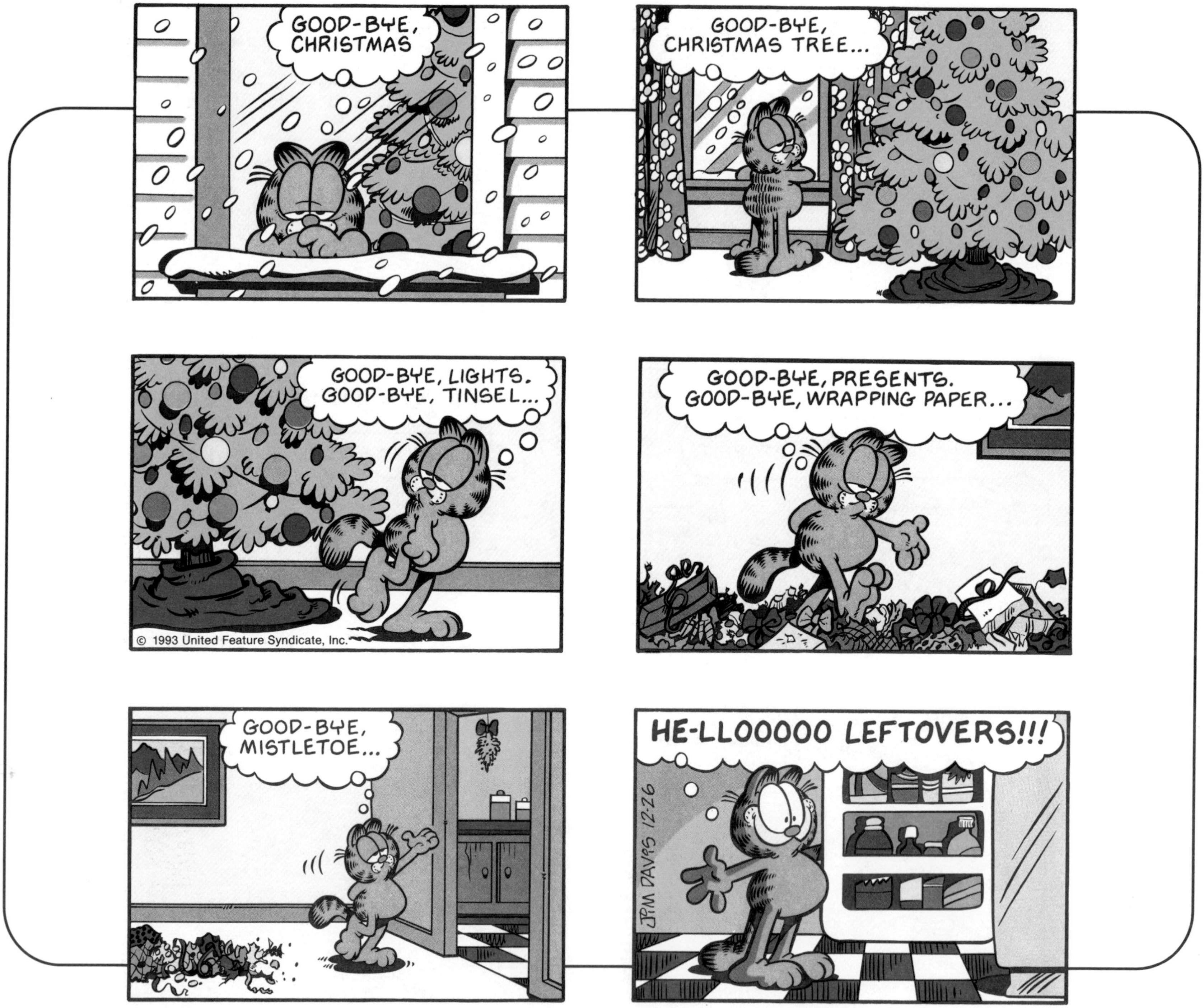
GOOD-BYE, CHRISTMAS
GOOD-BYE, CHRISTMAS TREE...
GOOD-BYE, LIGHTS. GOOD-BYE, TINSEL...
GOOD-BYE, PRESENTS. GOOD-BYE, WRAPPING PAPER...
GOOD-BYE, MISTLETOE...
HE-LLOOOOO LEFTOVERS!!!
JPM DAVPS 12-26
© 1993 United Feature Syndicate, Inc.

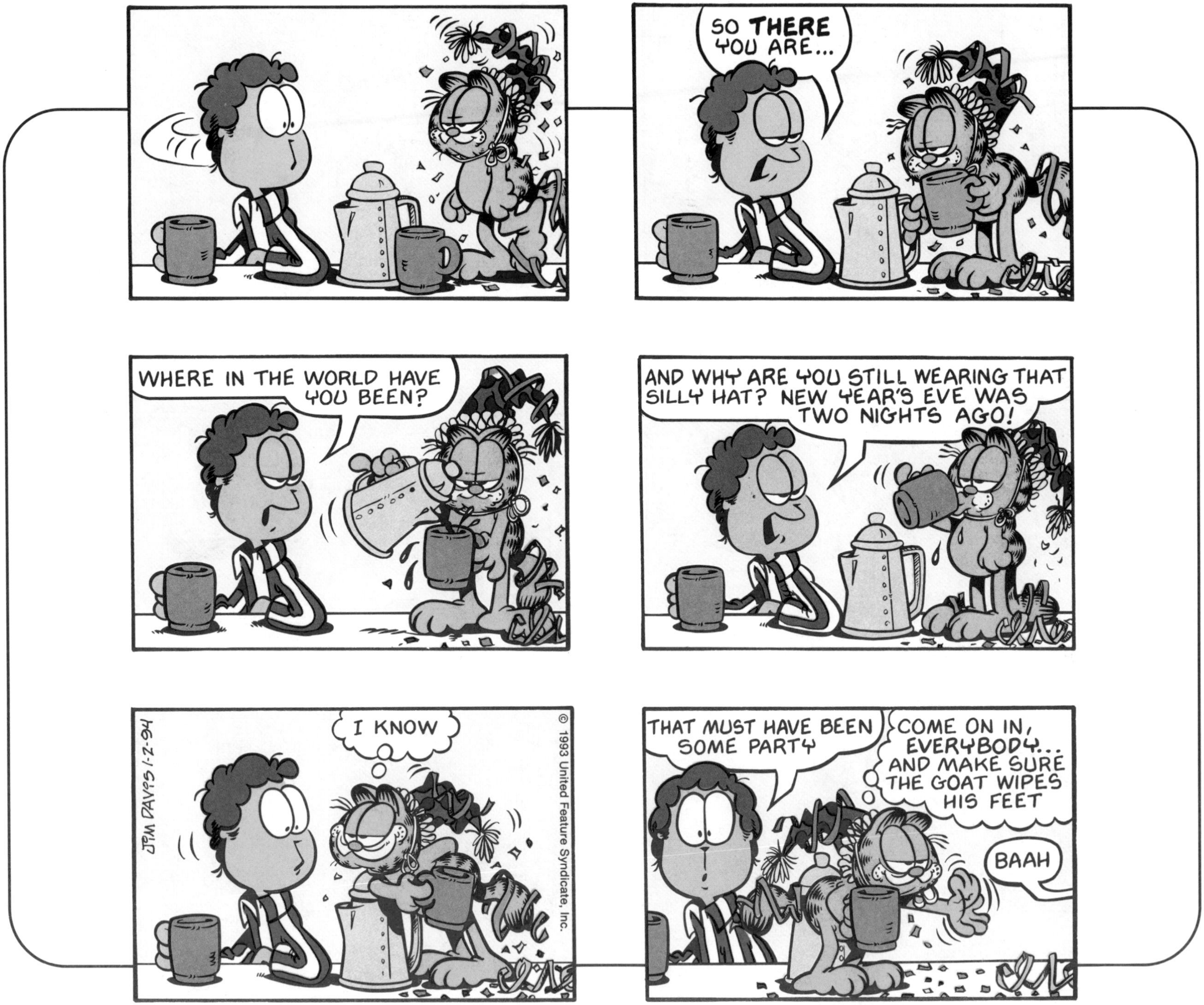
SO THERE YOU ARE...
WHERE IN THE WORLD HAVE YOU BEEN?
AND WHY ARE YOU STILL WEARING THAT SILLY HAT? NEW YEAR'S EVE WAS TWO NIGHTS AGO!
JIM DAVIS 1-2-94
I KNOW
© 1993 United Feature Syndicate, Inc.
THAT MUST HAVE BEEN SOME PARTY
COME ON IN, EVERYBODY... AND MAKE SURE THE GOAT WIPES HIS FEET
BAAH

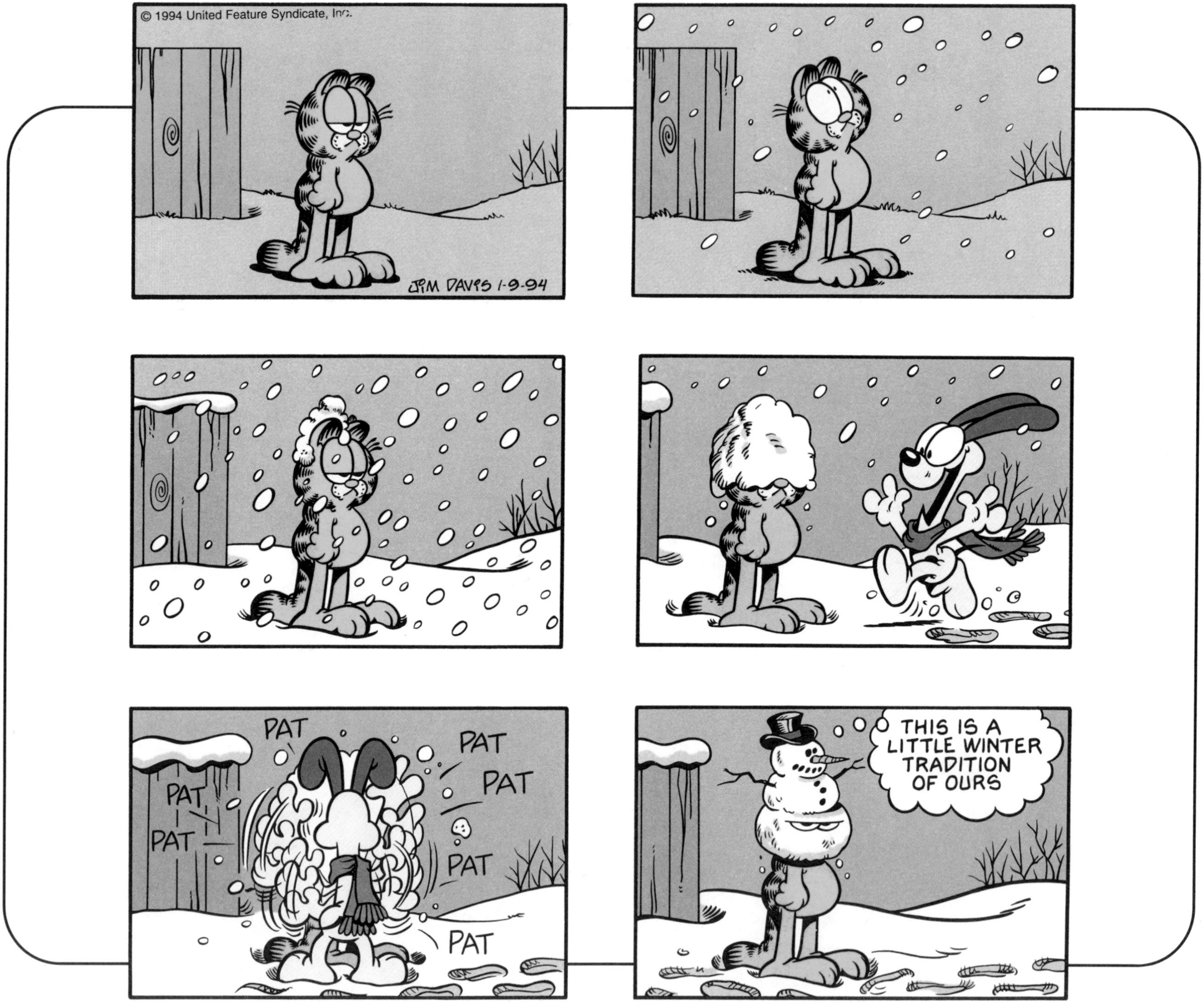
© 1994 United Feature Syndicate, Inc.
JIM DAVIS 1-9-94
PAT
PAT
PAT
PAT
PAT
PAT
PAT
THIS IS A LITTLE WINTER TRADITION OF OURS

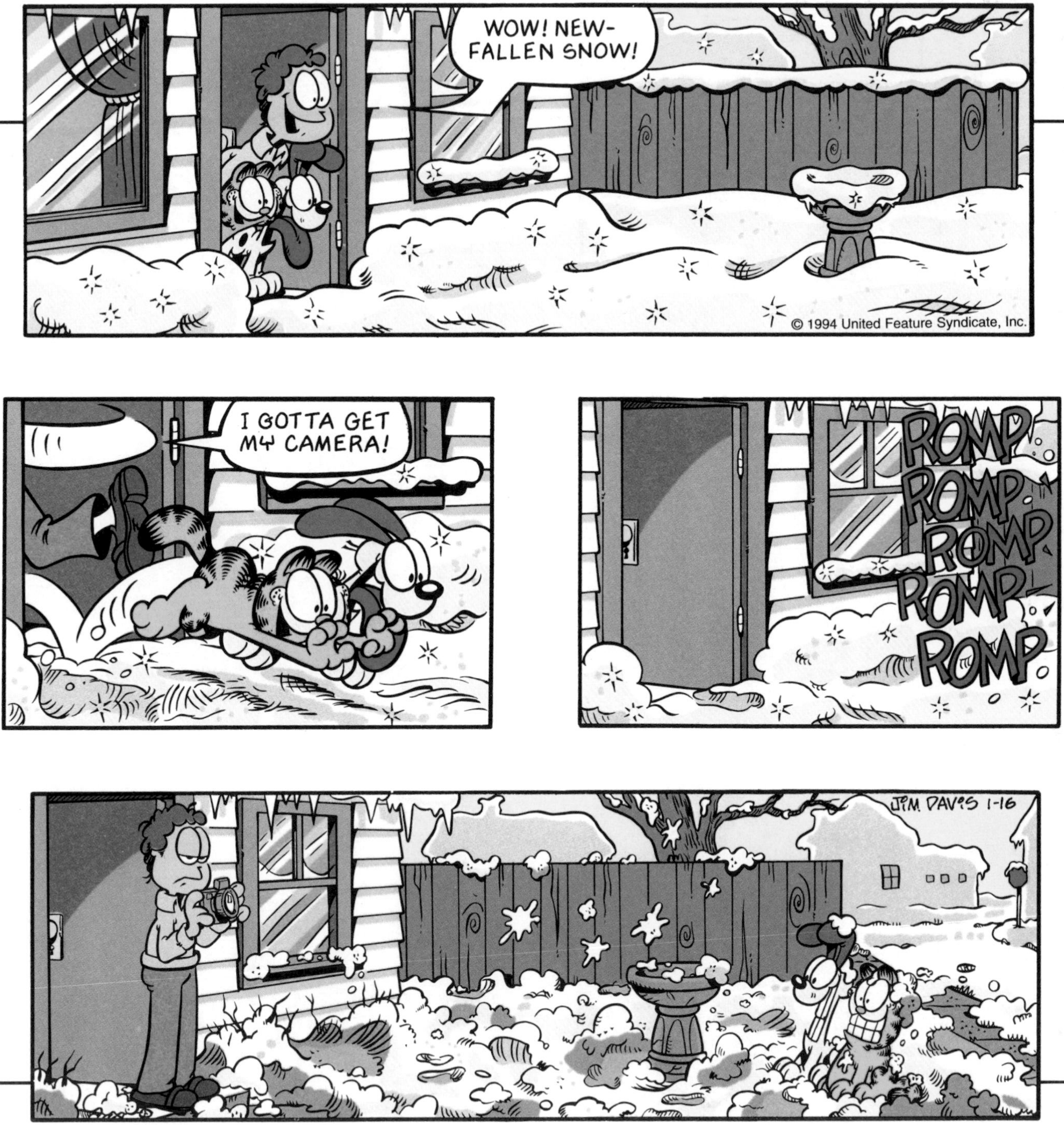
WOW! NEW-FALLEN SNOW!
© 1994 United Feature Syndicate, Inc.
I GOTTA GET MY CAMERA!
ROMP ROMP ROMP ROMP ROMP
JIM DAVIS 1-16

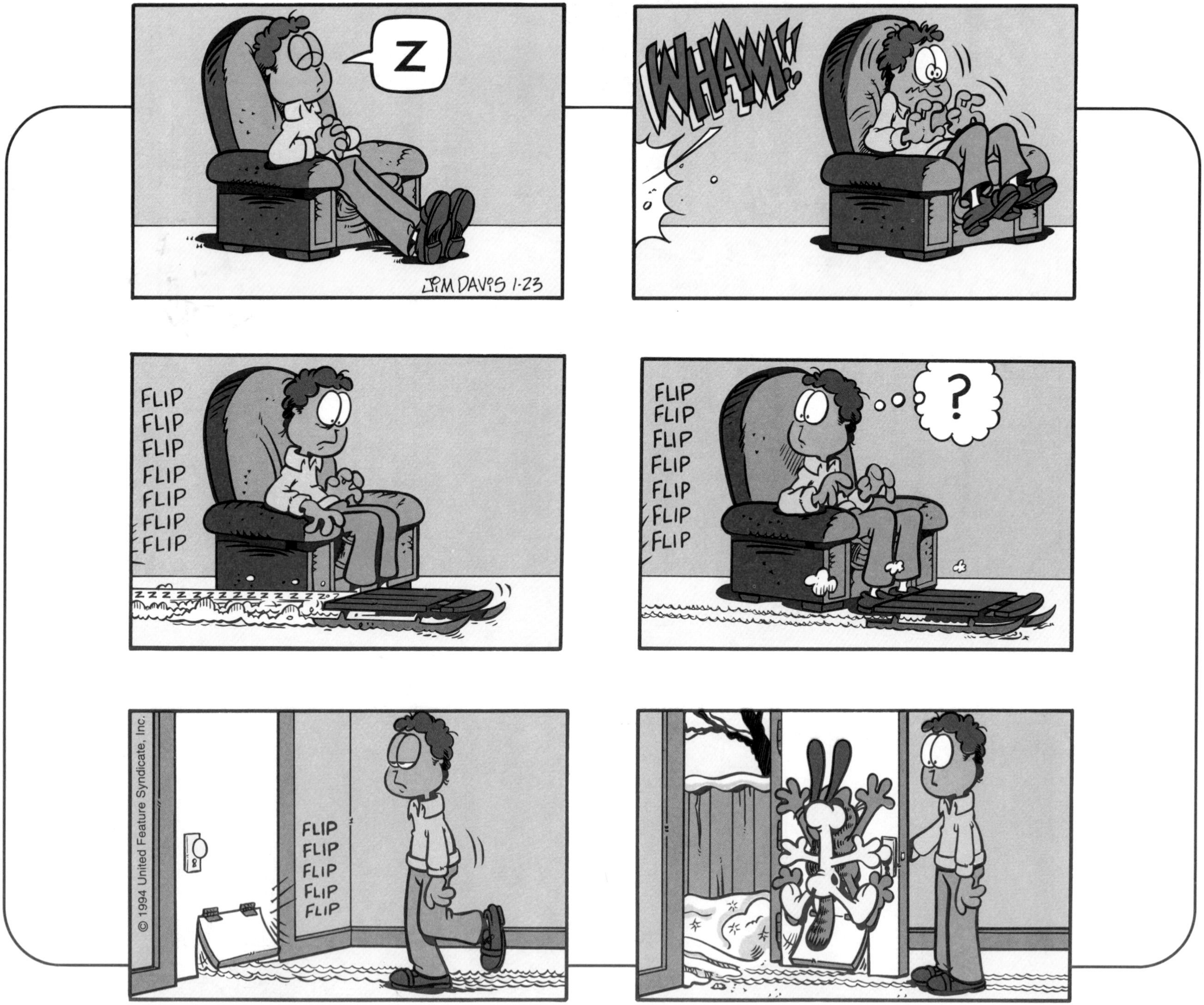
Z
JIM DAVIS 1-23
WHAM!!
FLIP
FLIP
FLIP
FLIP
FLIP
FLIP
FLIP
FLIP
FLIP
FLIP
FLIP
FLIP
FLIP
FLIP
?
© 1994 United Feature Syndicate, Inc.
FLIP
FLIP
FLIP
FLIP
FLIP

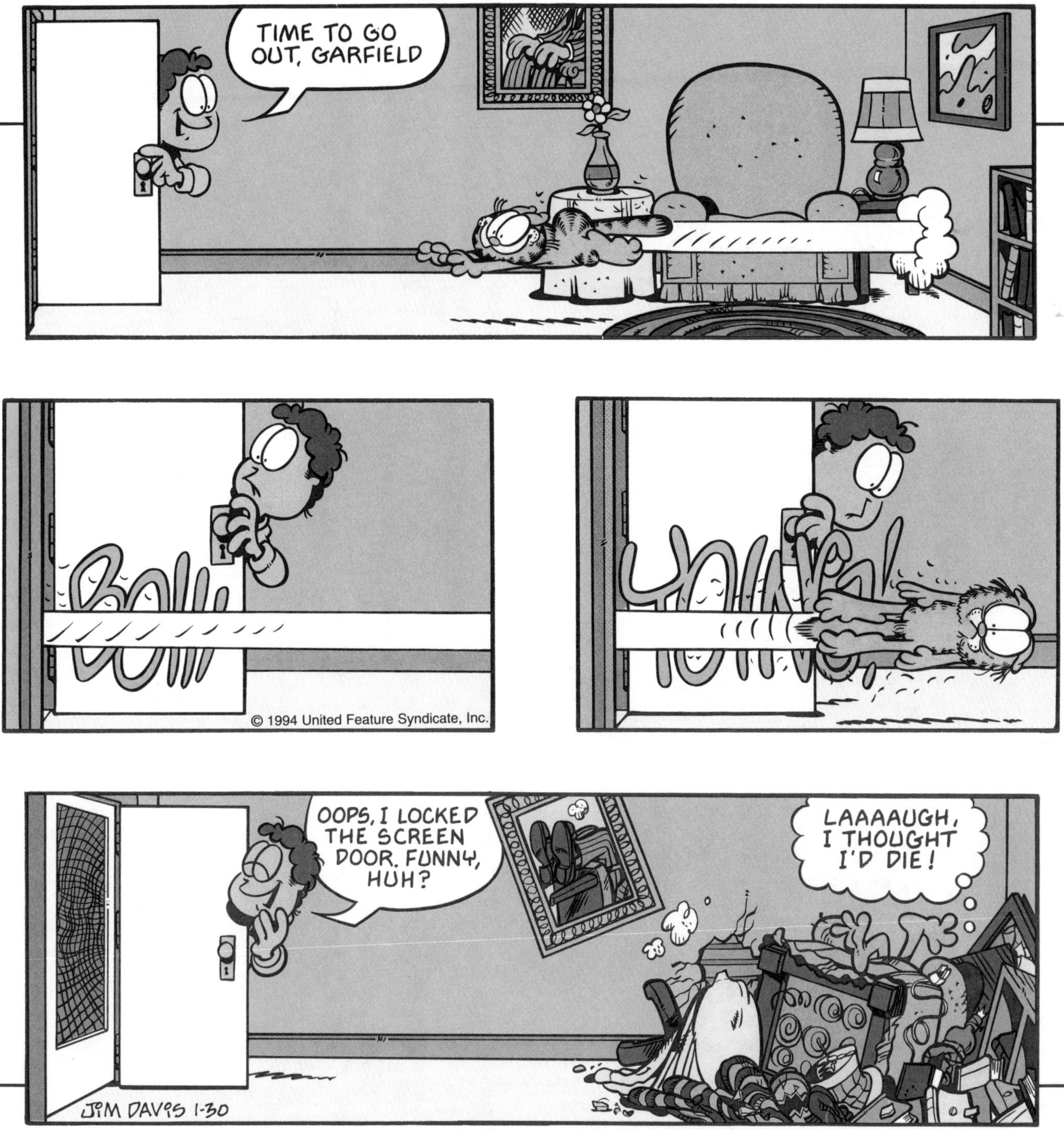
TIME TO GO OUT, GARFIELD
OOPS, I LOCKED THE SCREEN DOOR. FUNNY, HUH?
LAAAAUGH, I THOUGHT I'D DIE!
JIM DAVIS 1-30

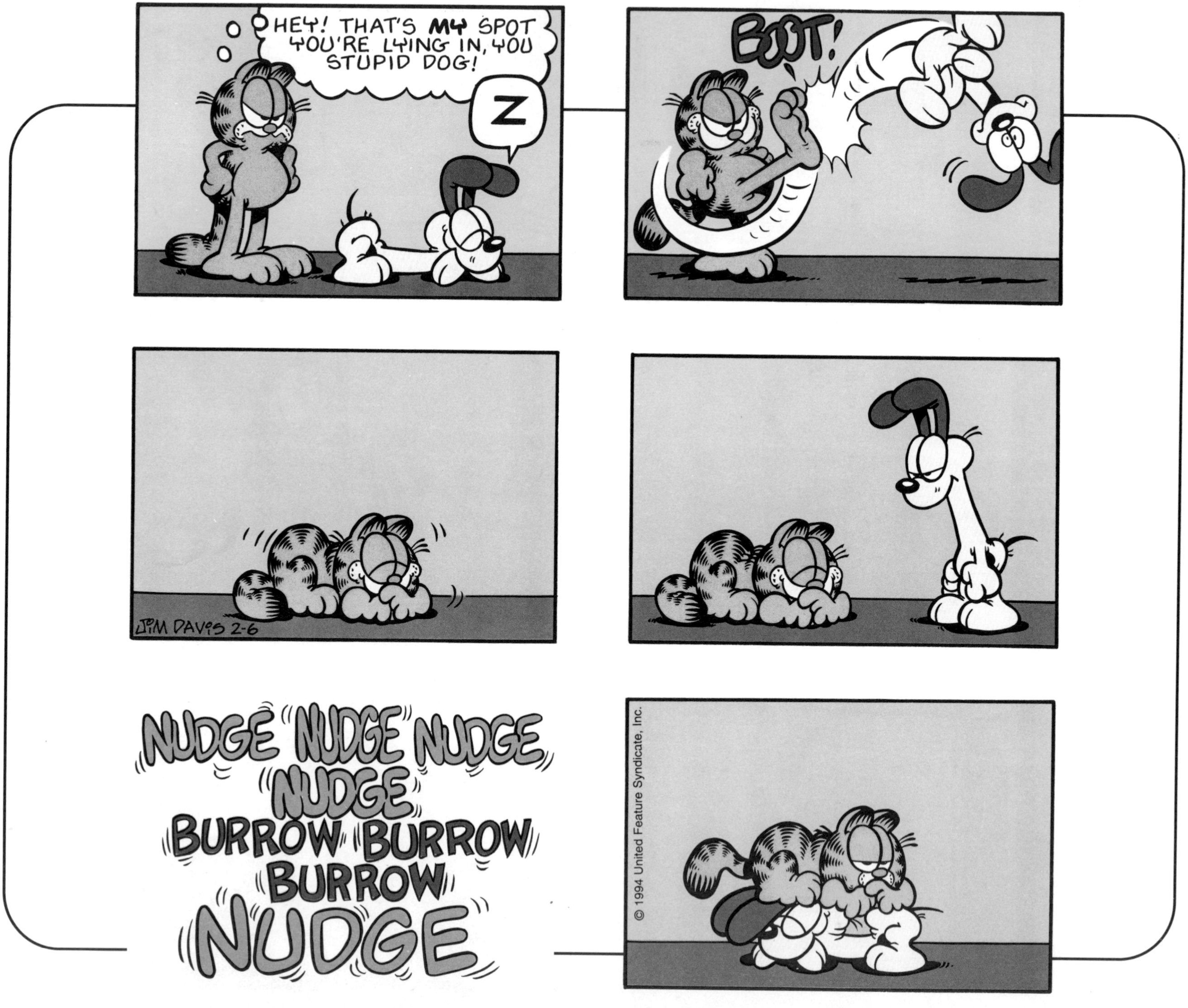
HEY! THAT'S MY SPOT YOU'RE LYING IN, YOU STUPID DOG!
Z
BOOT!
JIM DAVIS 2-6
NUDGE NUDGE NUDGE
NUDGE
BURROW BURROW
BURROW
NUDGE
© 1994 United Feature Syndicate, Inc.

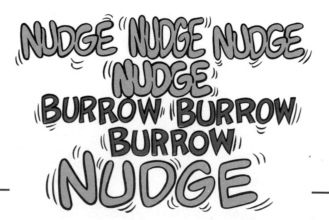

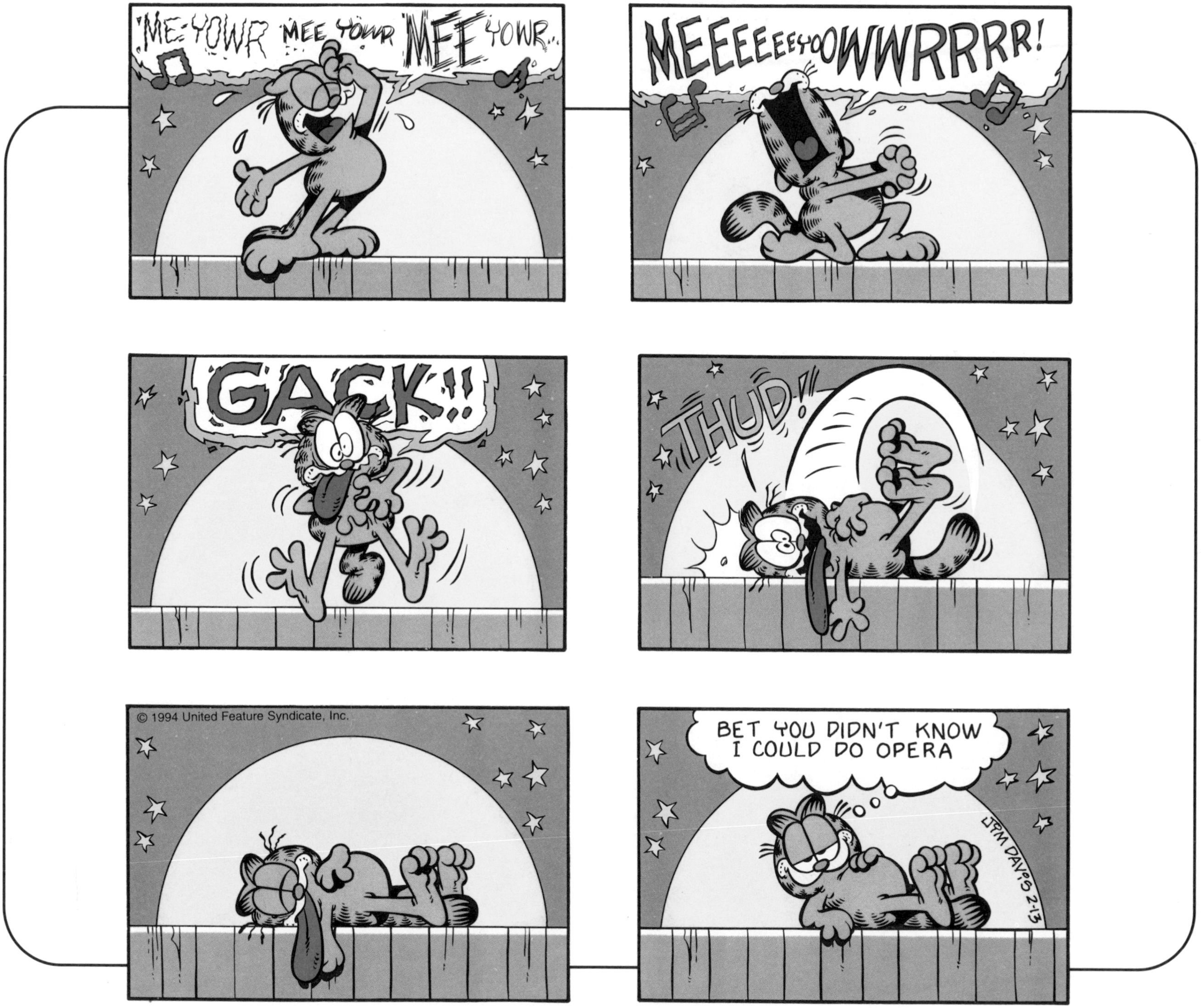
ME-YOWR MEE YOWR MEE YOWR..
MEEEEEEEYOOWWRRRRR!
GACK!!
THUD!
© 1994 United Feature Syndicate, Inc.
BET YOU DIDN'T KNOW I COULD DO OPERA
JIM DAVIS 2-13

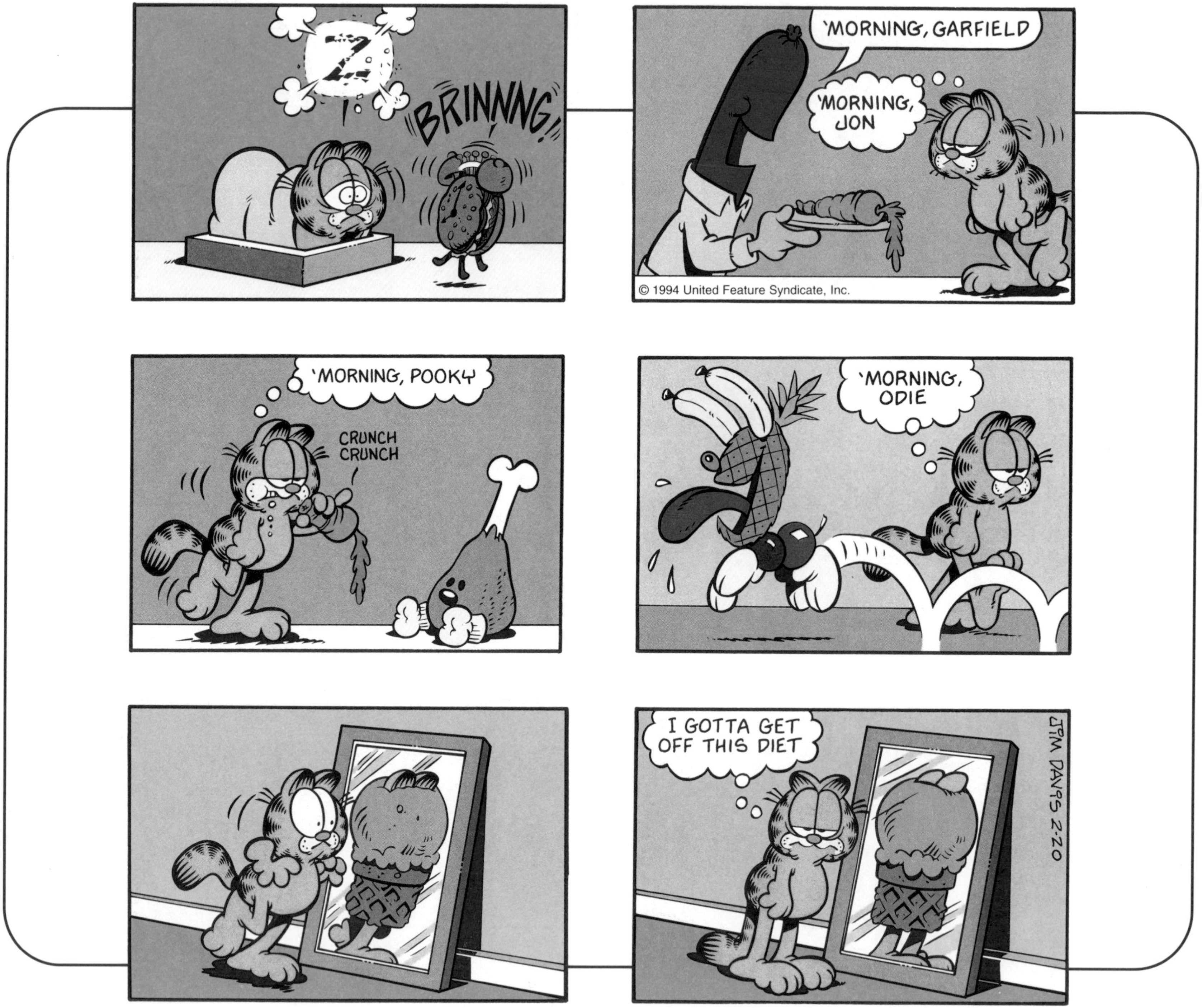
Z
BRINNNG!
'MORNING, GARFIELD
'MORNING, JON
© 1994 United Feature Syndicate, Inc.
'MORNING, POOKY
CRUNCH CRUNCH
'MORNING, ODIE
I GOTTA GET OFF THIS DIET
JIM DAVIS 2-20

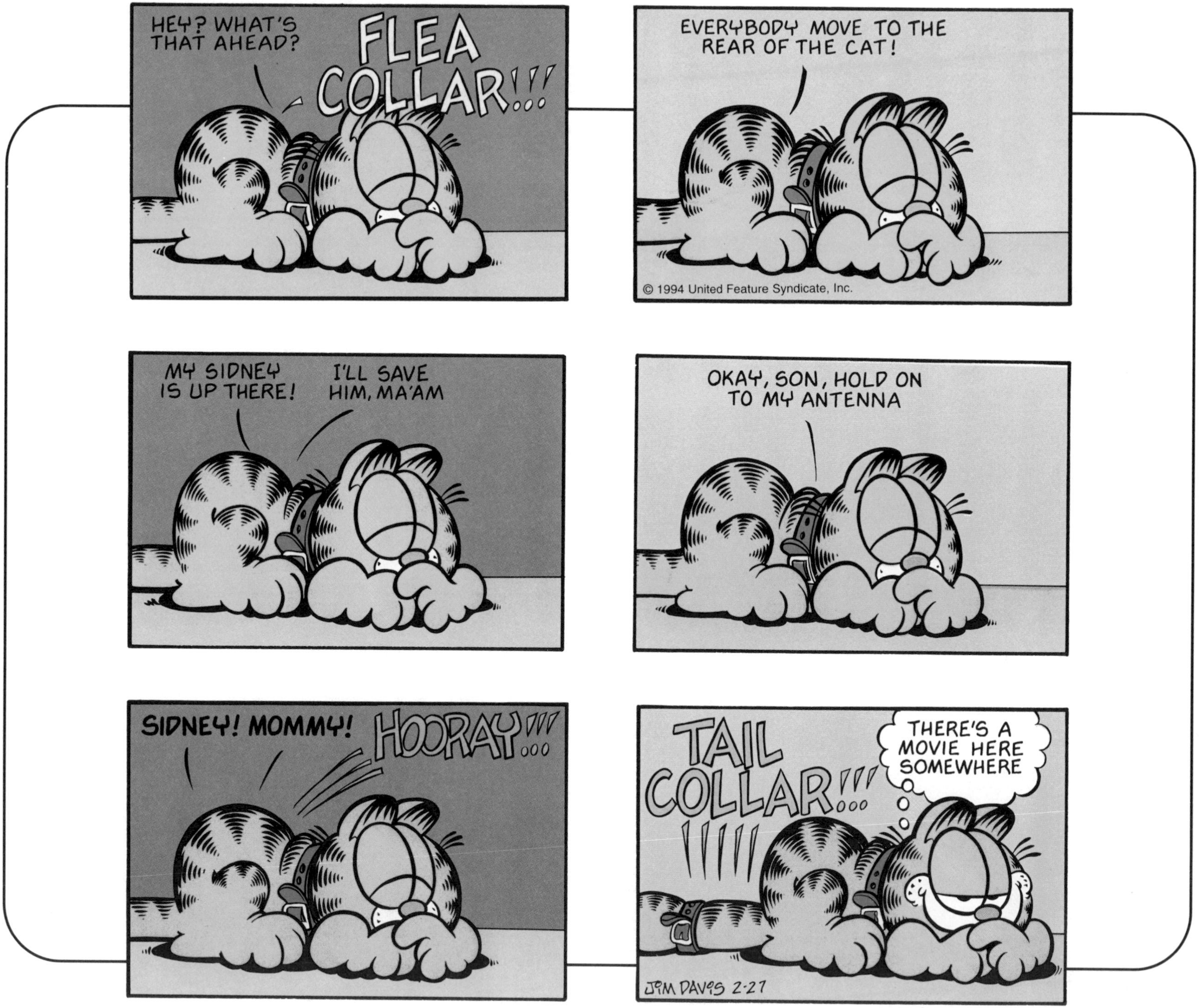
HEY? WHAT'S THAT AHEAD?
FLEA COLLAR!!!
EVERYBODY MOVE TO THE REAR OF THE CAT!
MY SIDNEY IS UP THERE!
I'LL SAVE HIM, MA'AM
OKAY, SON, HOLD ON TO MY ANTENNA
SIDNEY! MOMMY!
HOORAY!!!
TAIL COLLAR!!!
THERE'S A MOVIE HERE SOMEWHERE
JIM DAVIS 2-27

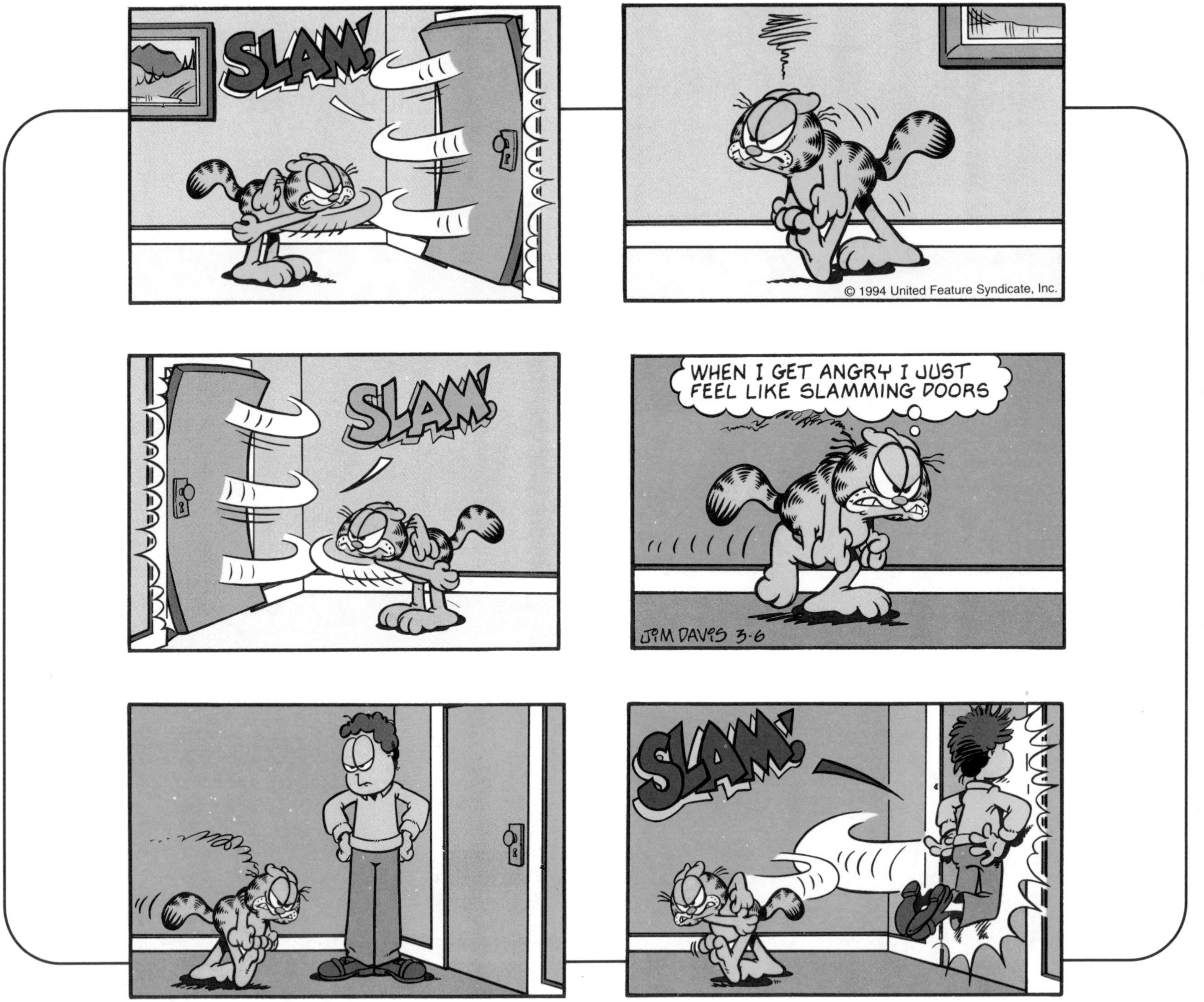
SLAM!
© 1994 United Feature Syndicate, Inc.
SLAM!
WHEN I GET ANGRY I JUST FEEL LIKE SLAMMING DOORS
JIM DAVIS 3-6
SLAM!

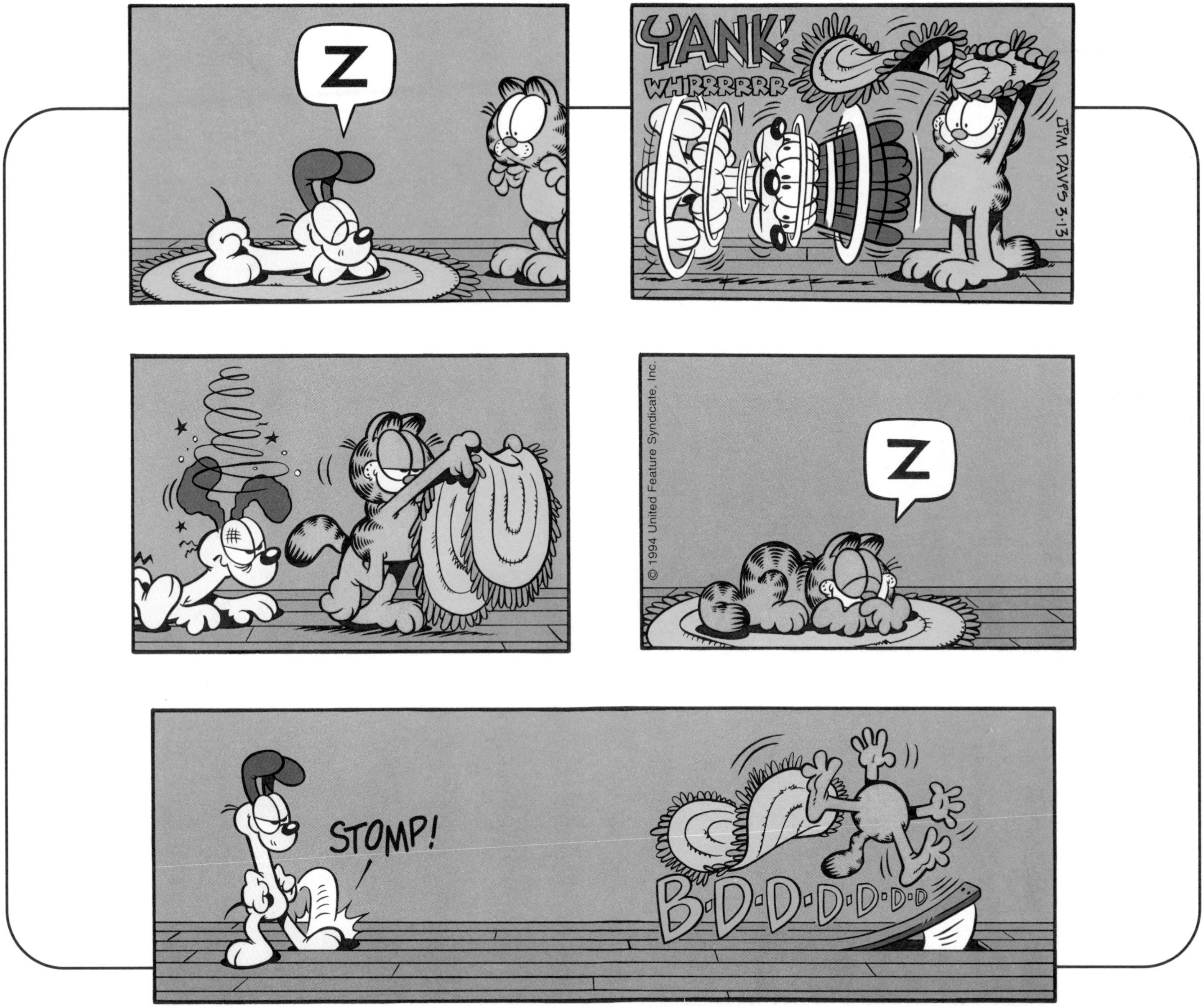
Z
YANK!
WHIRRRRRR
JIM DAVIS 3-13
© 1994 United Feature Syndicate, Inc.
Z
STOMP!
B-D-D-D-D-D-D

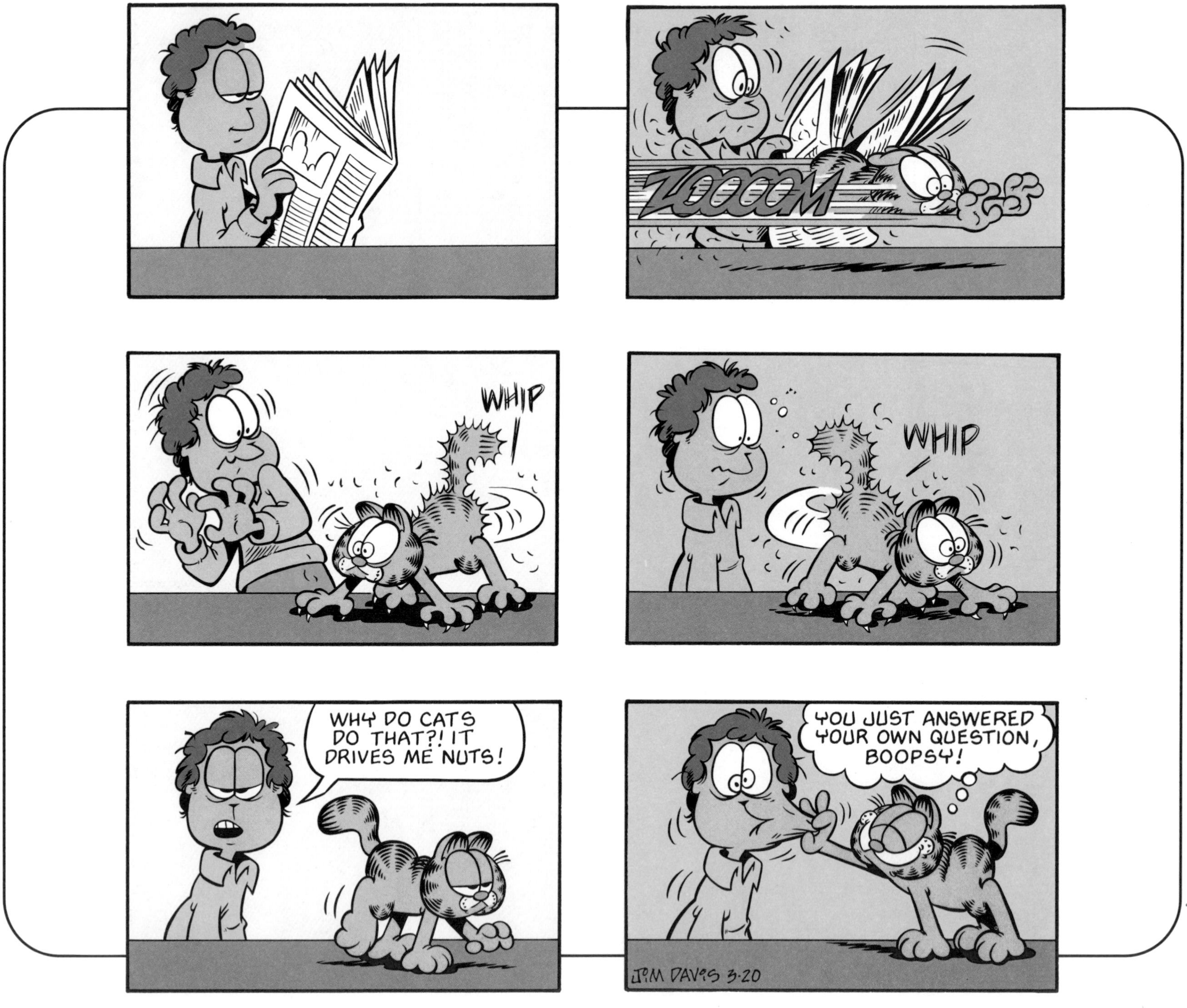
ZOOOOM
WHIP
WHIP
WHY DO CATS DO THAT?! IT DRIVES ME NUTS!
YOU JUST ANSWERED YOUR OWN QUESTION, BOOPSY!
JIM DAVIS 3-20

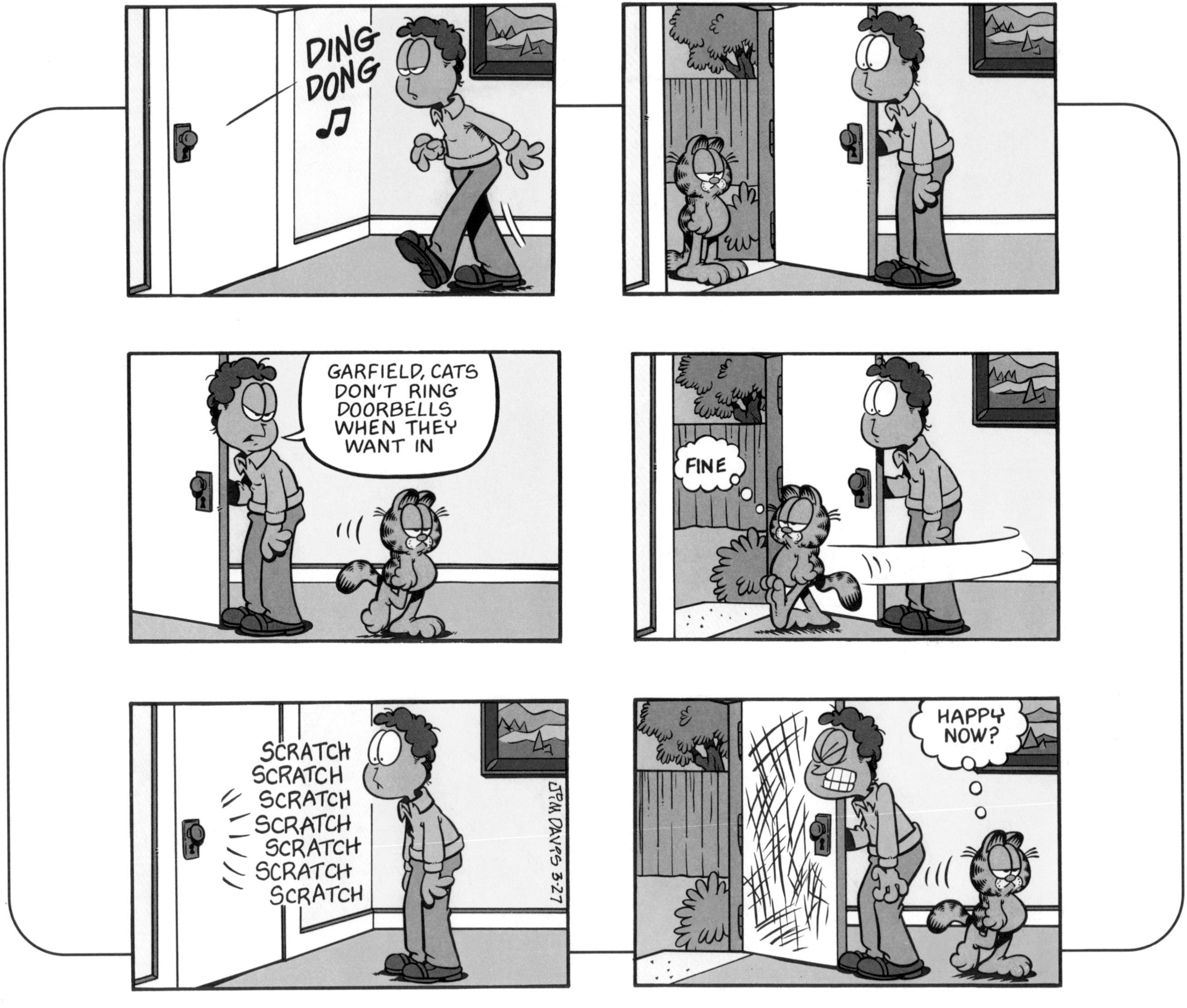
DING DONG ♫
GARFIELD, CATS DON'T RING DOORBELLS WHEN THEY WANT IN
FINE
SCRATCH SCRATCH SCRATCH SCRATCH SCRATCH SCRATCH SCRATCH
JPM DAVPS 3-27
HAPPY NOW?

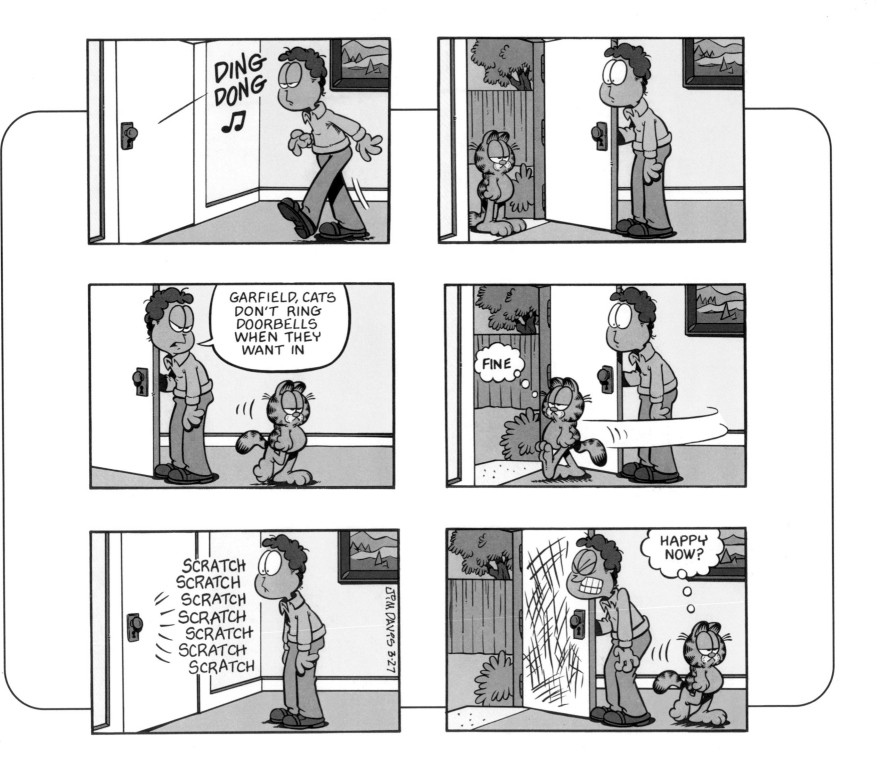

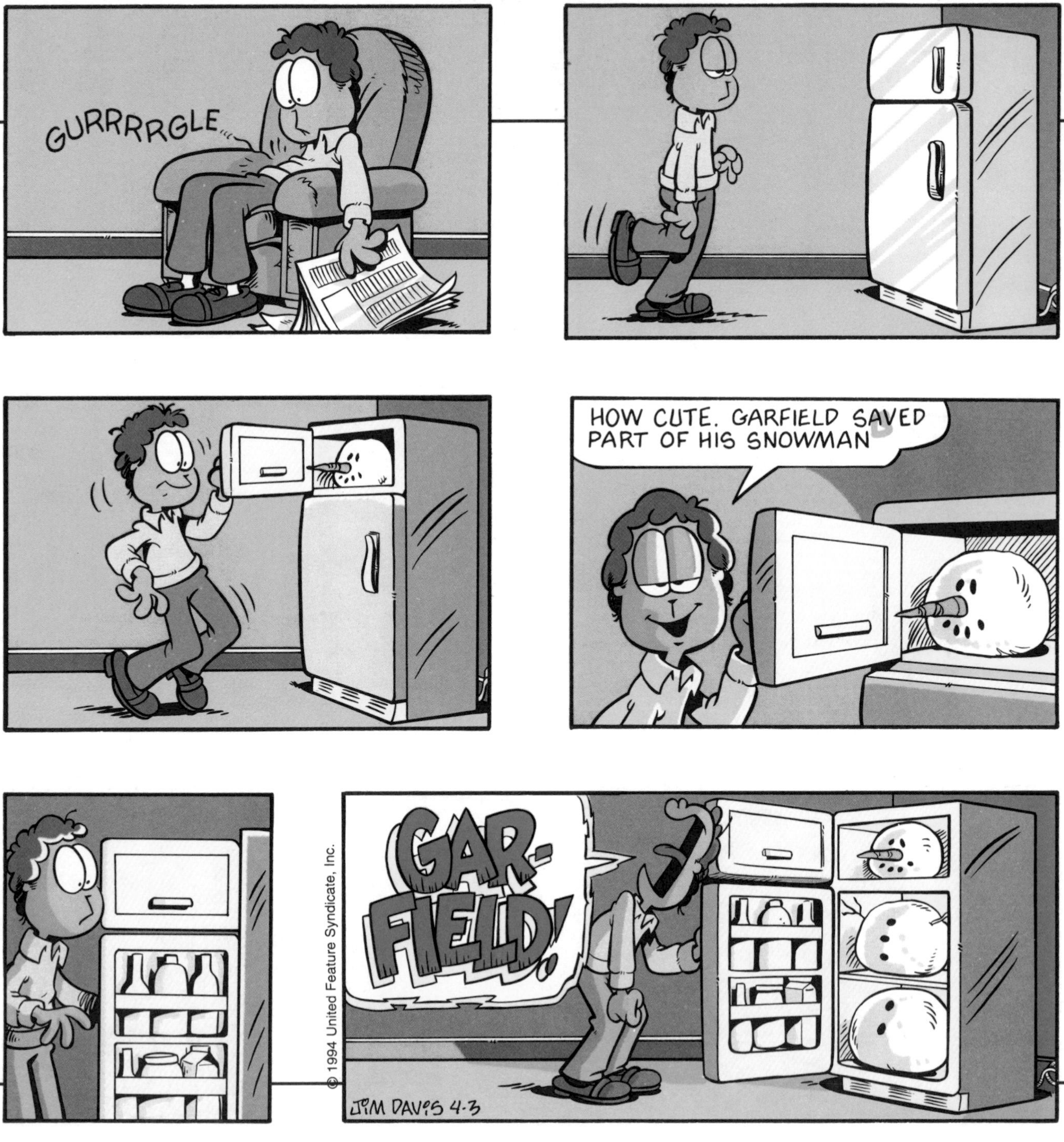
GURRRRGLE
HOW CUTE. GARFIELD SAVED PART OF HIS SNOWMAN
GAR-FIELD!
© 1994 United Feature Syndicate, Inc.
JIM DAVIS 4-3

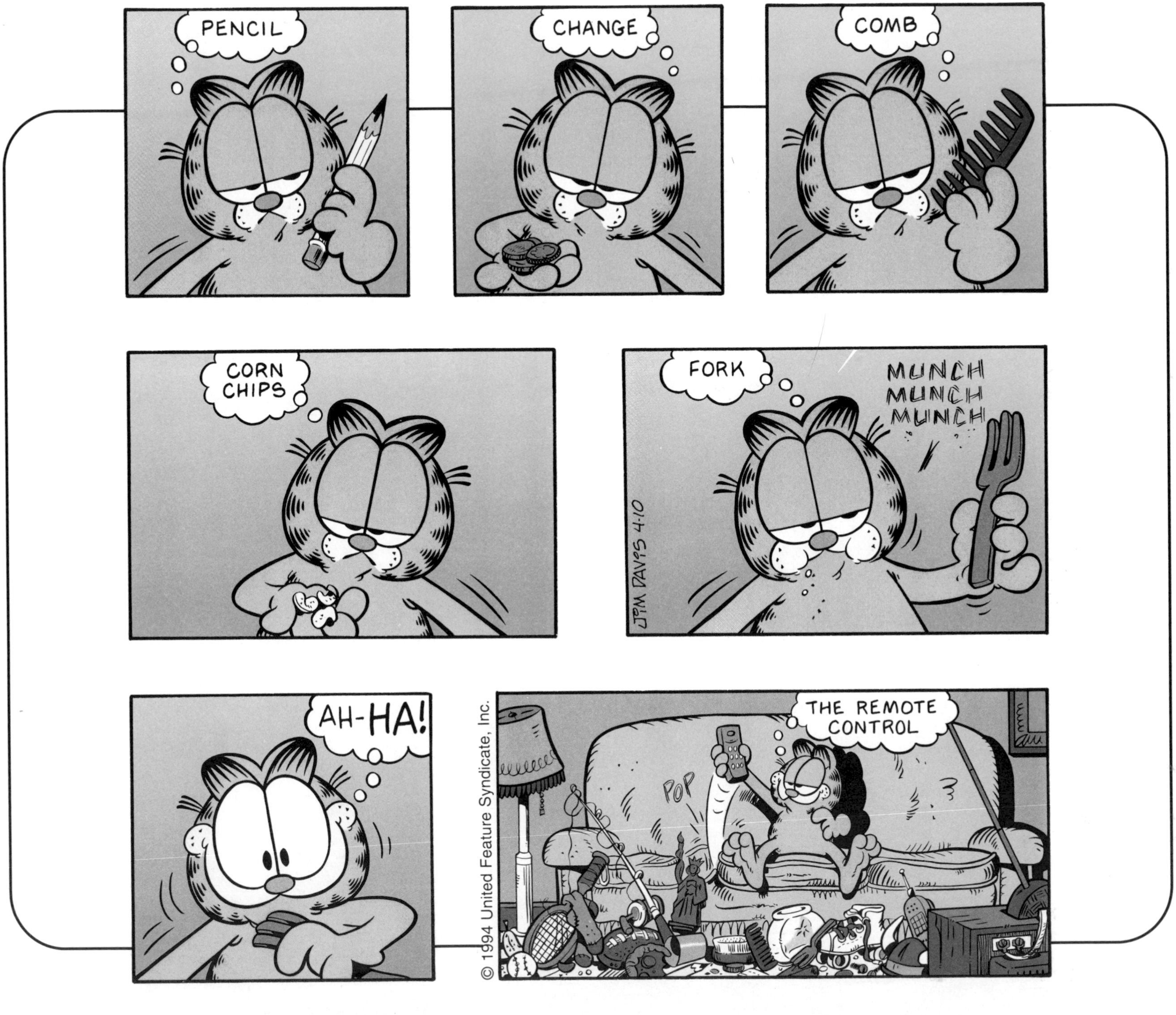
PENCIL
CHANGE
COMB
CORN CHIPS
FORK
MUNCH MUNCH MUNCH
JIM DAVIS 4-10
AH-HA!
THE REMOTE CONTROL
POP

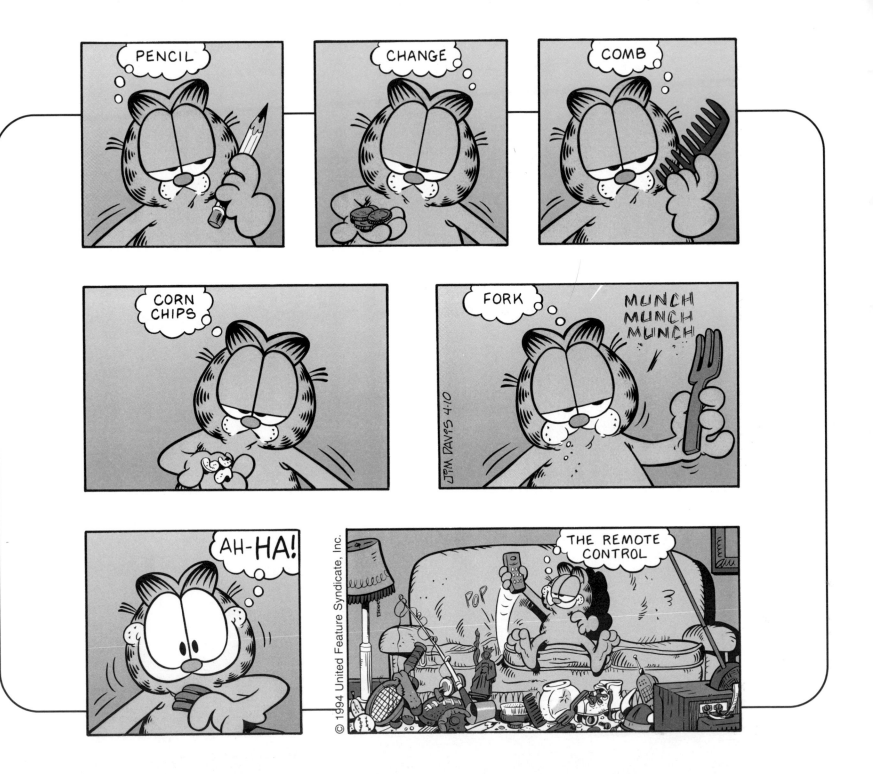

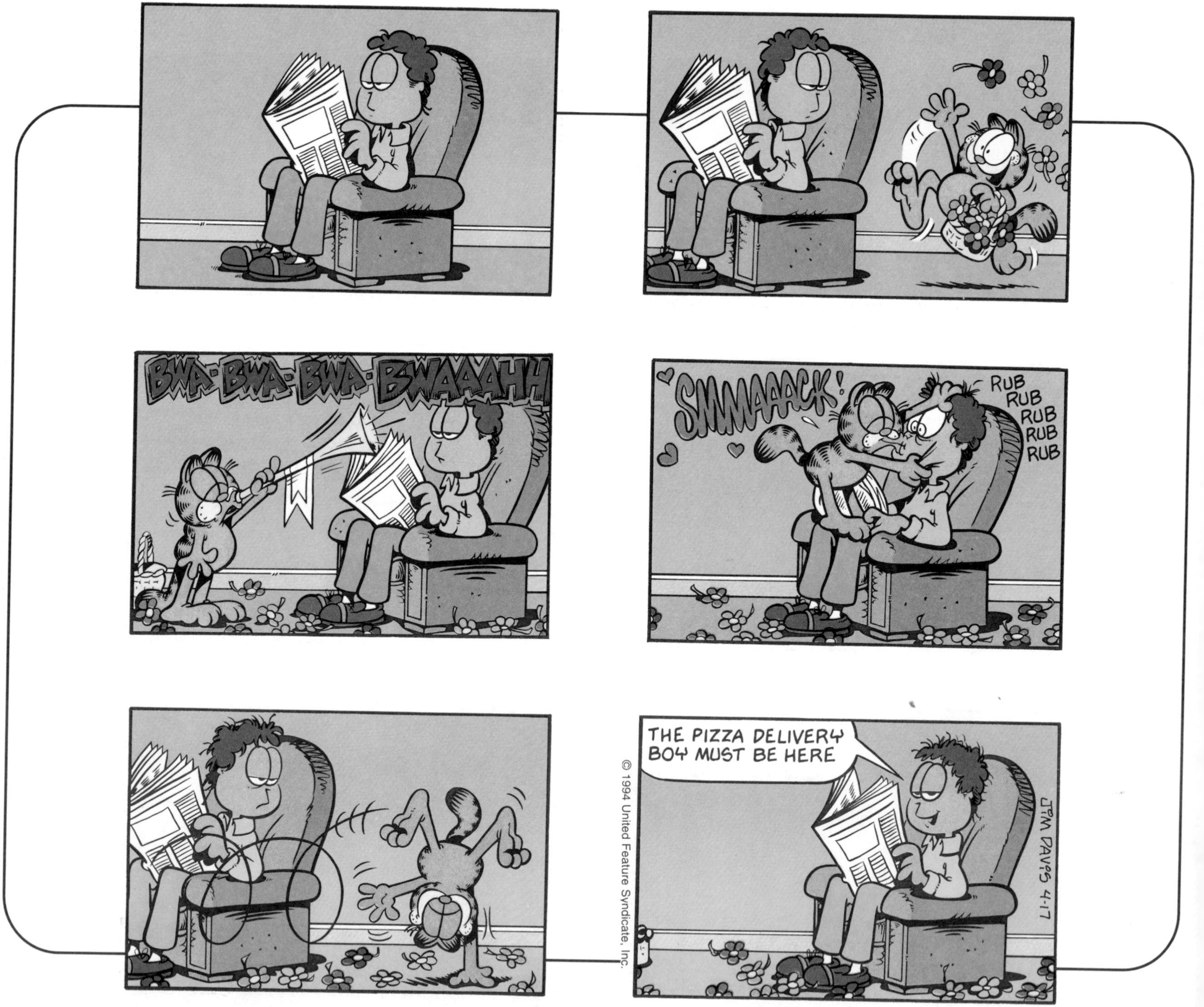
BWA-BWA-BWA-BWAAAHH
SMMAAACK!
RUB
RUB
RUB
RUB
RUB
THE PIZZA DELIVERY BOY MUST BE HERE
JIM DAVIS 4-17

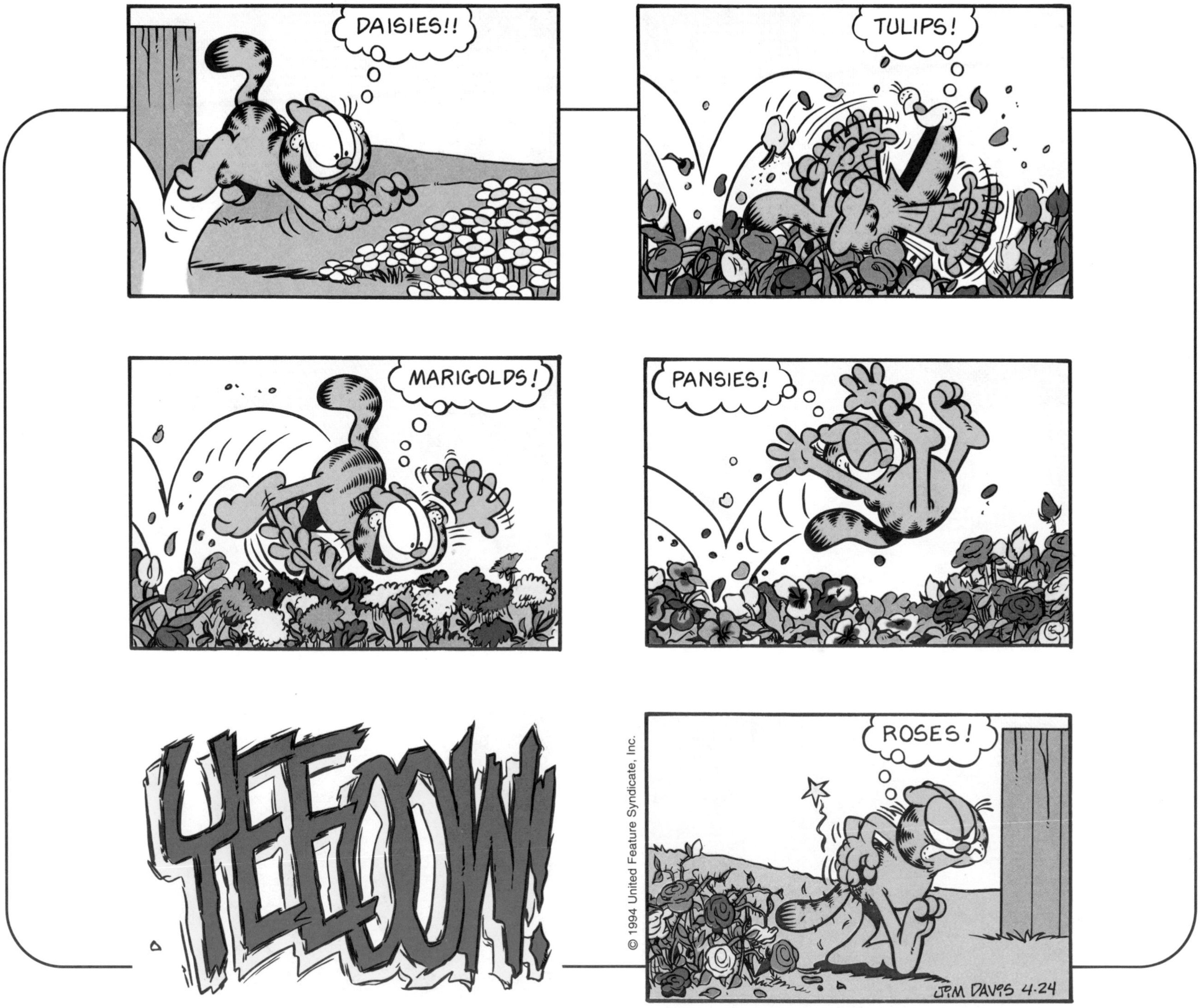
DAISIES!!
TULIPS!
MARIGOLDS!
PANSIES!
YEEOOW!
© 1994 United Feature Syndicate, Inc.
ROSES!
JIM DAVIS 4-24

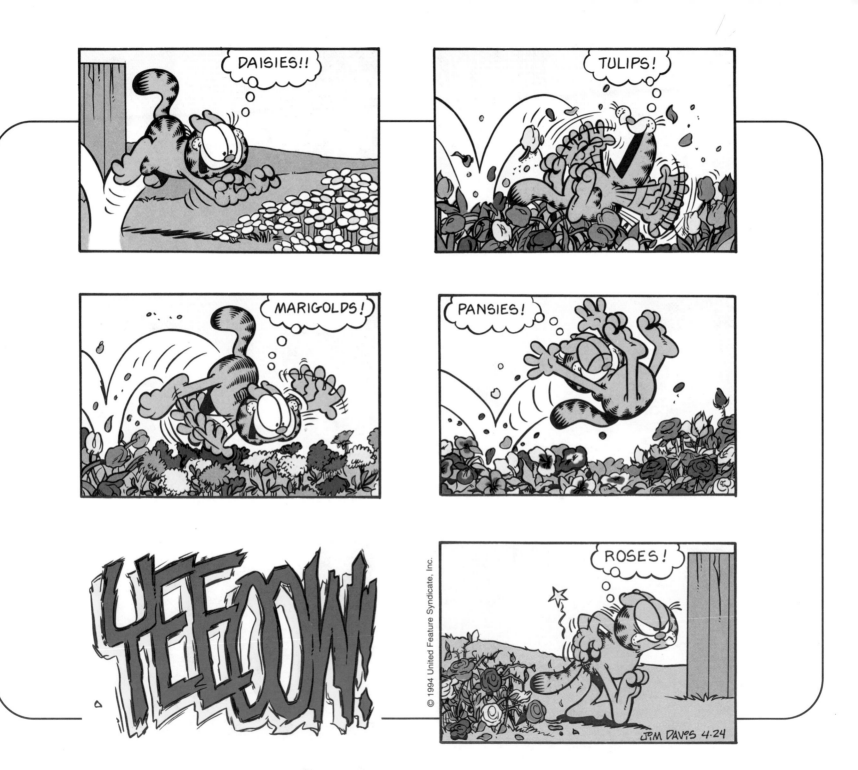

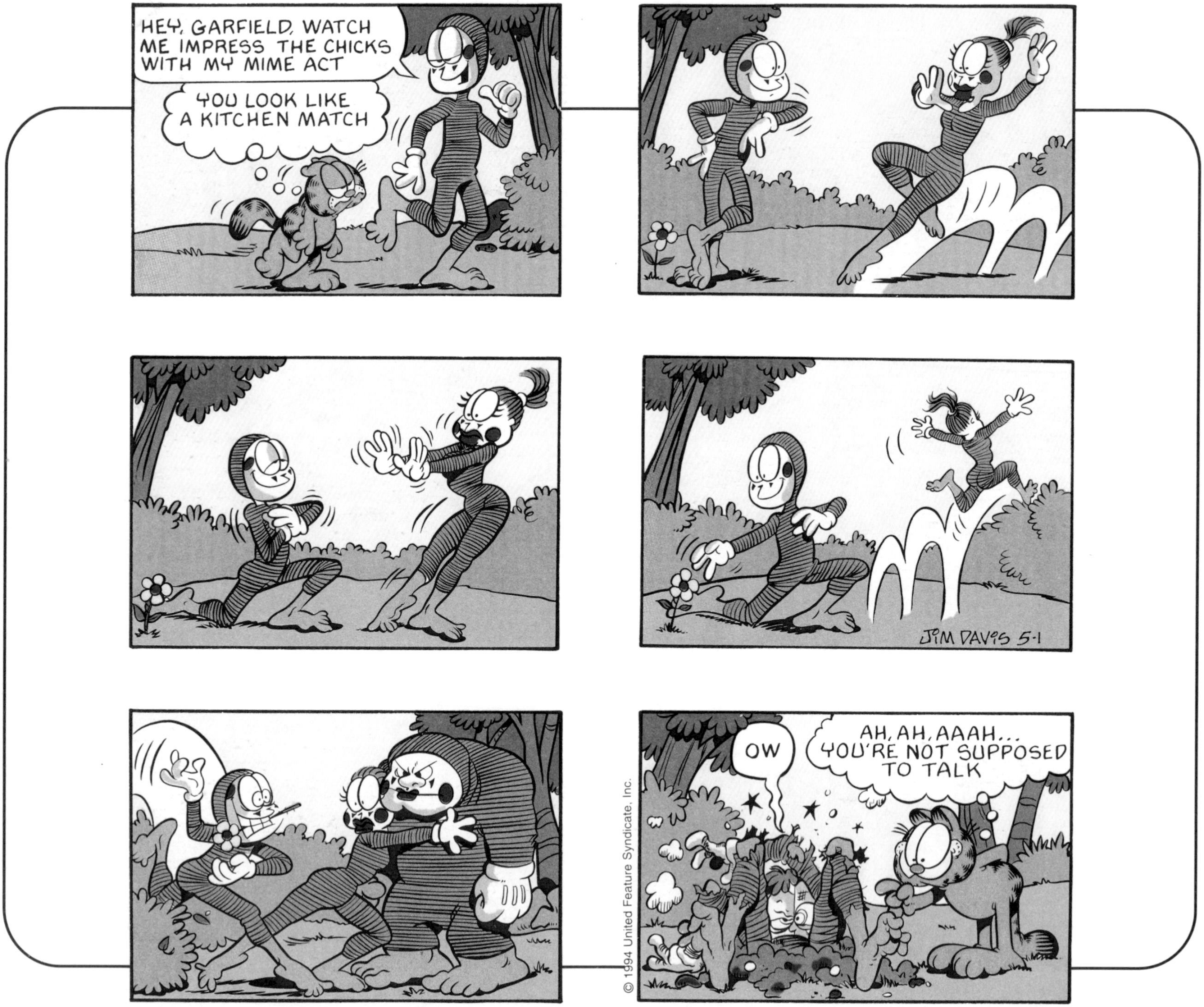
HEY, GARFIELD, WATCH ME IMPRESS THE CHICKS WITH MY MIME ACT
YOU LOOK LIKE A KITCHEN MATCH
JIM DAVIS 5-1
OW
AH, AH, AAAH... YOU'RE NOT SUPPOSED TO TALK

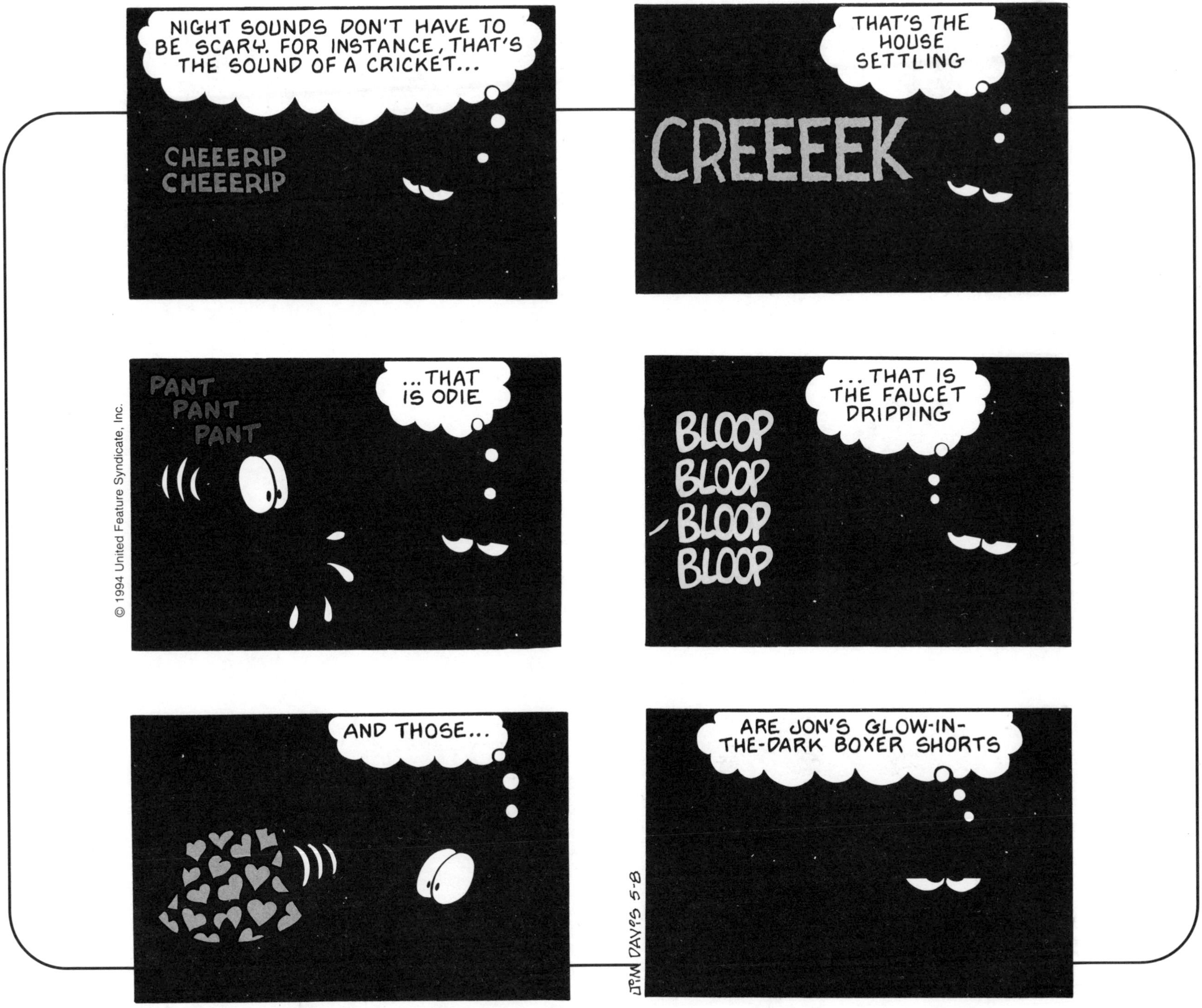
NIGHT SOUNDS DON'T HAVE TO BE SCARY. FOR INSTANCE, THAT'S THE SOUND OF A CRICKET...
CHEEERIP CHEEERIP
THAT'S THE HOUSE SETTLING
CREEEEK
PANT PANT PANT
...THAT IS ODIE
BLOOP BLOOP BLOOP BLOOP
...THAT IS THE FAUCET DRIPPING
AND THOSE...
ARE JON'S GLOW-IN-THE-DARK BOXER SHORTS
JIM DAVIS 5-8

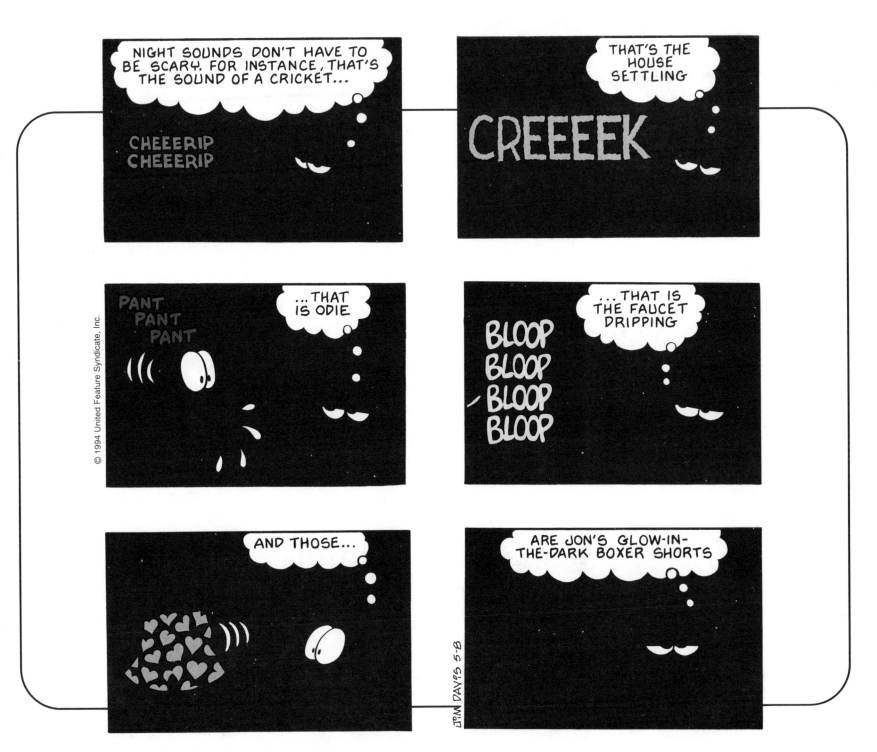

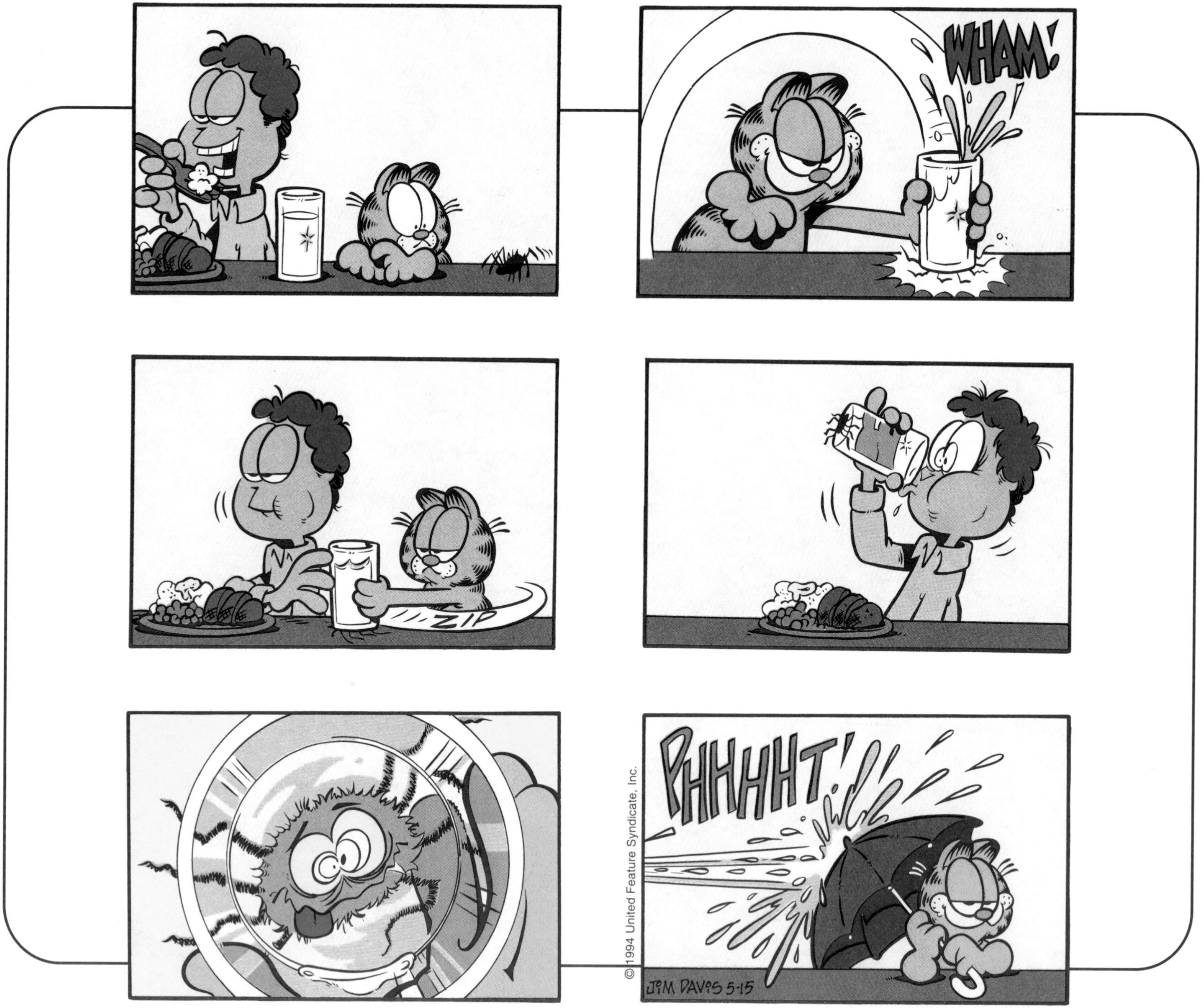
WHAM!
ZIP
PHHHT!
JIM DAVIS 5-15

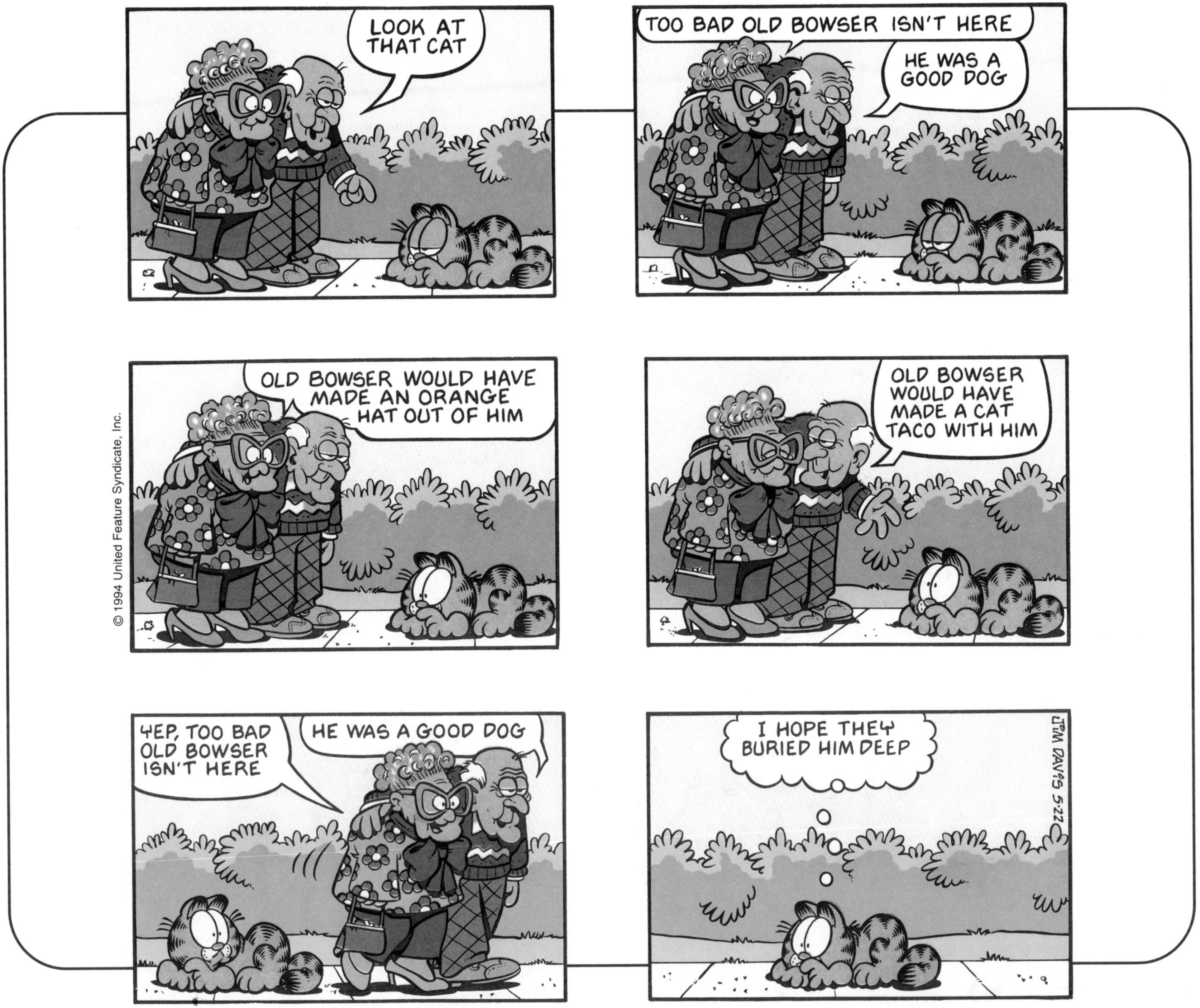
LOOK AT THAT CAT
TOO BAD OLD BOWSER ISN'T HERE
HE WAS A GOOD DOG
OLD BOWSER WOULD HAVE MADE AN ORANGE HAT OUT OF HIM
OLD BOWSER WOULD HAVE MADE A CAT TACO WITH HIM
YEP, TOO BAD OLD BOWSER ISN'T HERE
HE WAS A GOOD DOG
I HOPE THEY BURIED HIM DEEP
JIM DAVIS 5-22

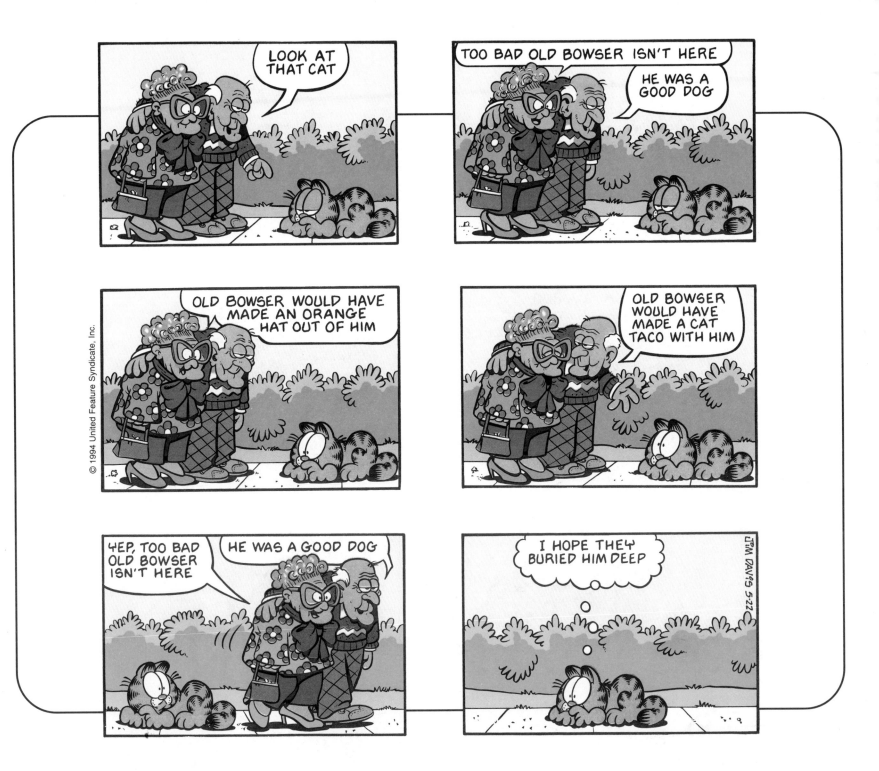

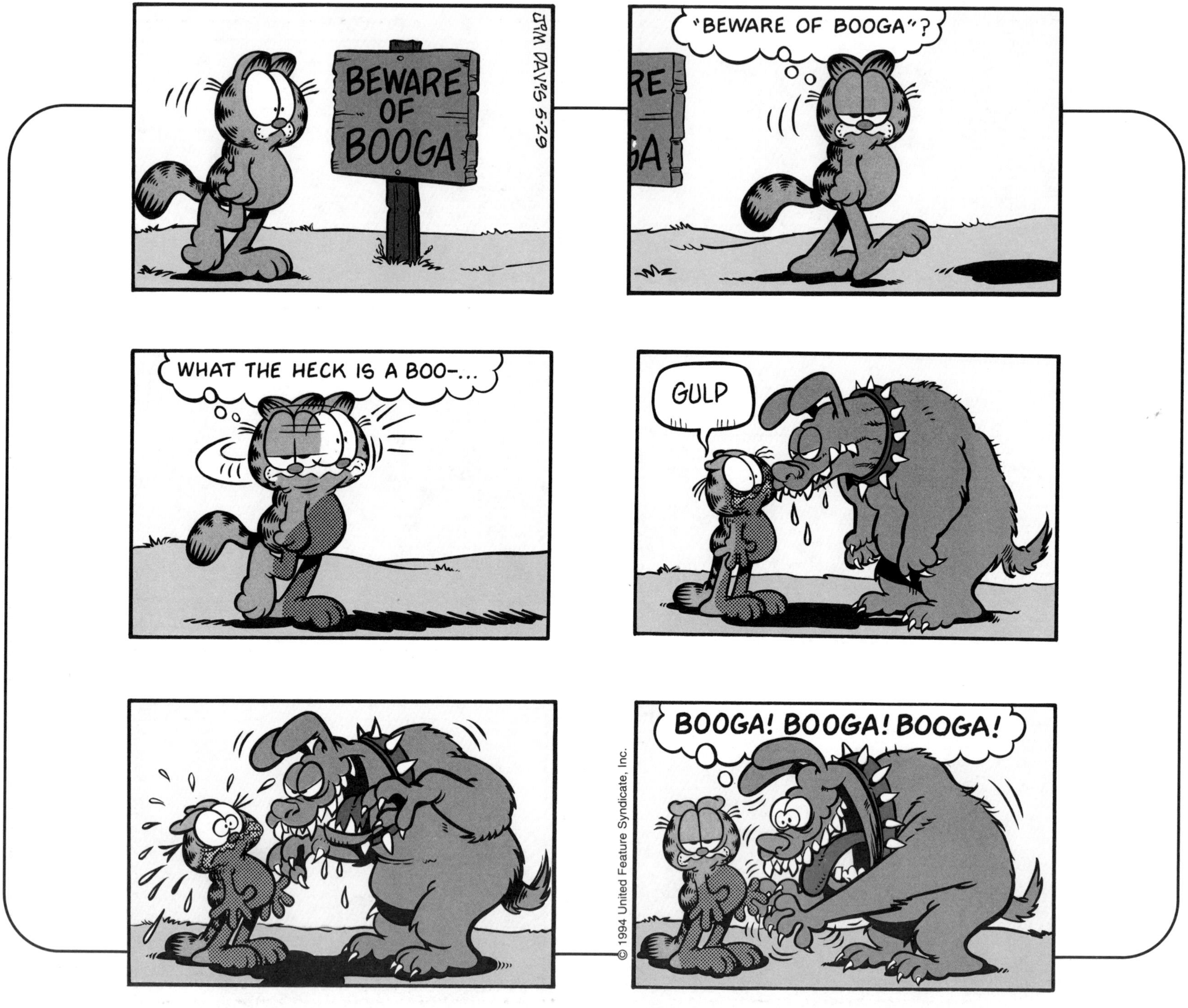
BEWARE OF BOOGA
JIM DAVIS 5-29
"BEWARE OF BOOGA"?
WHAT THE HECK IS A BOO-...
GULP
BOOGA! BOOGA! BOOGA!

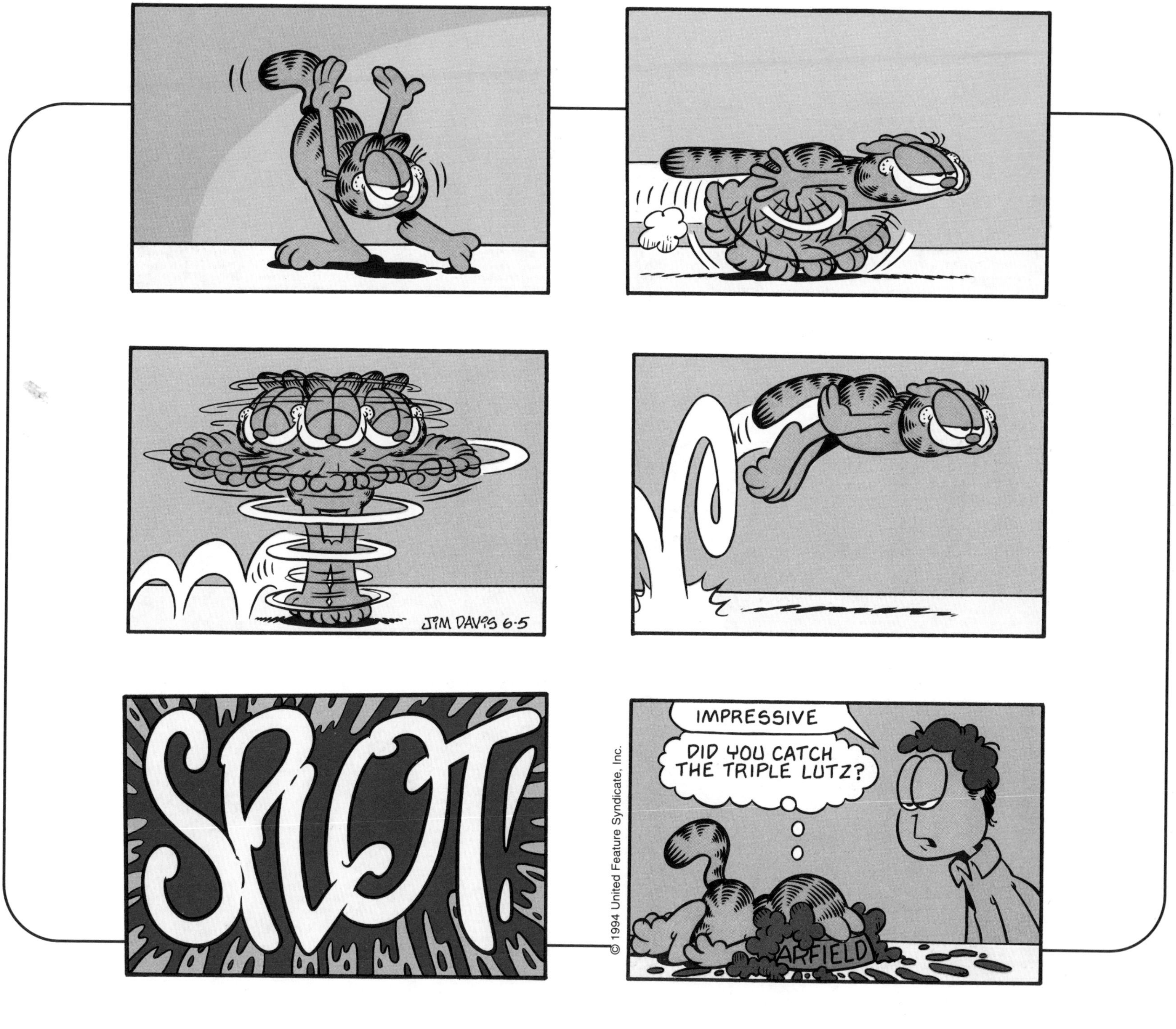
JIM DAVIS 6-5
SPLOT!
IMPRESSIVE
DID YOU CATCH THE TRIPLE LUTZ?
ARFIELD

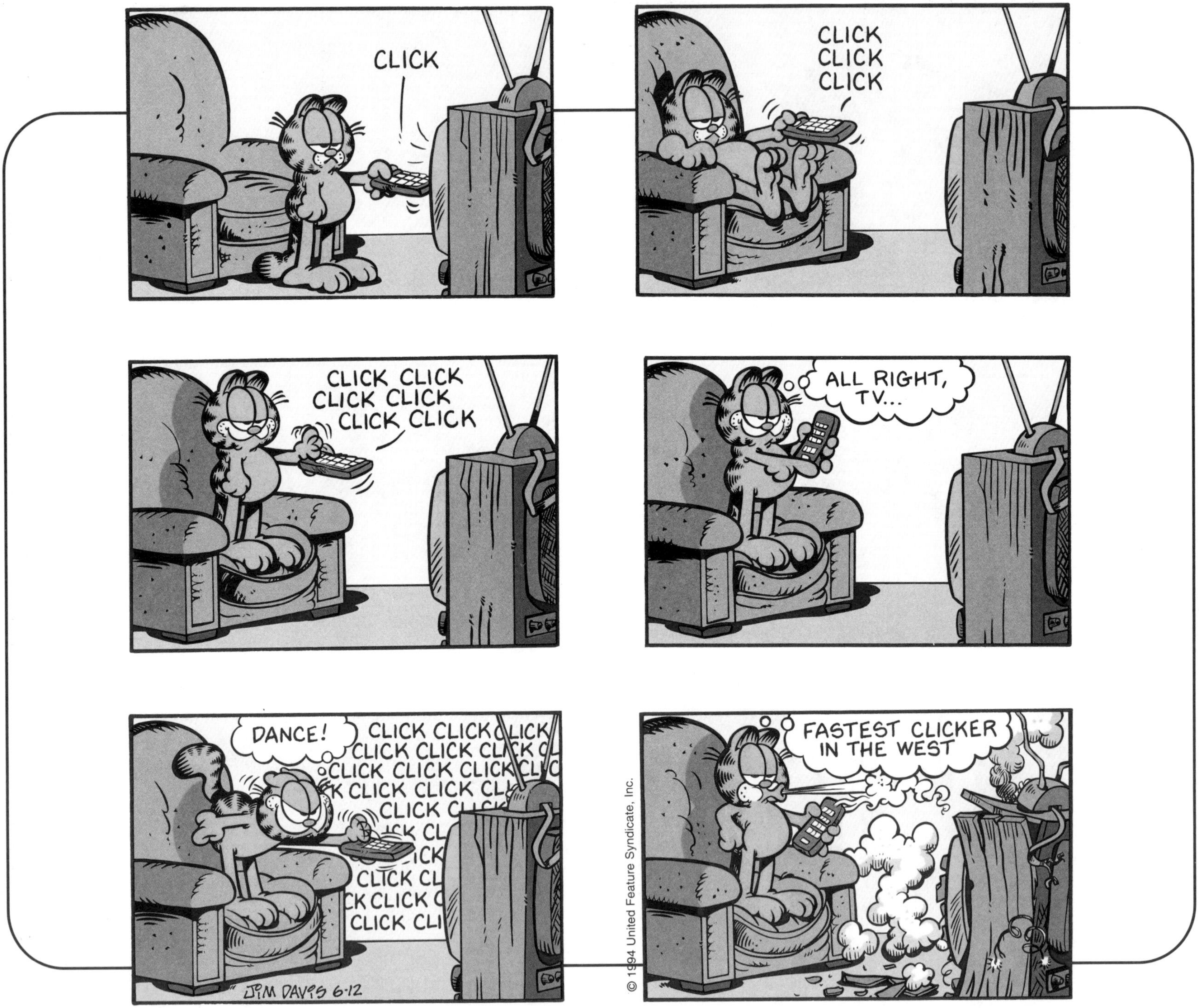
CLICK
CLICK
CLICK
CLICK
CLICK CLICK
CLICK CLICK
CLICK CLICK
ALL RIGHT, TV...
DANCE!
CLICK CLICK
CLICK CLICK
CLICK CLICK CLICK
CLICK CLICK
CLICK
CLICK
CLICK
CLICK
JIM DAVIS 6-12
FASTEST CLICKER IN THE WEST

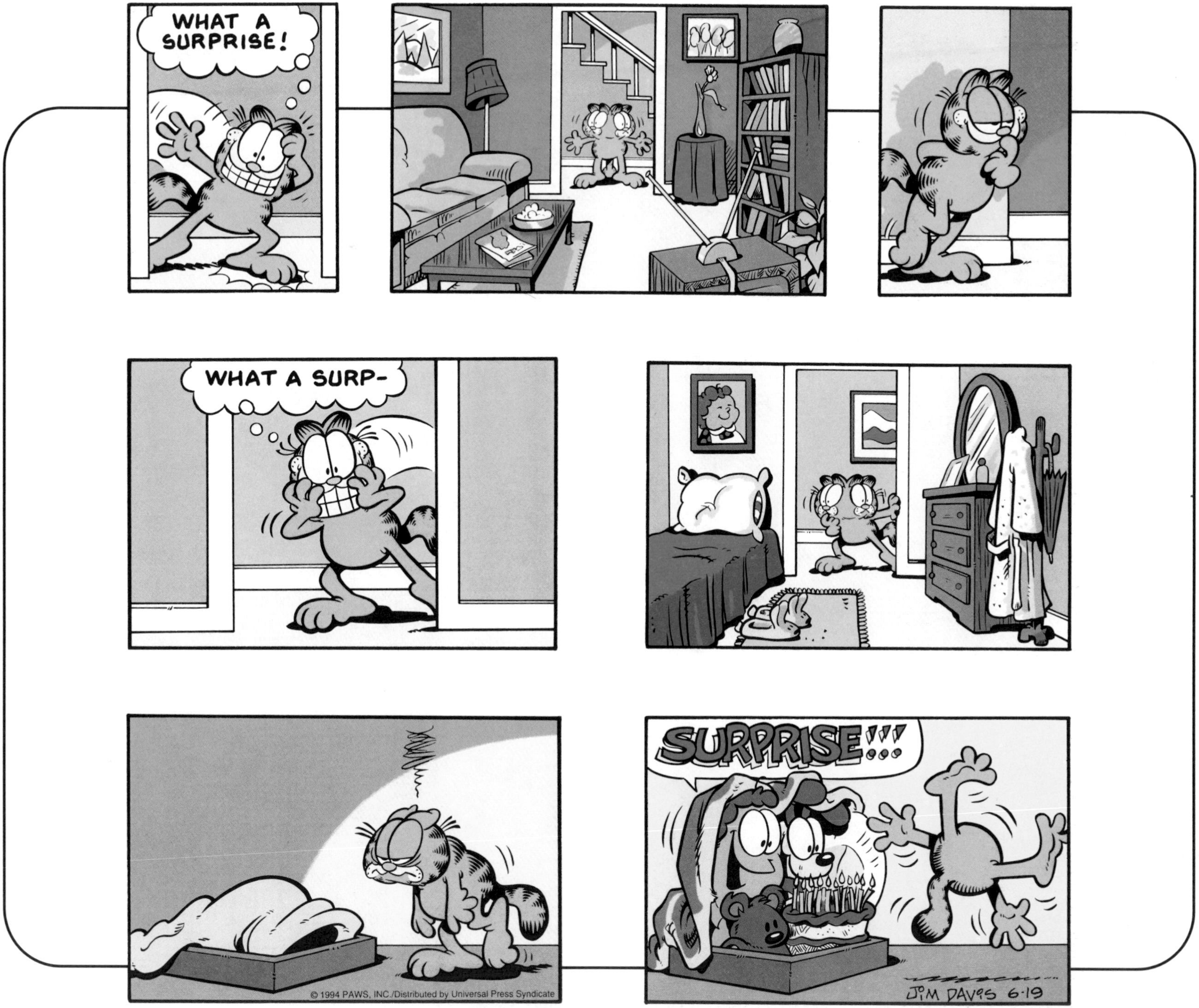
WHAT A SURPRISE!
WHAT A SURP-
SURPRISE!!!
© 1994 PAWS, INC./Distributed by Universal Press Syndicate
JIM DAVIS 6-19

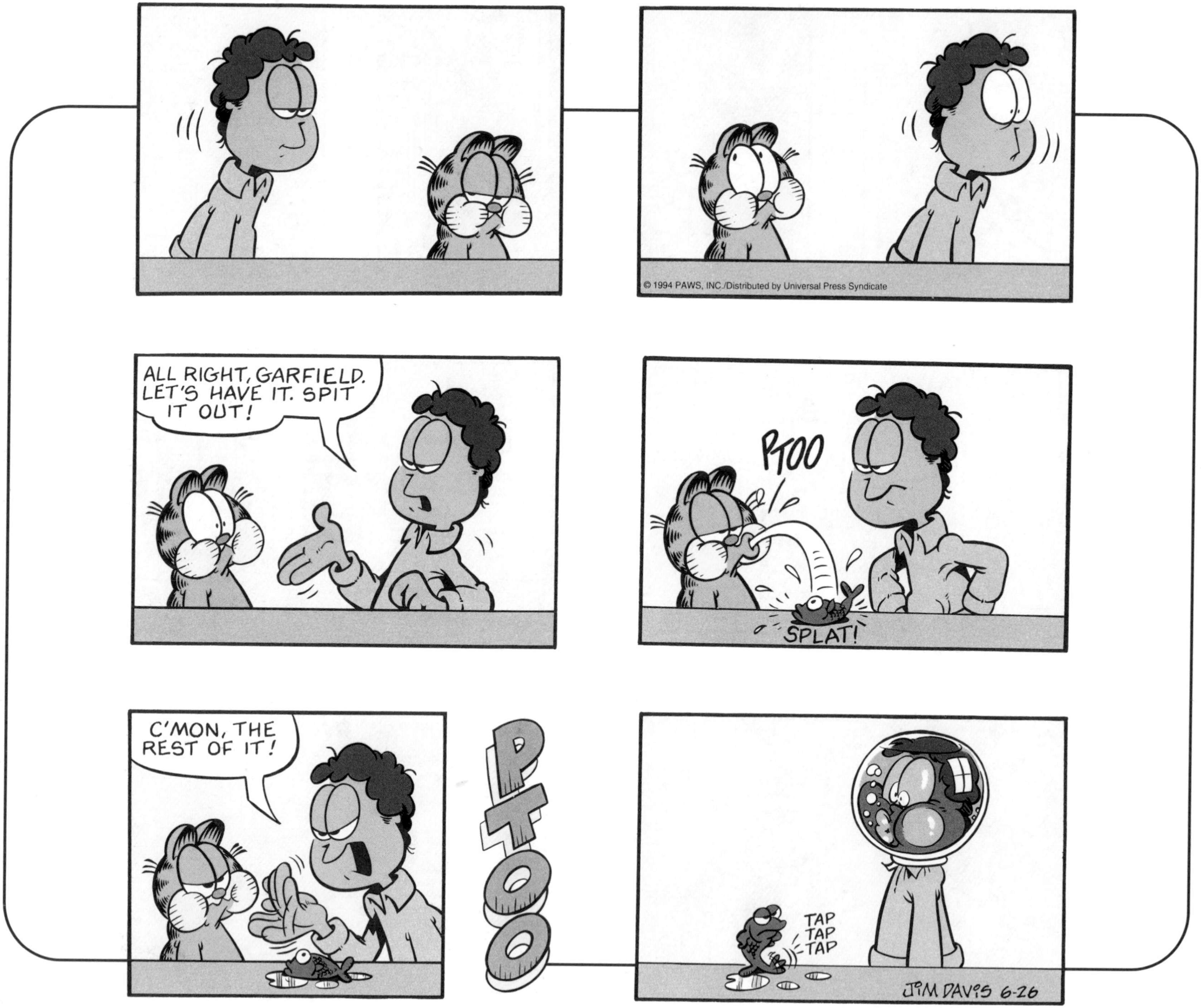

© 1994 PAWS, INC./Distributed by Universal Press Syndicate
ALL RIGHT, GARFIELD. LET'S HAVE IT. SPIT IT OUT!
PTOO
SPLAT!
C'MON, THE REST OF IT!
PTOO
TAP TAP TAP
JIM DAVIS 6-26

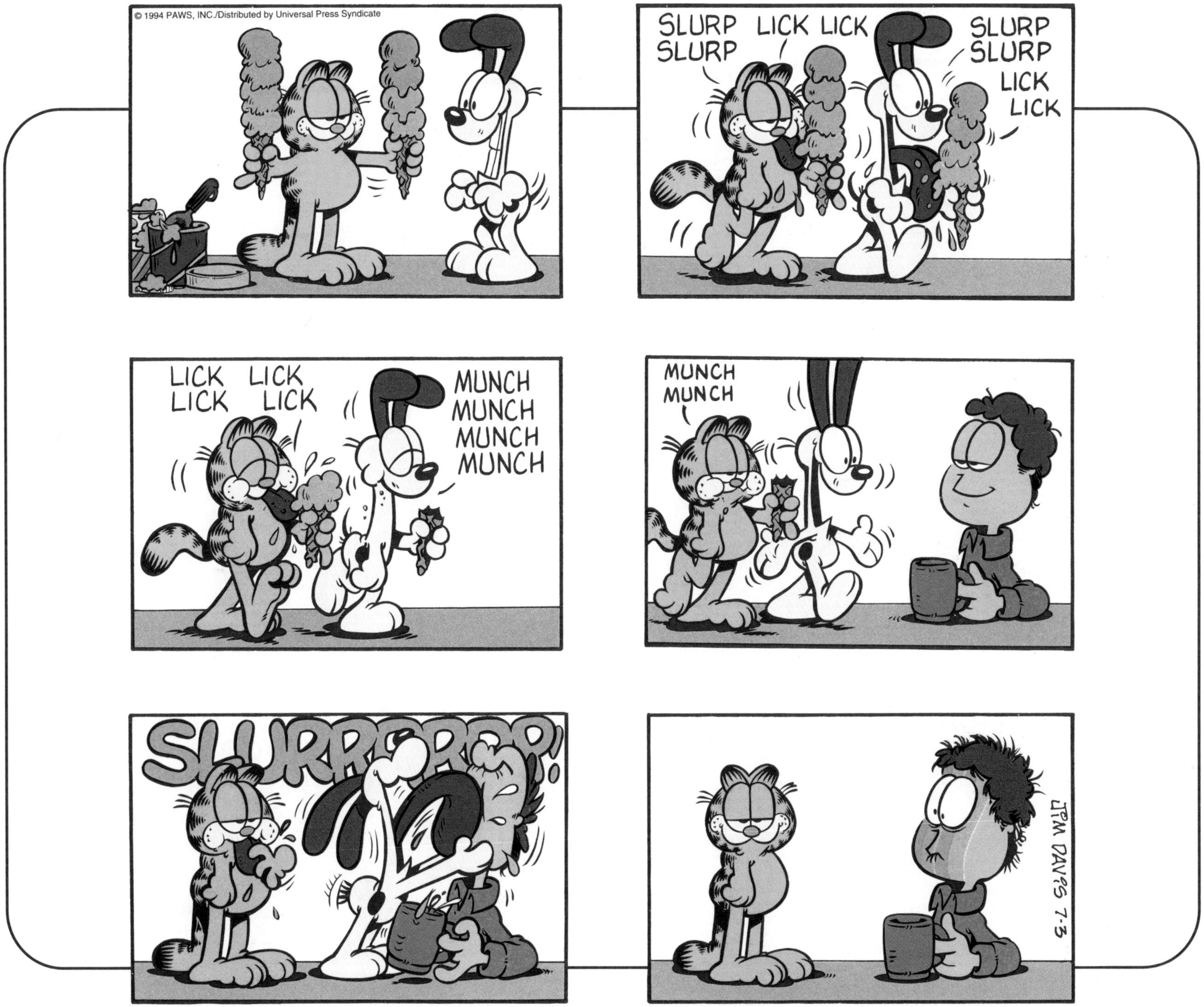

© 1994 PAWS, INC./Distributed by Universal Press Syndicate
SLURP SLURP
LICK LICK
SLURP SLURP
LICK LICK
LICK LICK
LICK LICK
MUNCH MUNCH MUNCH MUNCH
MUNCH MUNCH
SLURRRRRP!
JPM DAVPS 7-3

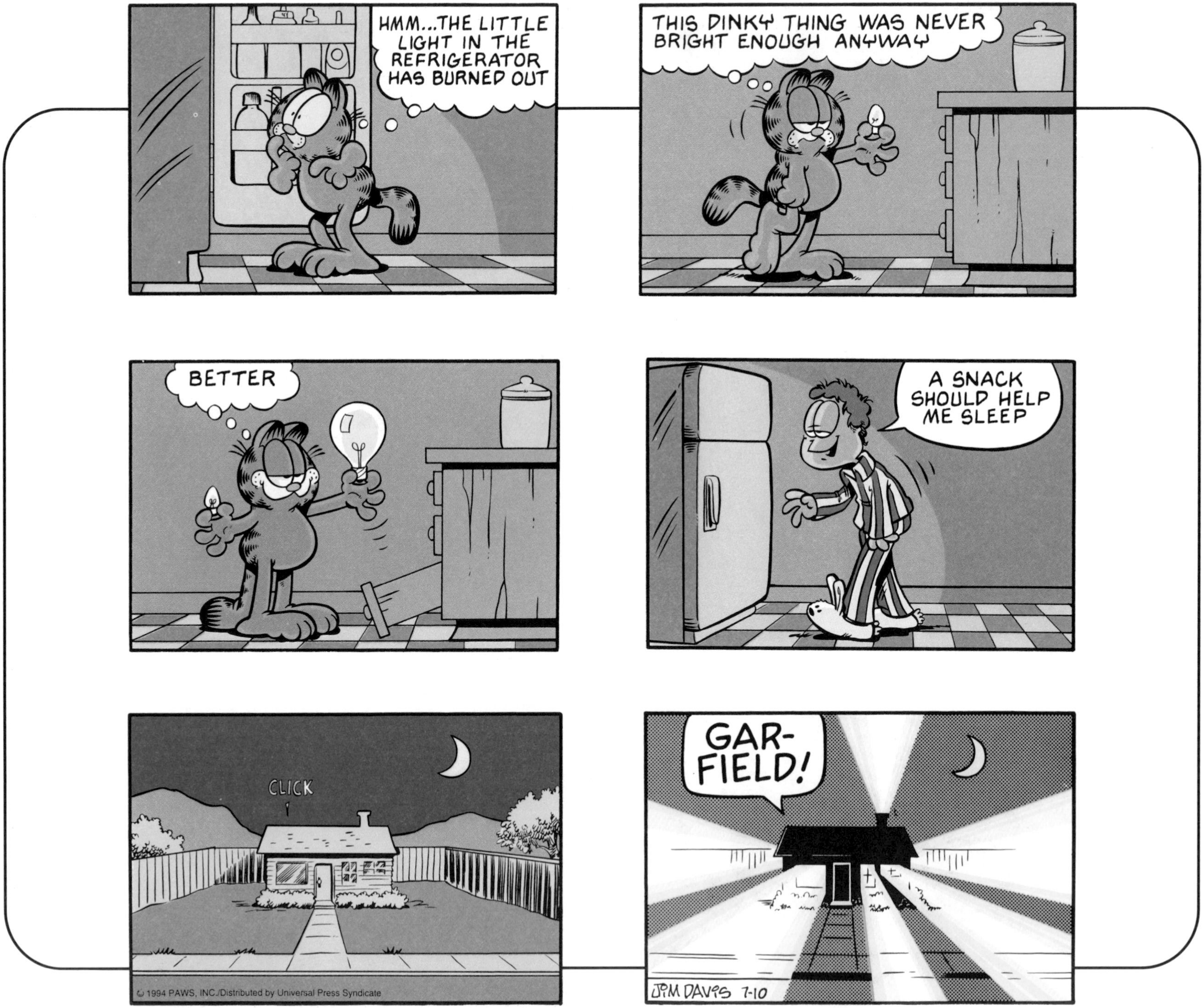
HMM...THE LITTLE LIGHT IN THE REFRIGERATOR HAS BURNED OUT
THIS DINKY THING WAS NEVER BRIGHT ENOUGH ANYWAY
BETTER
A SNACK SHOULD HELP ME SLEEP
CLICK
GAR-FIELD!
© 1994 PAWS, INC./Distributed by Universal Press Syndicate
JIM DAVIS 7-10

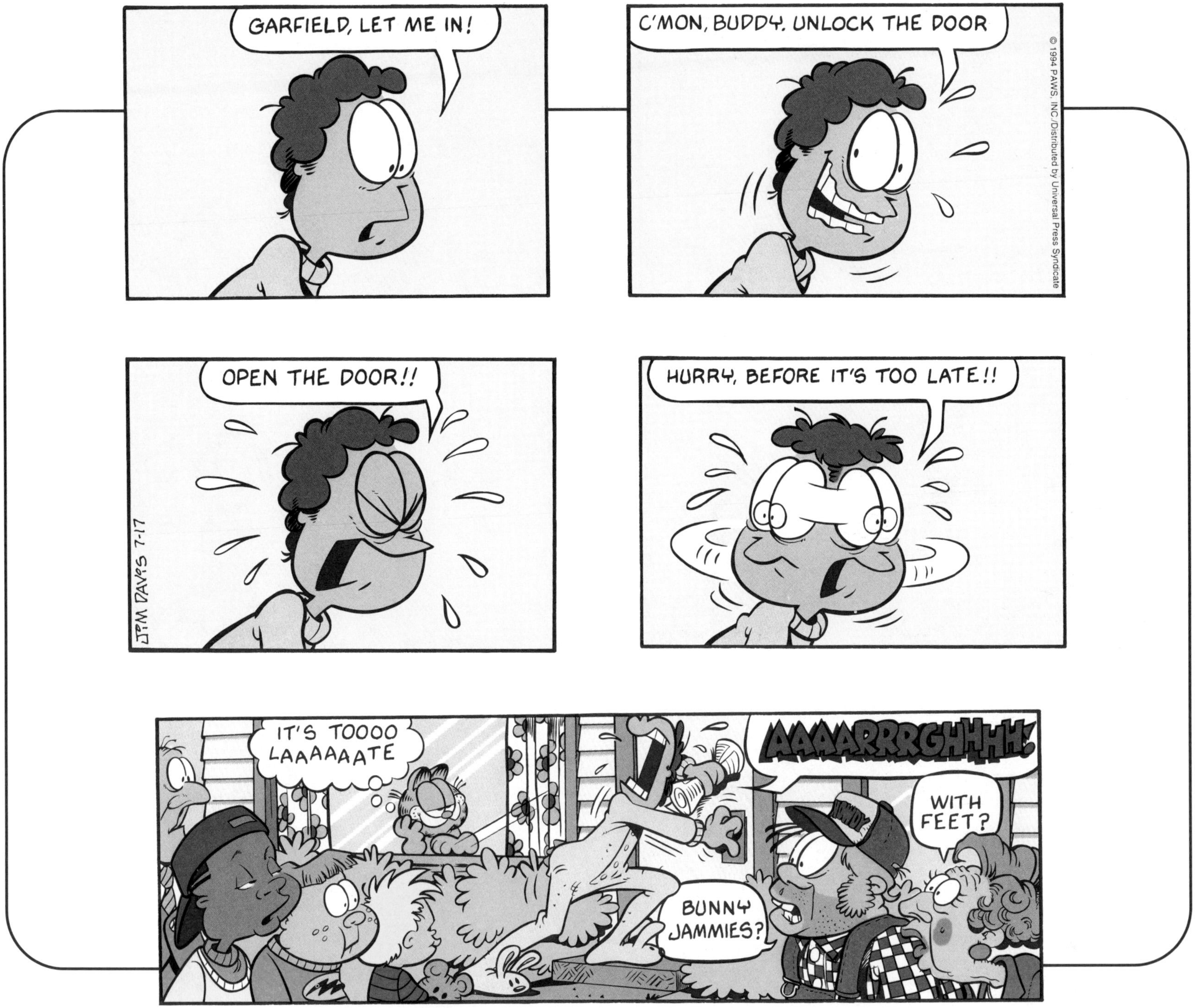
GARFIELD, LET ME IN!
C'MON, BUDDY. UNLOCK THE DOOR
© 1994 PAWS, INC./Distributed by Universal Press Syndicate
OPEN THE DOOR!!
JIM DAVIS 7-17
HURRY, BEFORE IT'S TOO LATE!!
IT'S TOOOO LAAAAAAATE
AAAARRRGHHHH!
WITH FEET?
BUNNY JAMMIES?

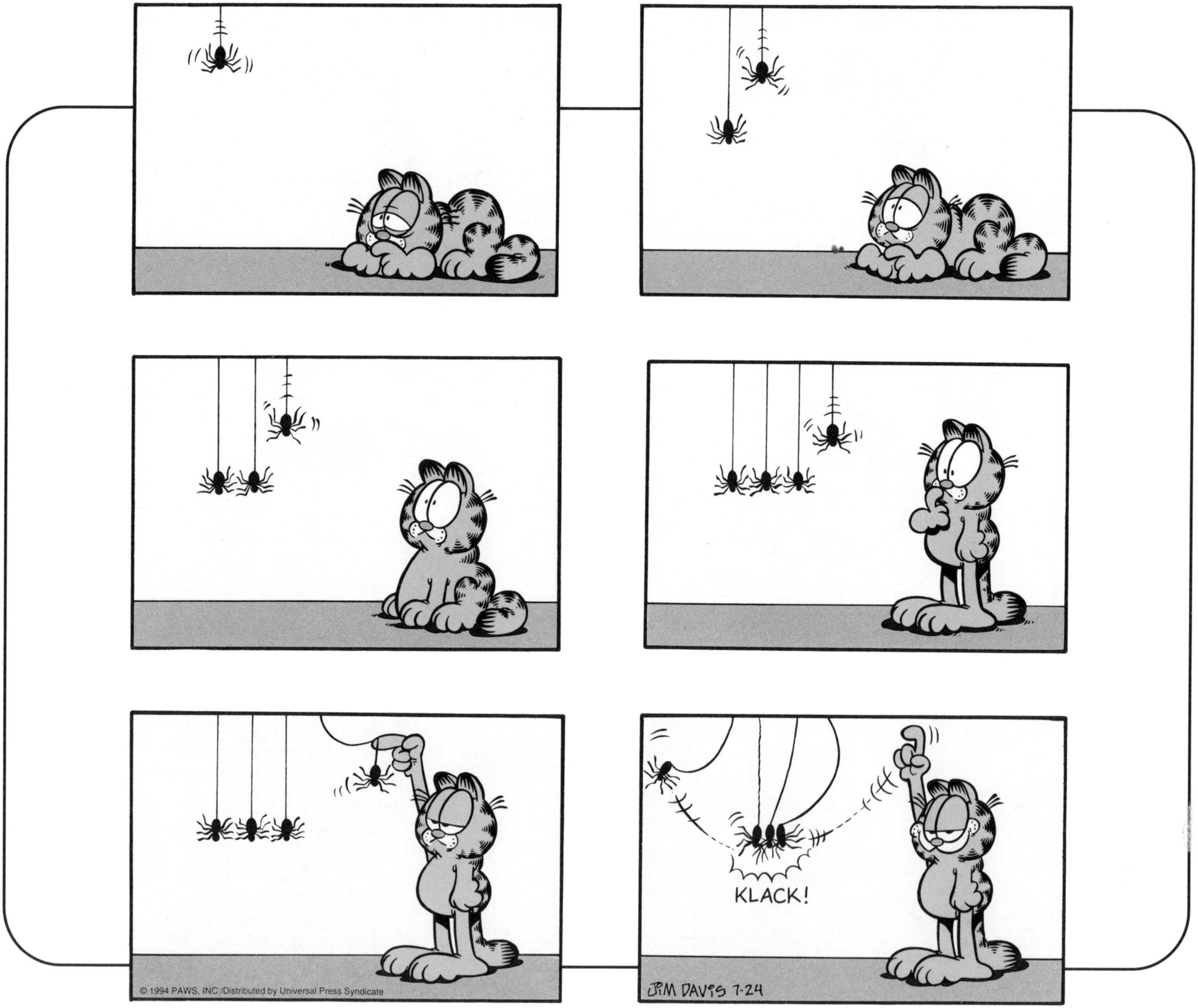
KLACK!
© 1994 PAWS, INC./Distributed by Universal Press Syndicate
JIM DAVIS 7-24

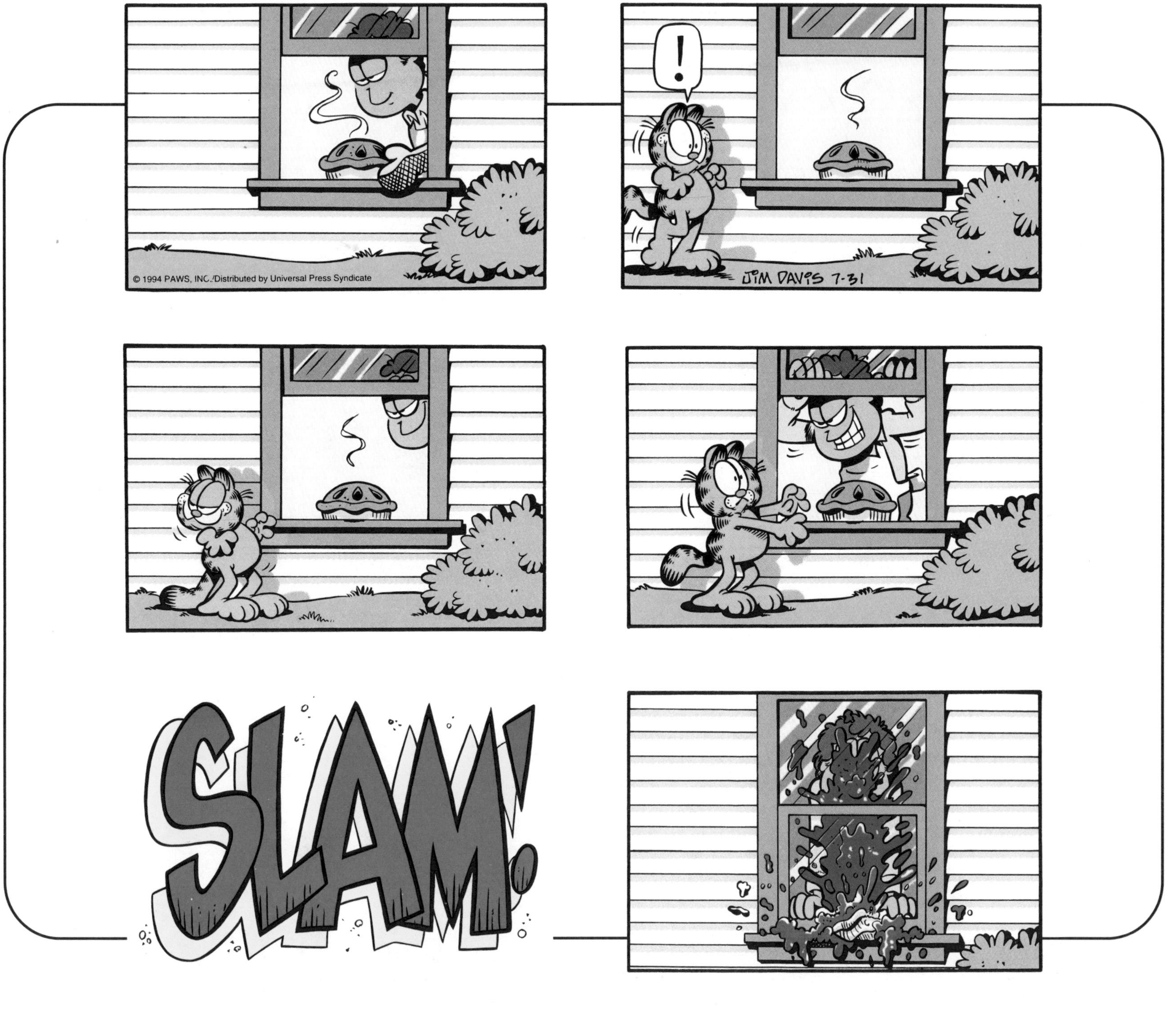
© 1994 PAWS, INC./Distributed by Universal Press Syndicate
!
JIM DAVIS 7-31
SLAM!

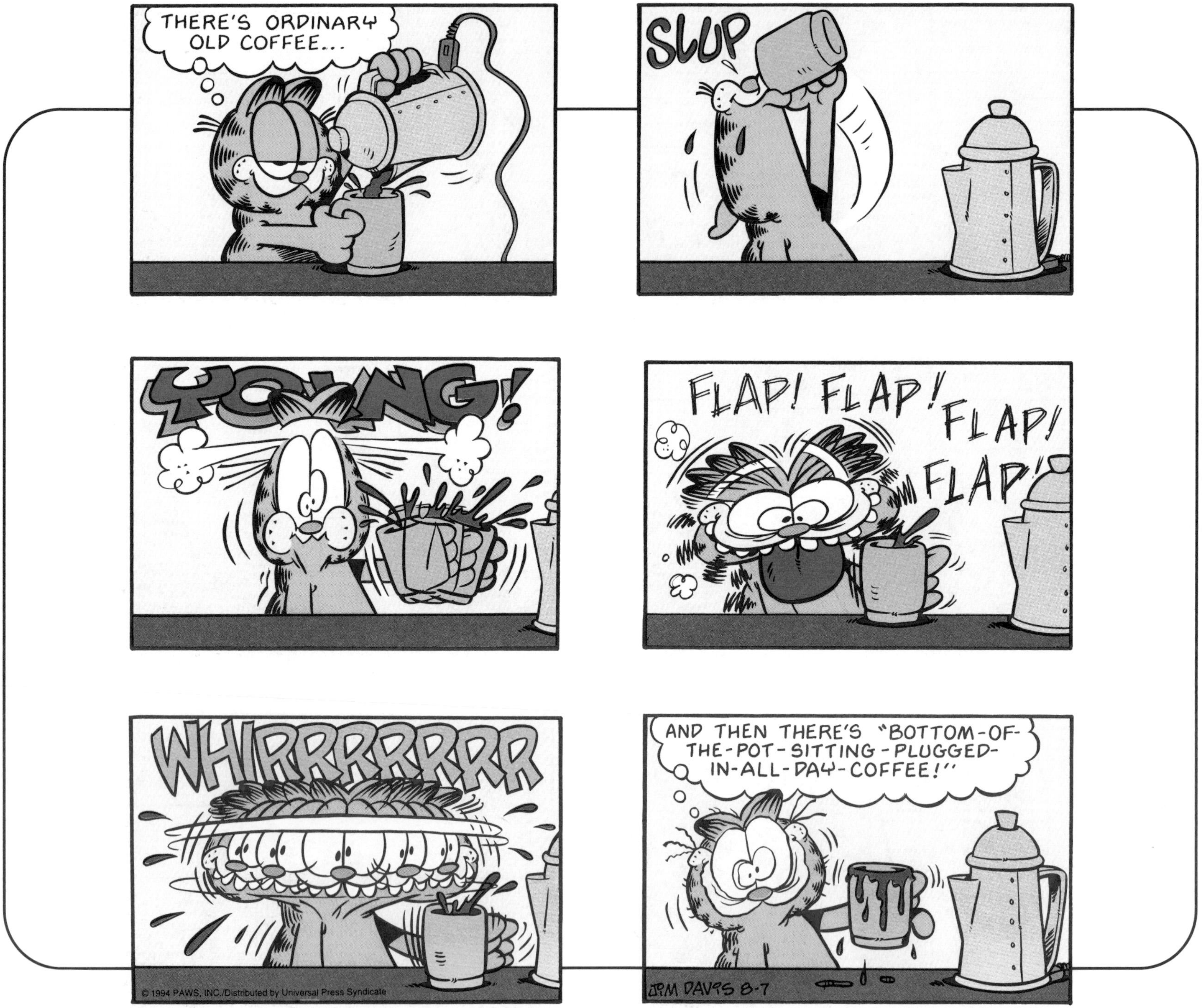
THERE'S ORDINARY OLD COFFEE...
SLUP
YOING!
FLAP! FLAP! FLAP! FLAP!
WHIRRRRRRRR
AND THEN THERE'S "BOTTOM-OF-THE-POT-SITTING-PLUGGED-IN-ALL-DAY-COFFEE!"
JIM DAVIS 8-7

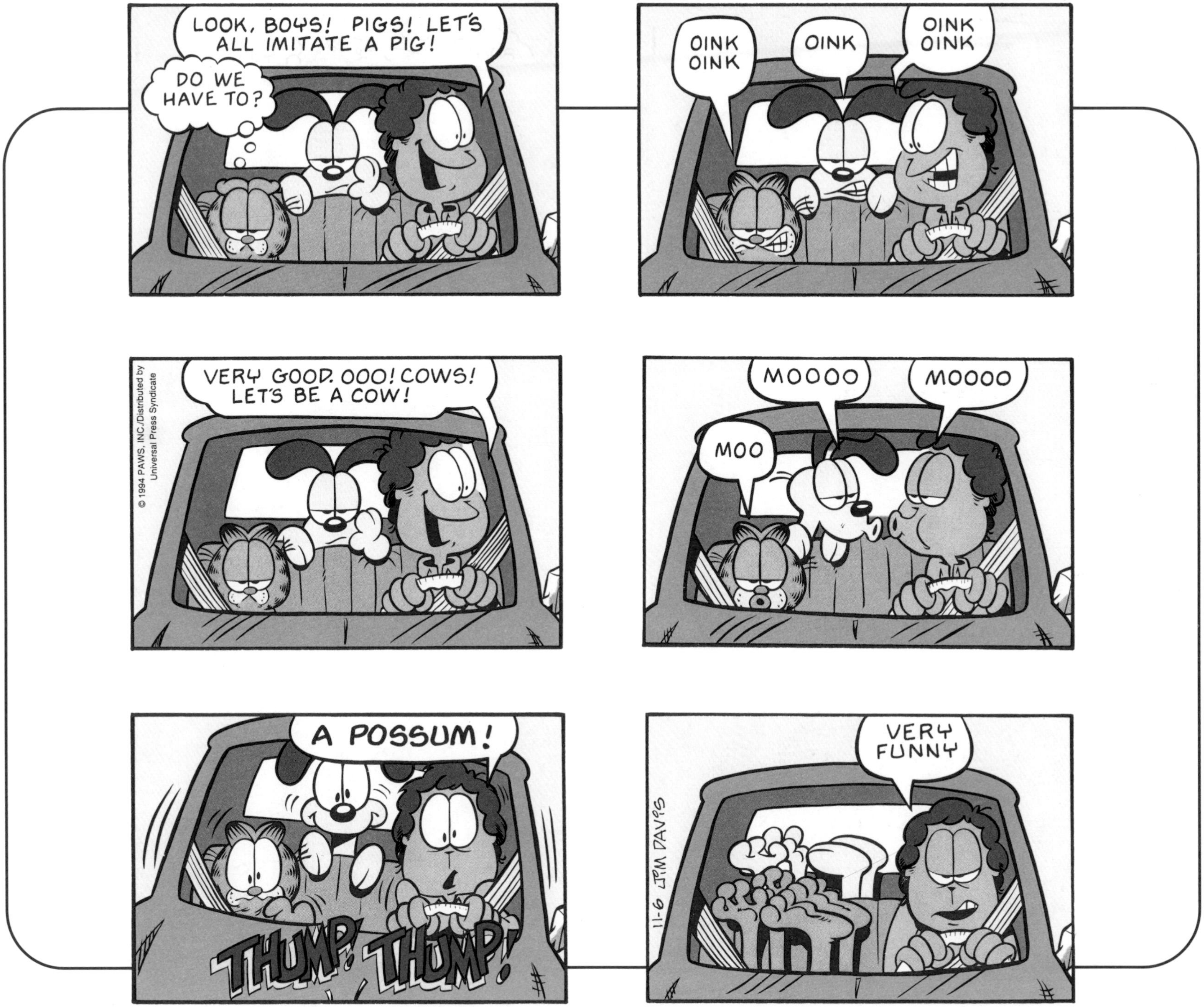
LOOK, BOYS! PIGS! LET'S ALL IMITATE A PIG!
DO WE HAVE TO?
OINK OINK
OINK
OINK OINK
VERY GOOD. OOO! COWS! LET'S BE A COW!
MOO
MOOOO
MOOOO
A POSSUM!
THUMP! THUMP!
JIM DAVIS 11-6
VERY FUNNY

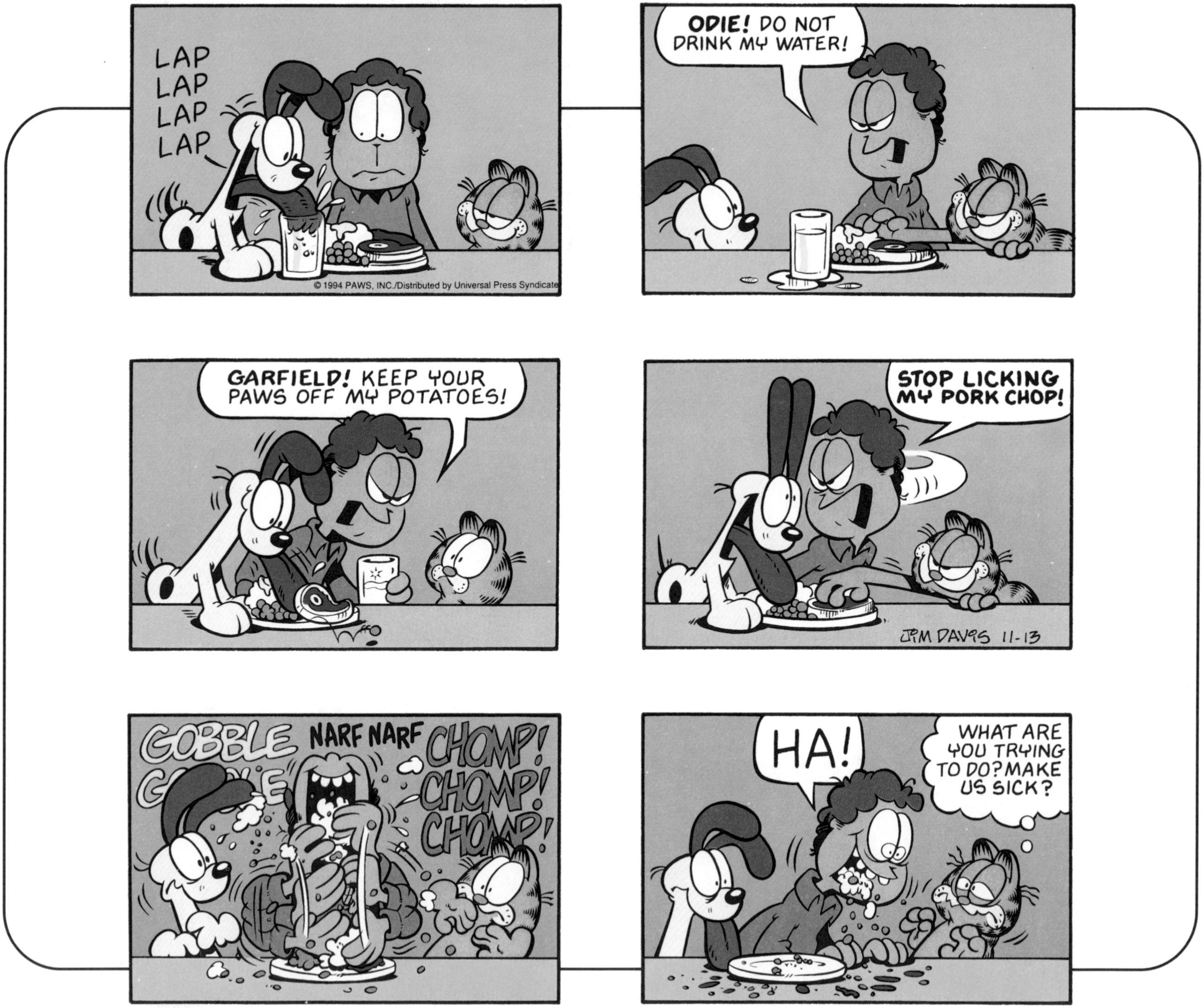
LAP
LAP
LAP
LAP
© 1994 PAWS, INC./Distributed by Universal Press Syndicate
ODIE! DO NOT DRINK MY WATER!
GARFIELD! KEEP YOUR PAWS OFF MY POTATOES!
STOP LICKING MY PORK CHOP!
JIM DAVIS 11-13
GOBBLE
NARF NARF
CHOMP!
CHOMP!
HA!
WHAT ARE YOU TRYING TO DO? MAKE US SICK?

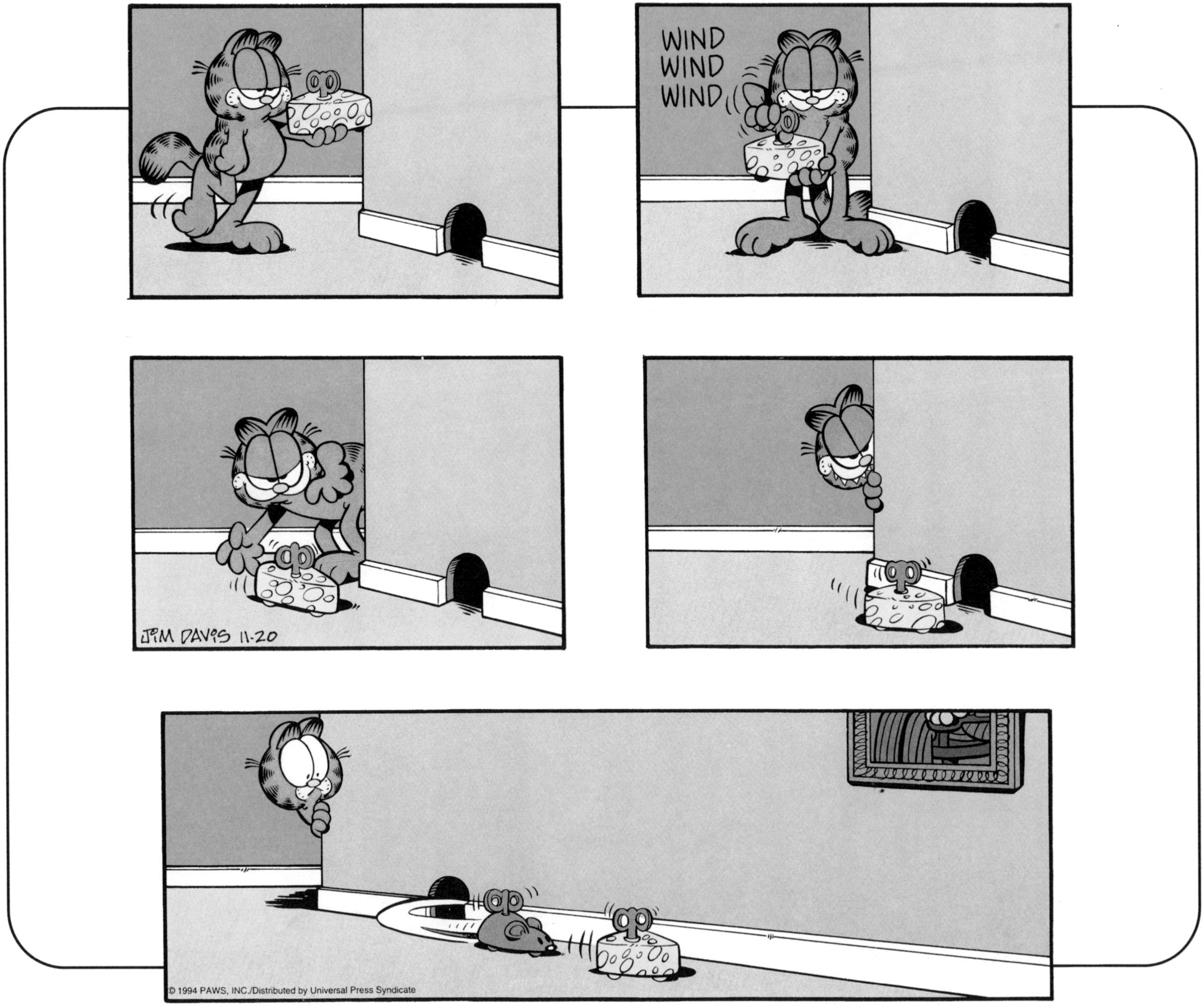
WIND
WIND
WIND
JIM DAVIS 11-20

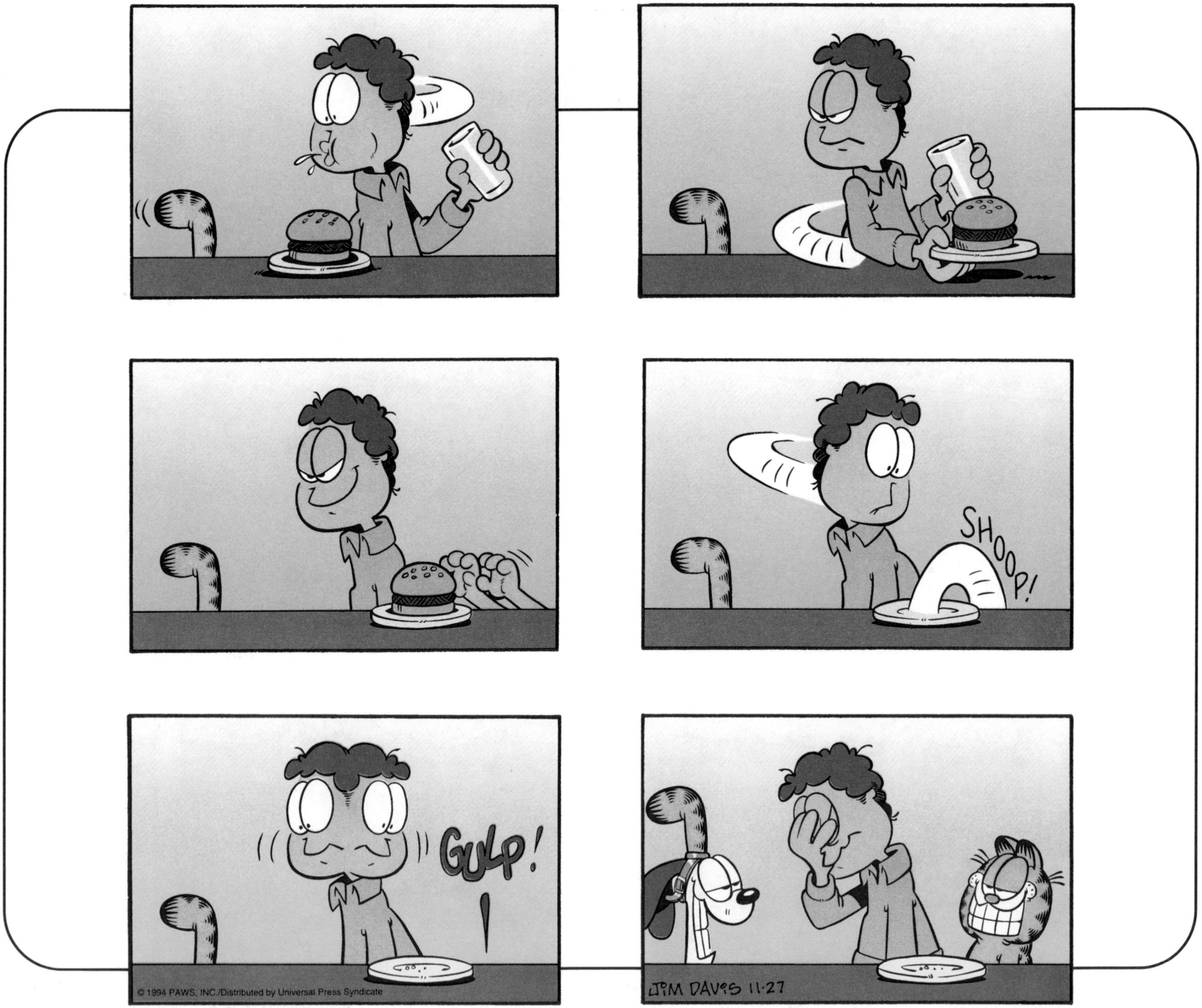
SHOOP!
GULP!
JIM DAVIS 11·27

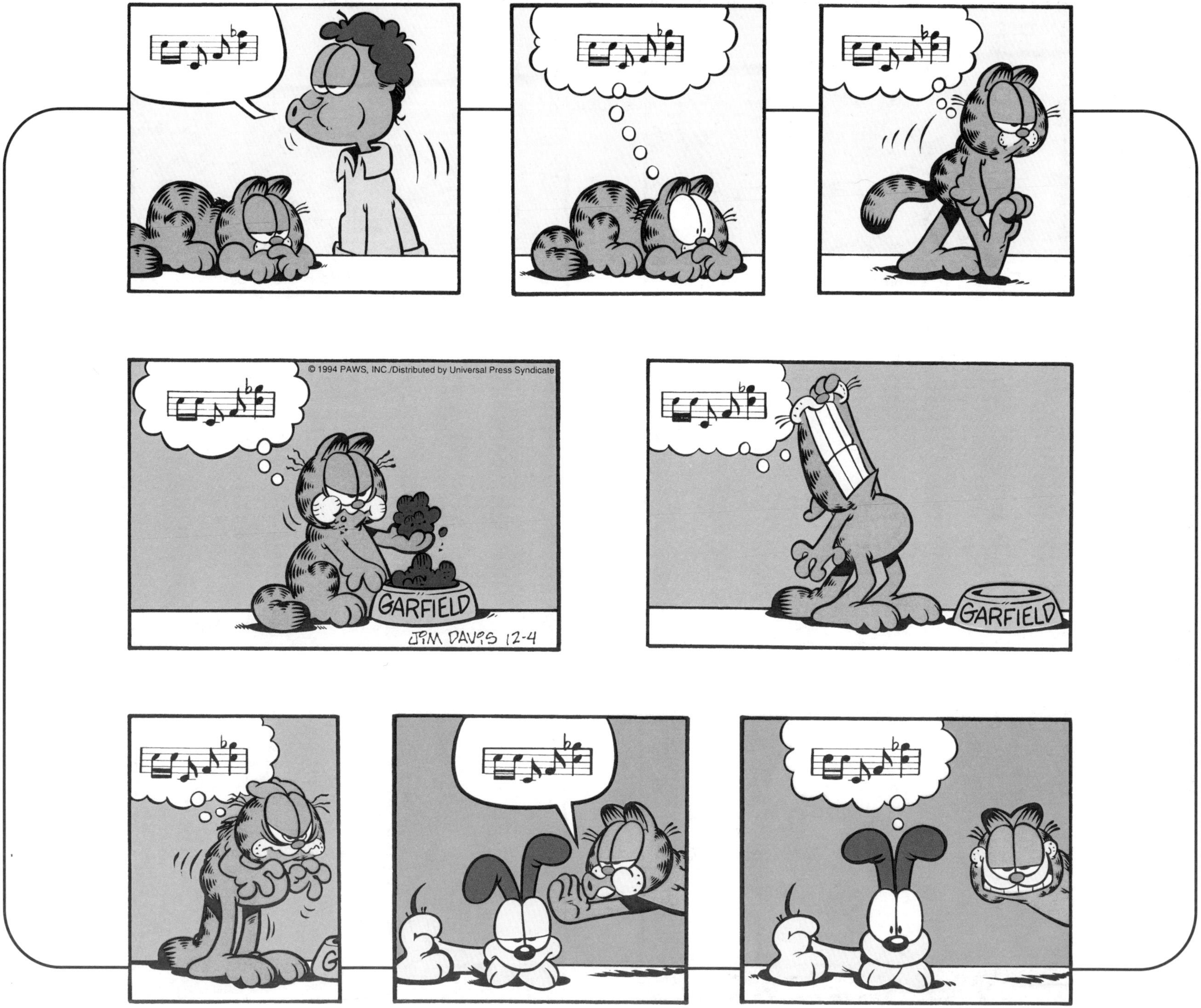
© 1994 PAWS, INC./Distributed by Universal Press Syndicate
GARFIELD
JIM DAVIS 12-4
GARFIELD

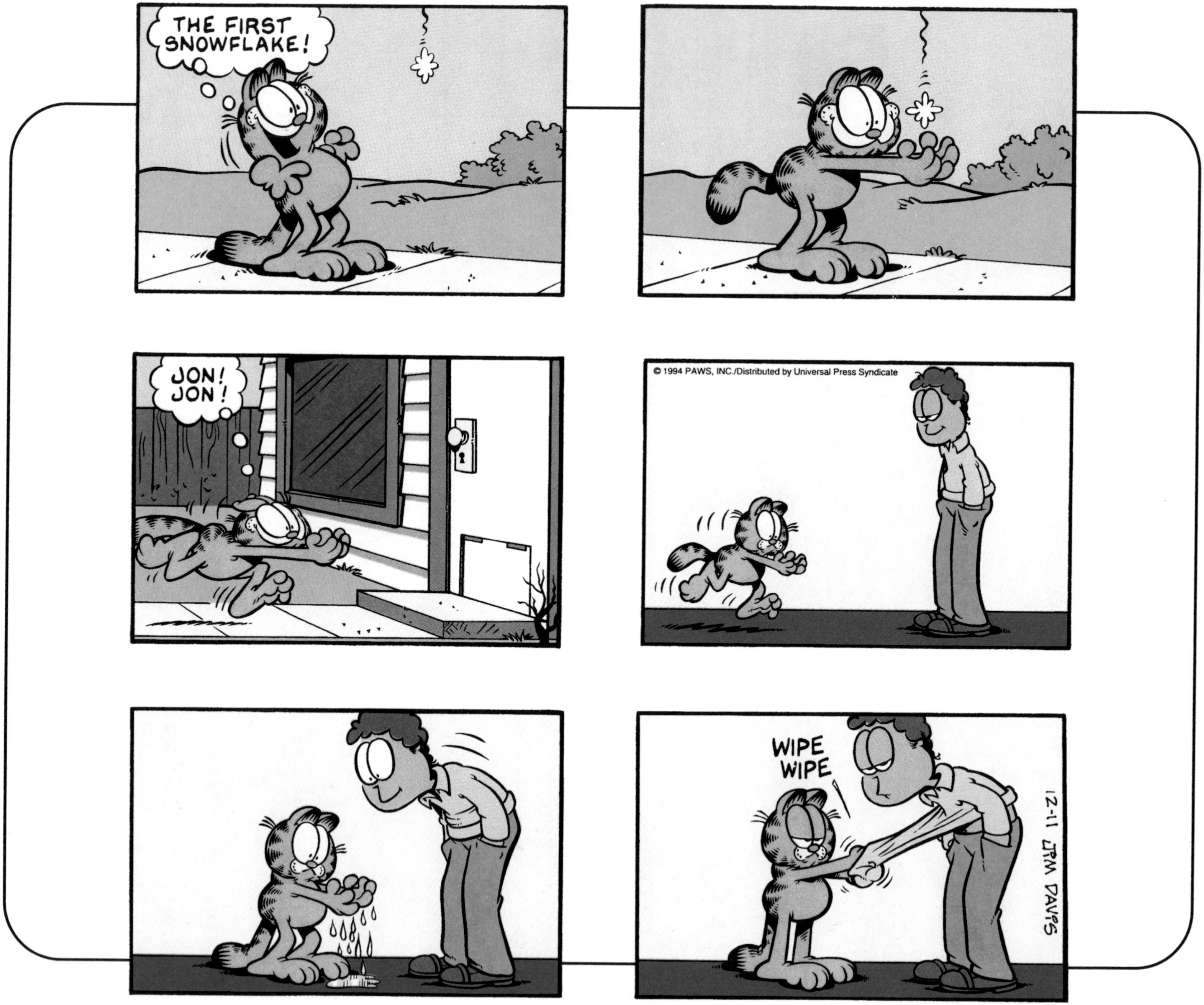
THE FIRST SNOWFLAKE!
JON! JON!
© 1994 PAWS, INC./Distributed by Universal Press Syndicate
WIPE WIPE
12-11 JPM DAVIS

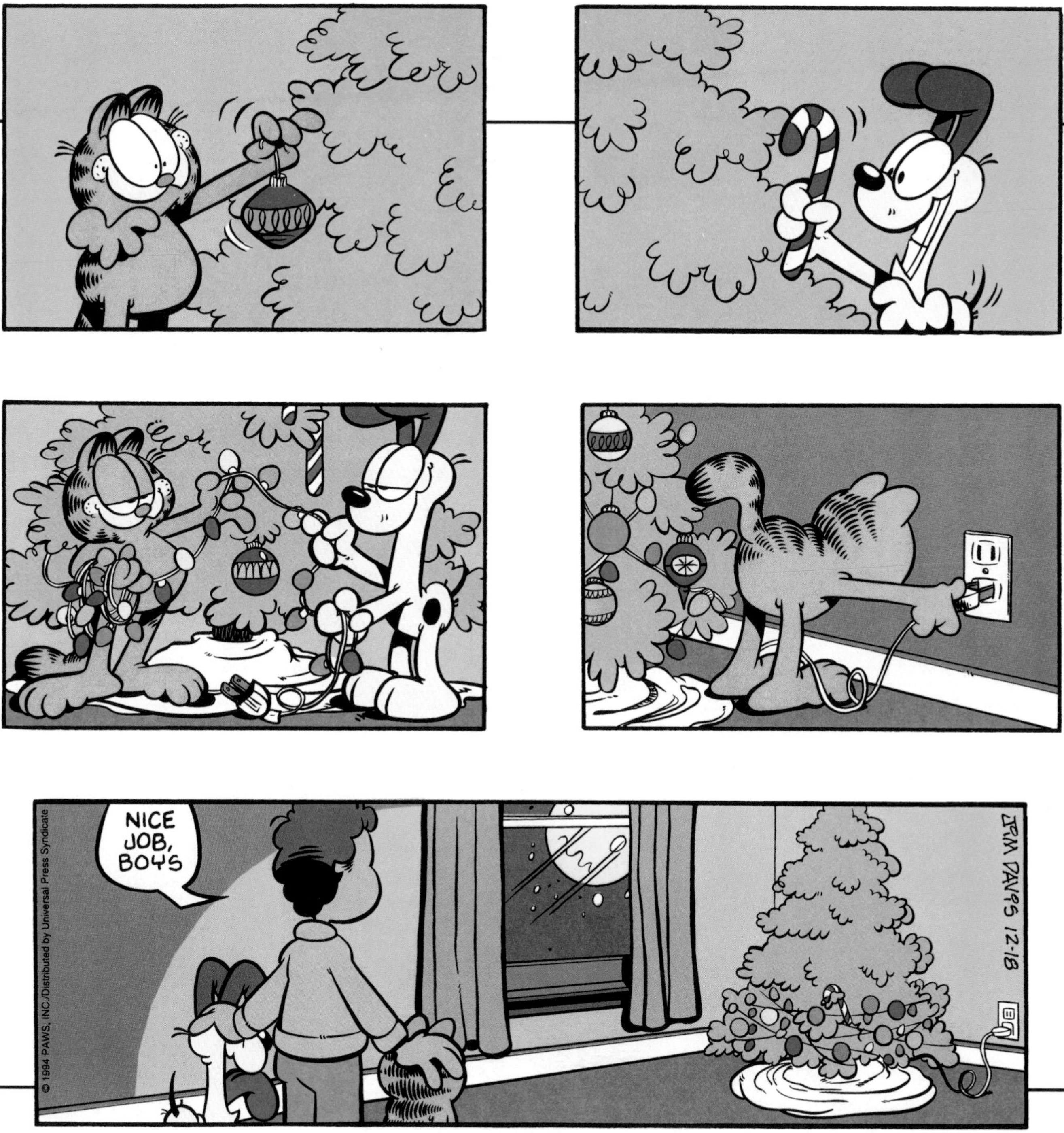
NICE JOB, BOYS
JPM DAVPS 12-18
© 1994 PAWS, INC./Distributed by Universal Press Syndicate

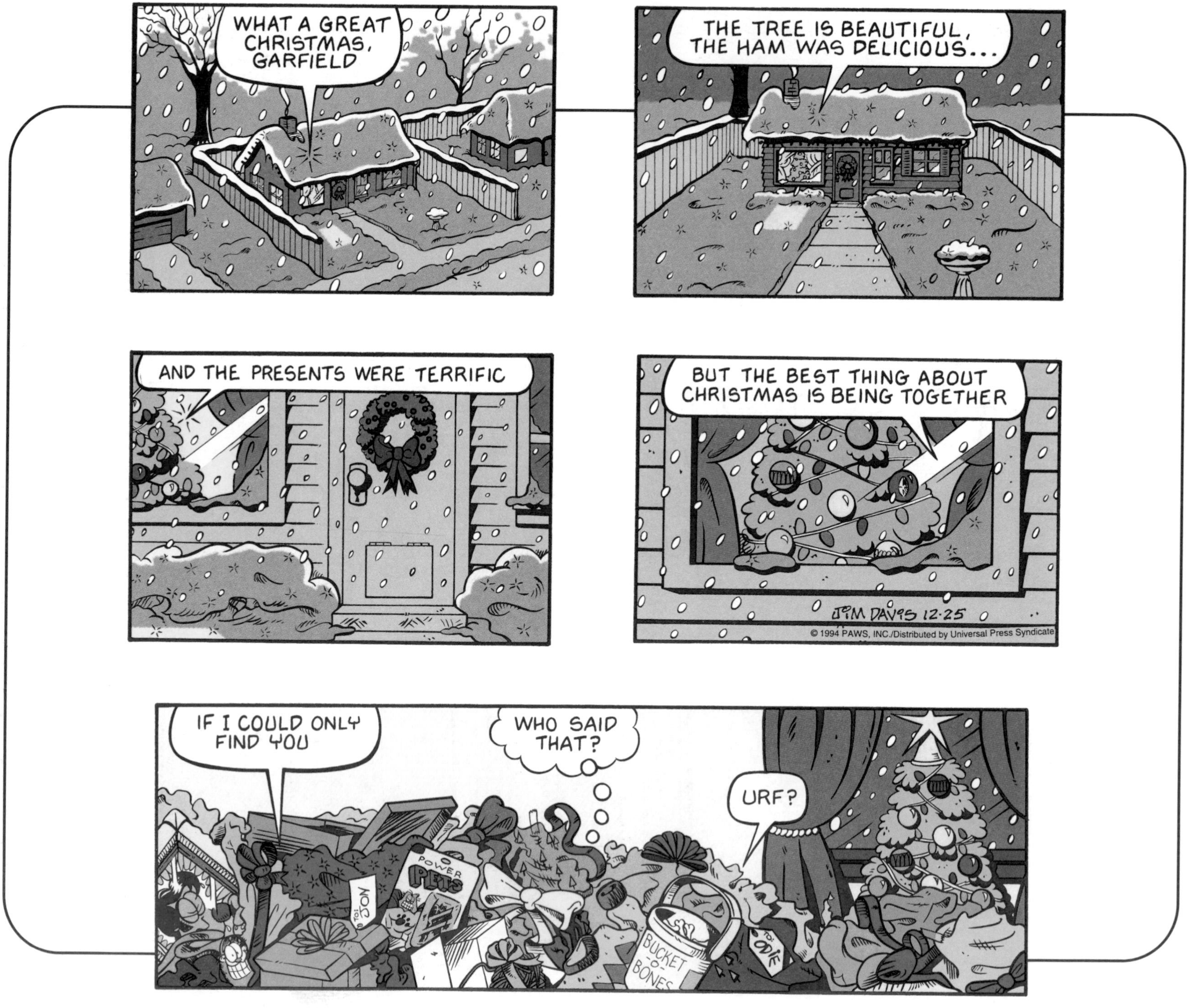

WHAT A GREAT CHRISTMAS, GARFIELD
THE TREE IS BEAUTIFUL, THE HAM WAS DELICIOUS...
AND THE PRESENTS WERE TERRIFIC
BUT THE BEST THING ABOUT CHRISTMAS IS BEING TOGETHER
JIM DAVIS 12-25
© 1994 PAWS, INC./Distributed by Universal Press Syndicate
IF I COULD ONLY FIND YOU
WHO SAID THAT?
URF?
TO: JON
POWER PETS
BUCKET -O- BONES
TO: ODIE

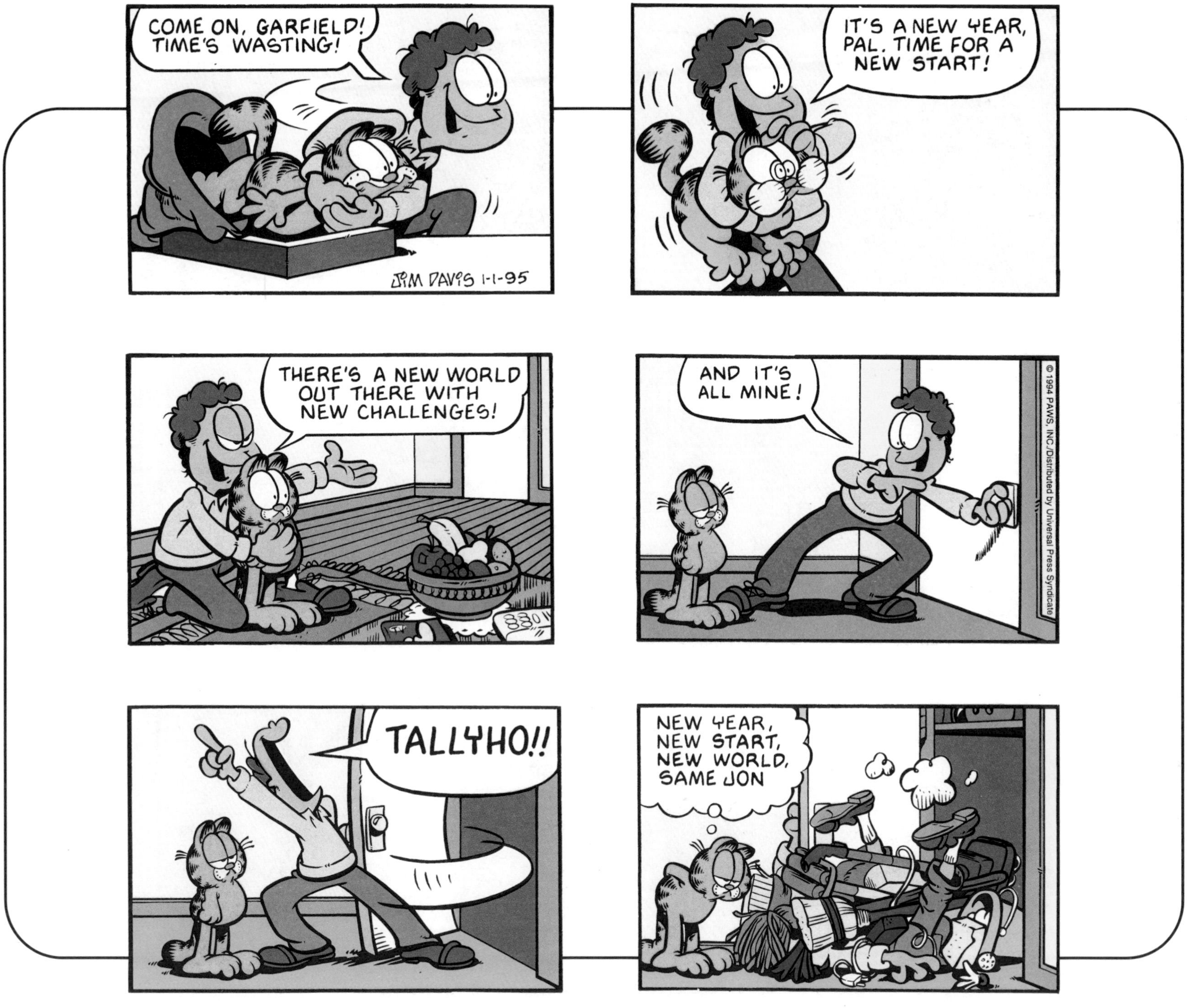
COME ON, GARFIELD! TIME'S WASTING!
JIM DAVIS 1-1-95
IT'S A NEW YEAR, PAL. TIME FOR A NEW START!
THERE'S A NEW WORLD OUT THERE WITH NEW CHALLENGES!
AND IT'S ALL MINE!
© 1994 PAWS, INC./Distributed by Universal Press Syndicate
TALLYHO!!
NEW YEAR, NEW START, NEW WORLD, SAME JON

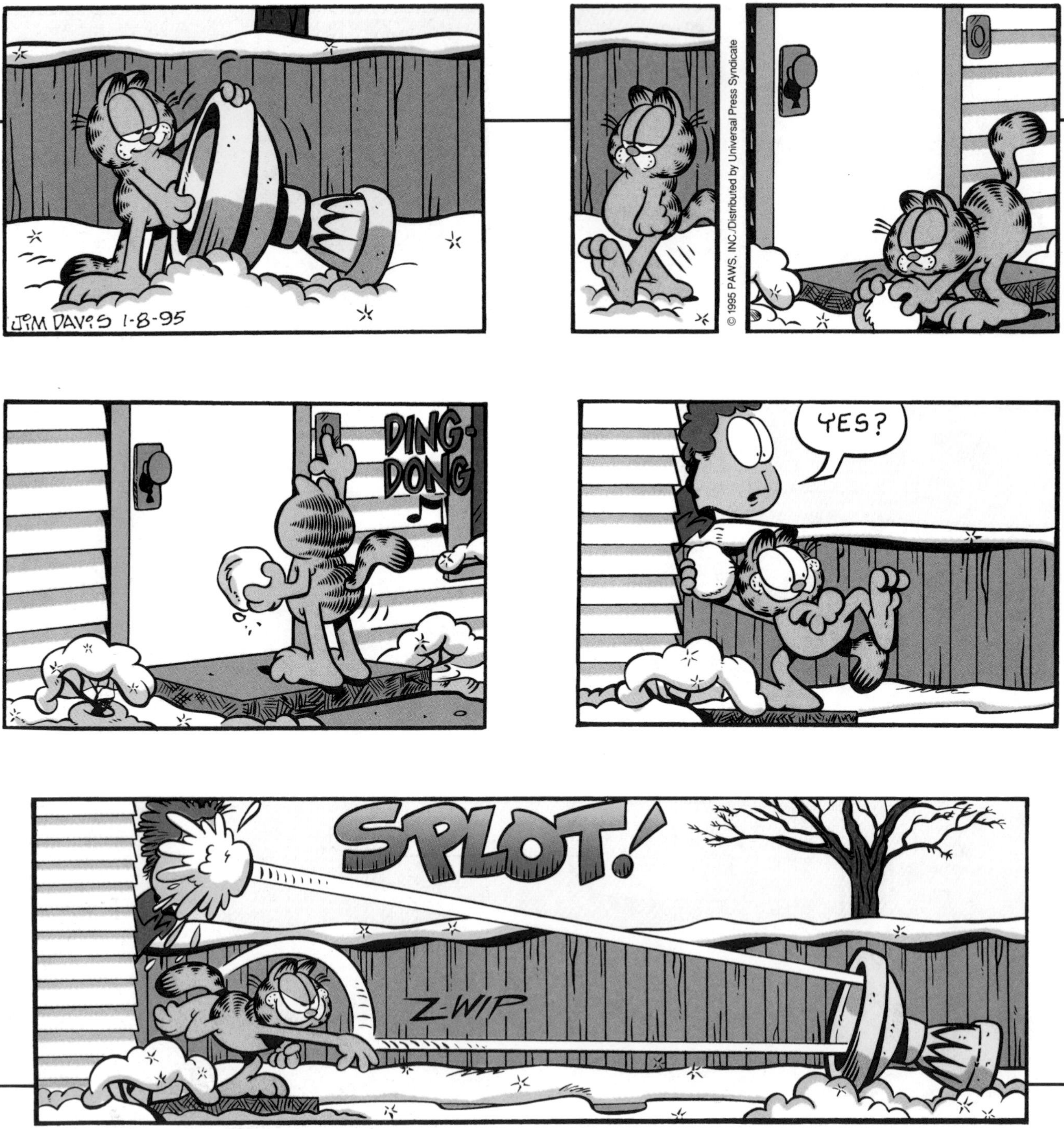
JIM DAVIS 1-8-95
© 1995 PAWS, INC./Distributed by Universal Press Syndicate
DING-DONG
YES?
SPLOT!
Z-WIP

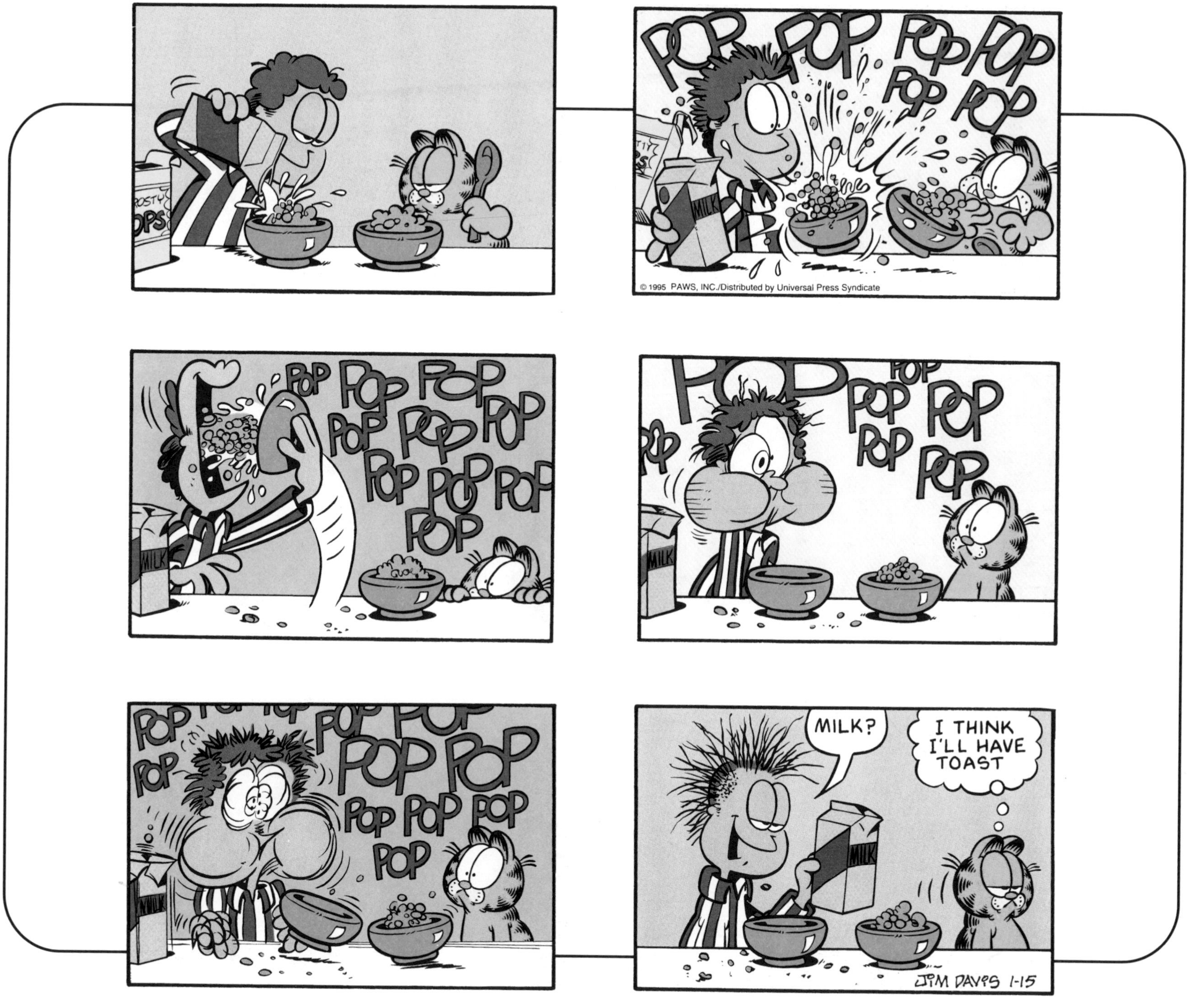
POPS
POP POP POP POP POP POP
MILK
POP POP POP POP POP POP POP POP POP POP POP
MILK
POP POP POP POP POP POP
MILK
POP POP POP POP POP POP POP POP POP POP POP
MILK
MILK?
I THINK I'LL HAVE TOAST
MILK
JIM DAVIS 1-15

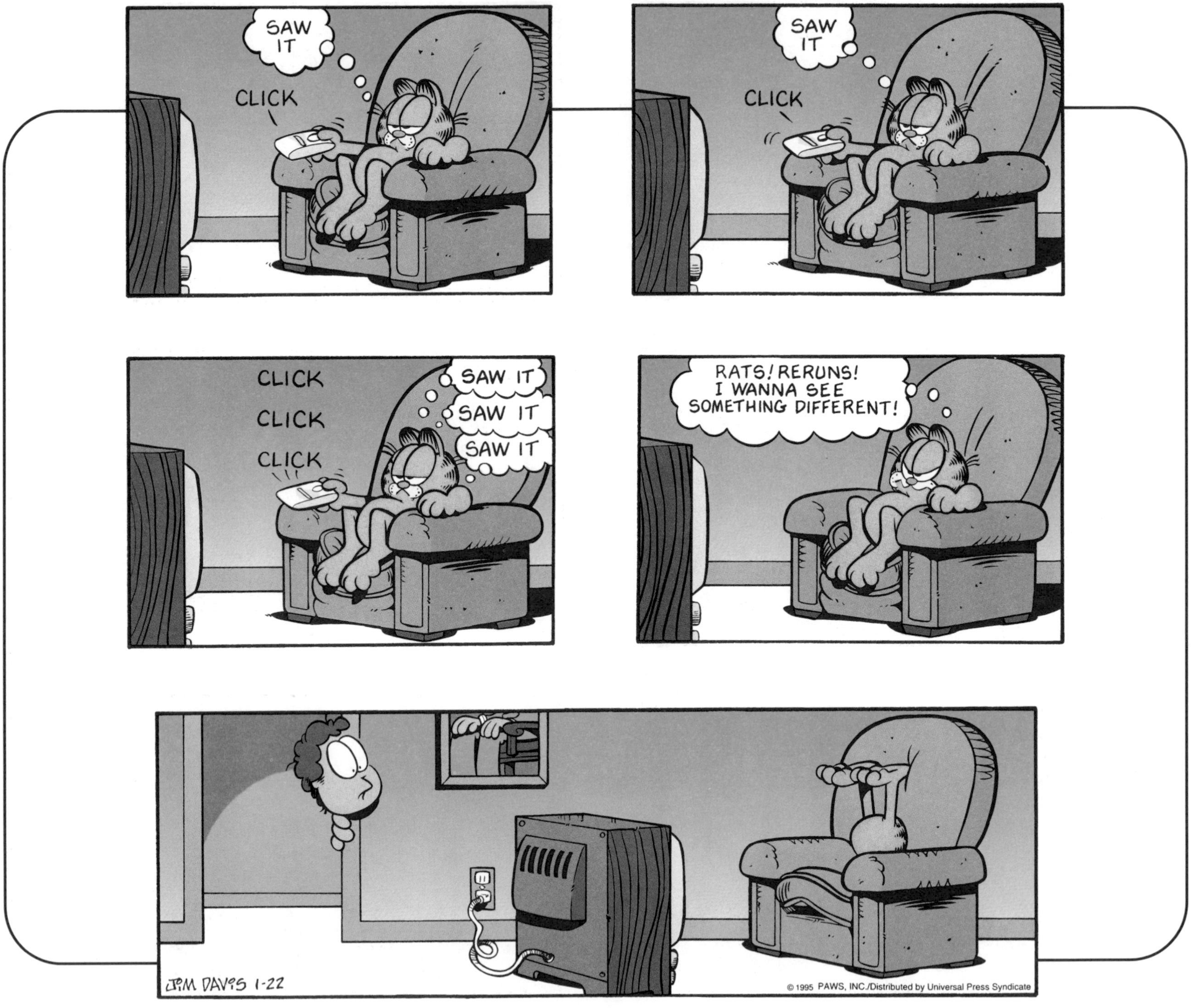
SAW IT
CLICK
SAW IT
CLICK
CLICK
CLICK
CLICK
SAW IT
SAW IT
SAW IT
RATS! RERUNS! I WANNA SEE SOMETHING DIFFERENT!
JIM DAVIS 1-22
© 1995 PAWS, INC./Distributed by Universal Press Syndicate

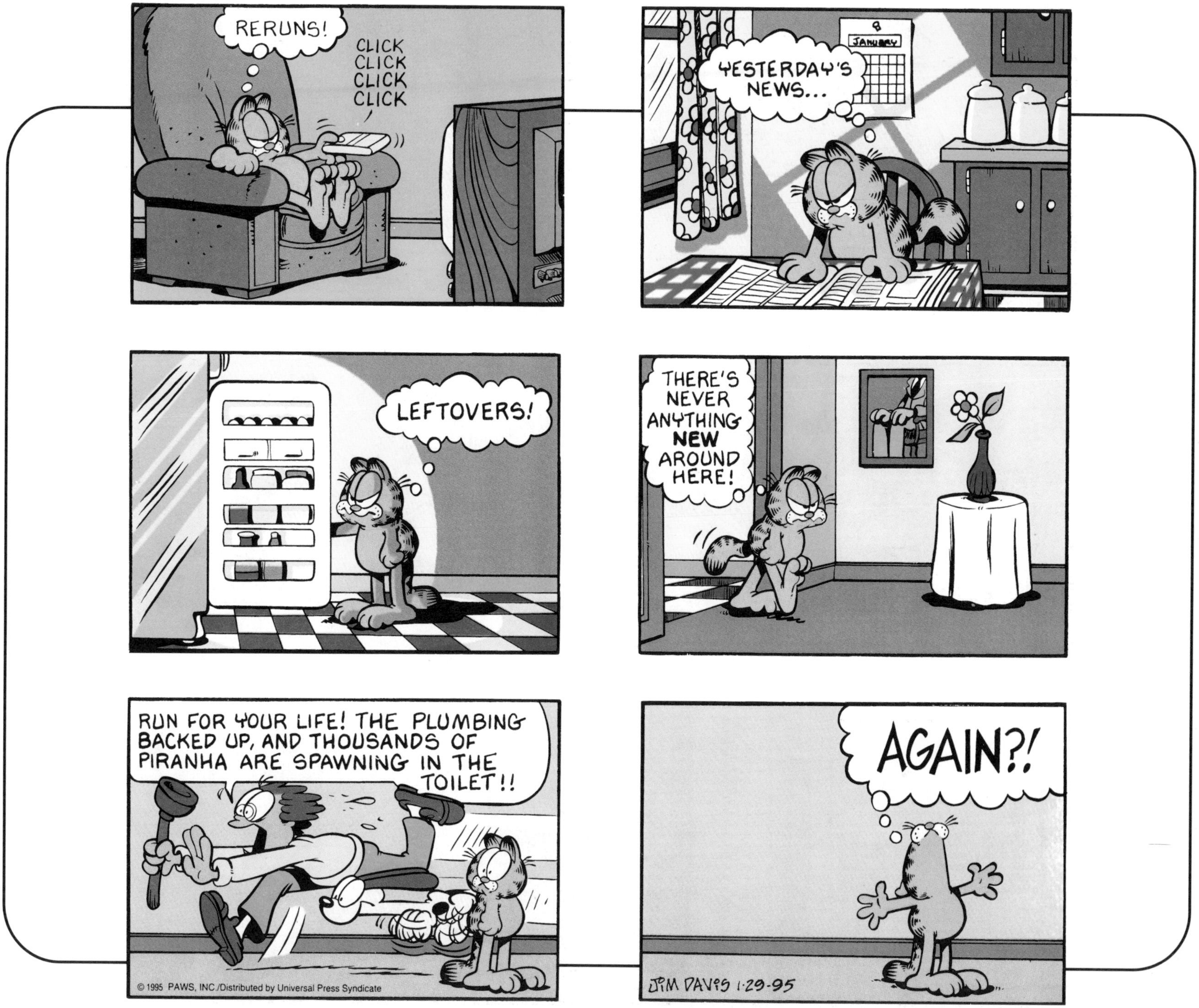
RERUNS!
CLICK CLICK CLICK CLICK
YESTERDAY'S NEWS...
JANUARY
LEFTOVERS!
THERE'S NEVER ANYTHING NEW AROUND HERE!
RUN FOR YOUR LIFE! THE PLUMBING BACKED UP, AND THOUSANDS OF PIRANHA ARE SPAWNING IN THE TOILET!!
AGAIN?!
JIM DAVIS 1-29-95
© 1995 PAWS, INC./Distributed by Universal Press Syndicate

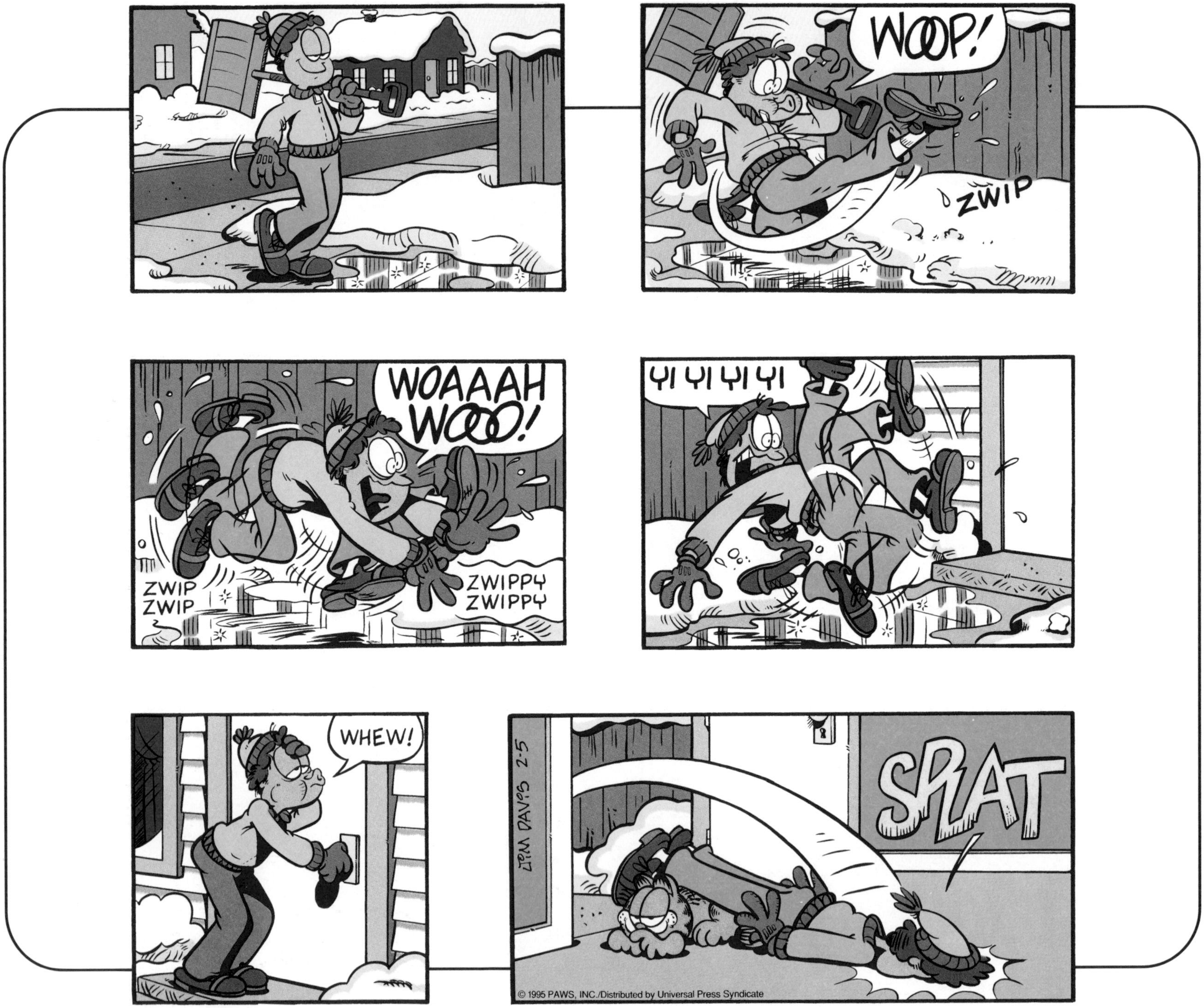
WOOP!
ZWIP
WOAAAH WOOO!
ZWIP ZWIP
ZWIPPY ZWIPPY
YI YI YI YI
WHEW!
JIM DAVIS 2-5
SPLAT
© 1995 PAWS, INC./Distributed by Universal Press Syndicate

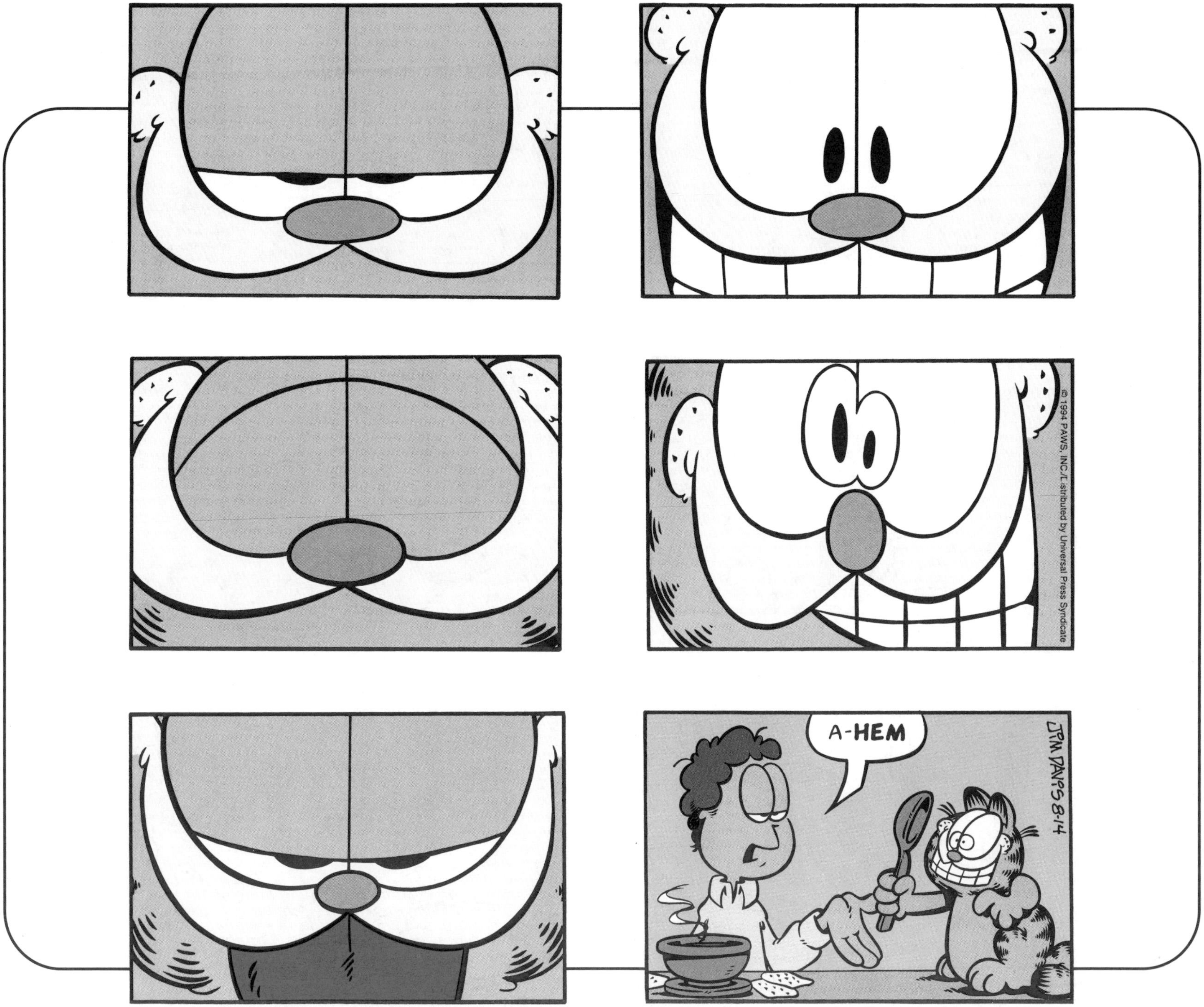
© 1994 PAWS, INC./Distributed by Universal Press Syndicate
JIM DAVIS 8-14
A-HEM

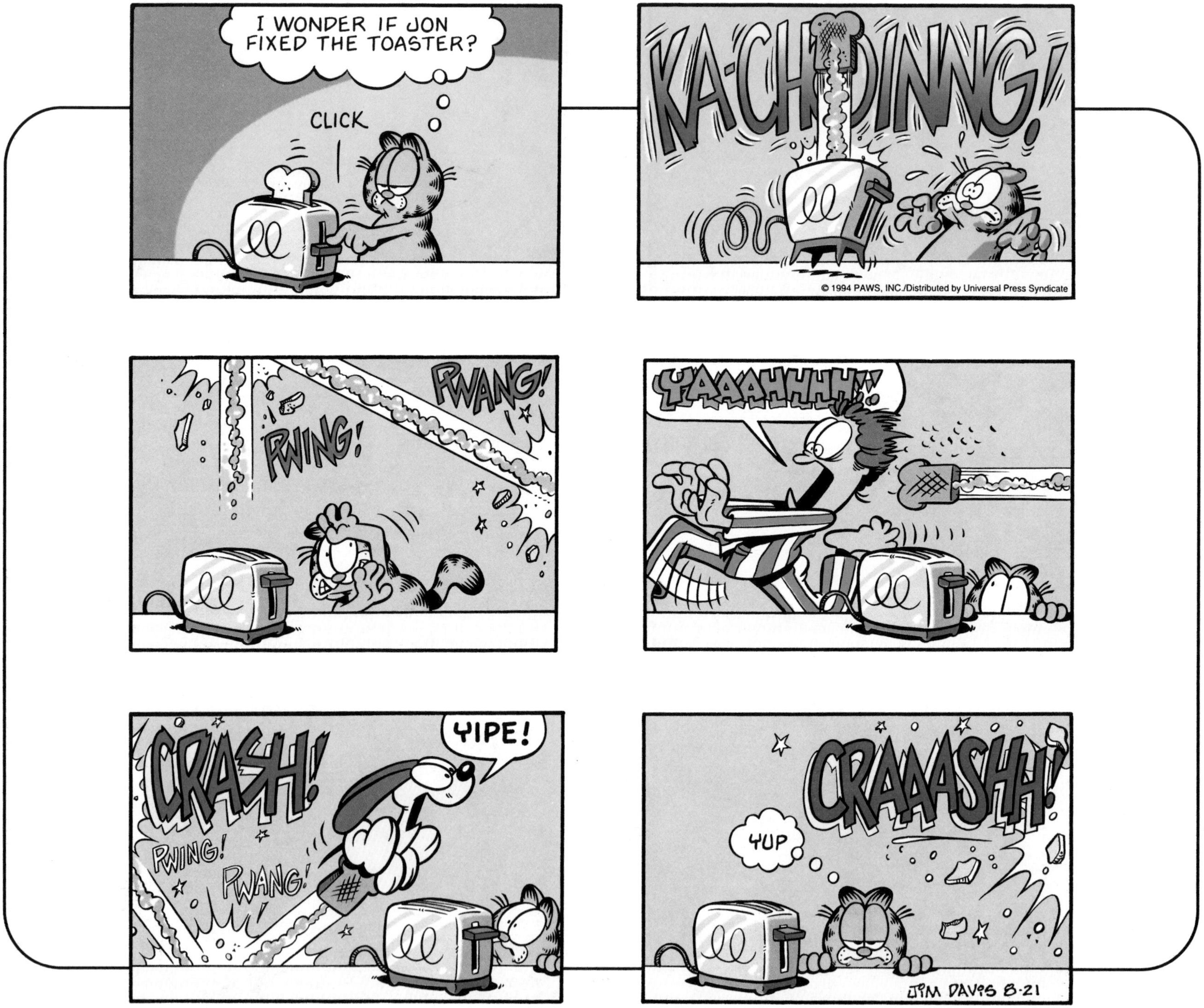
I WONDER IF JON FIXED THE TOASTER?
CLICK
KA-CHOINNG!
© 1994 PAWS, INC./Distributed by Universal Press Syndicate
PWANG!
PWING!
YAAAHHHH!!
CRASH!
YIPE!
PWING!
PWANG!
CRAAASHH!
YUP
JIM DAVIS 8-21

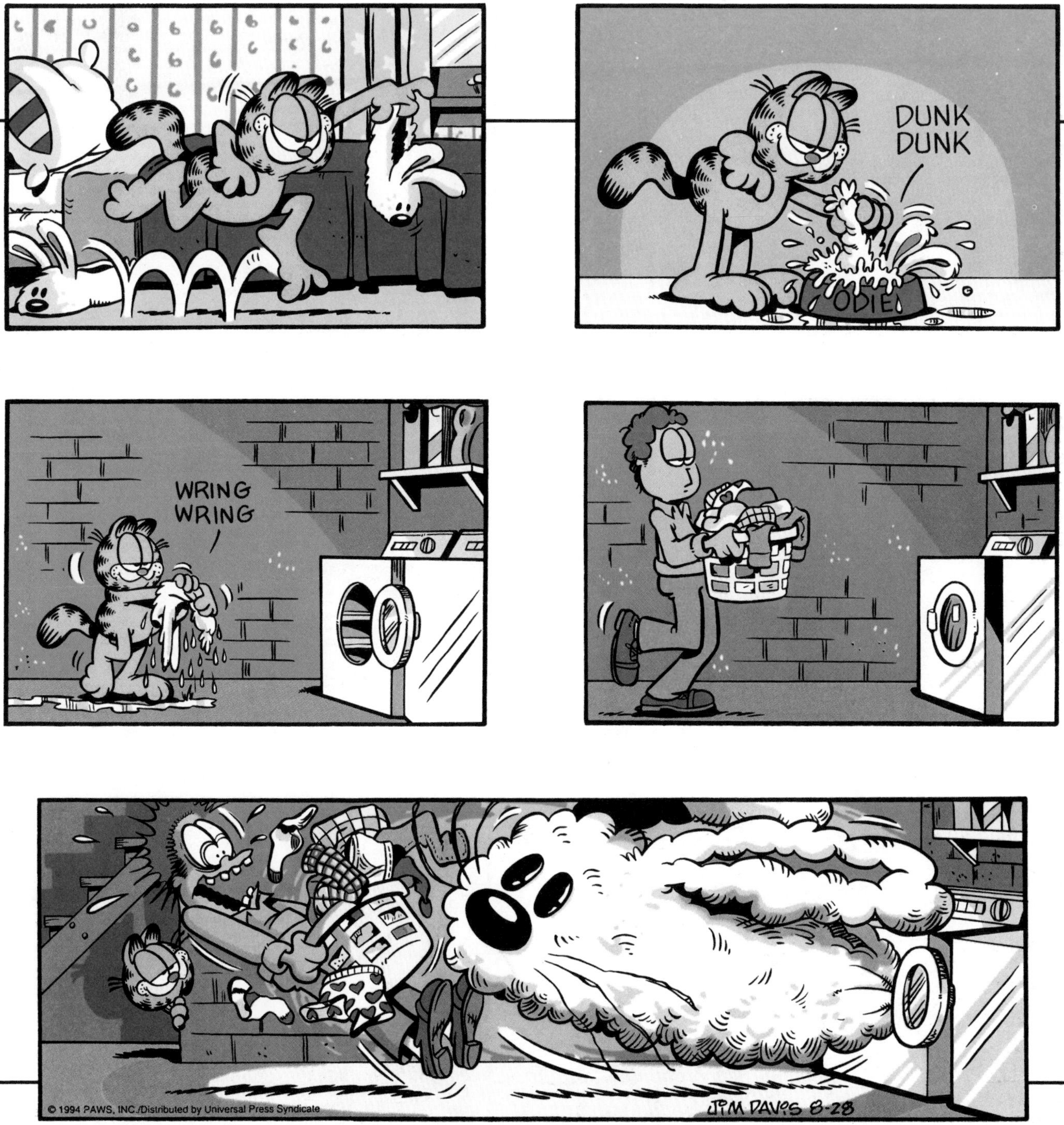
DUNK
DUNK
WRING
WRING
ODIE
© 1994 PAWS, INC./Distributed by Universal Press Syndicate
JIM DAVIS 8-28

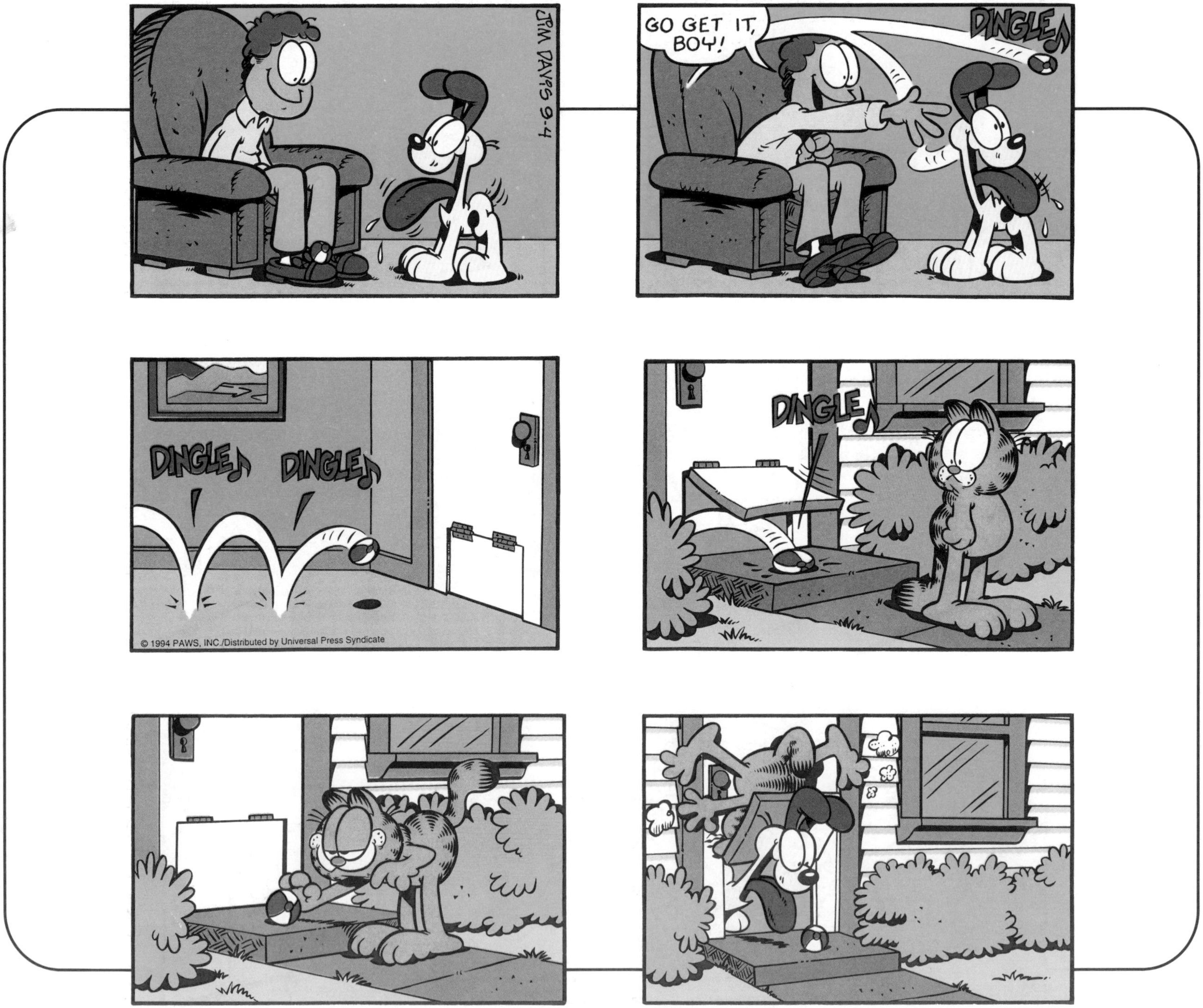
JIM DAVIS 9-4
GO GET IT, BOY!
DINGLE
DINGLE
DINGLE
DINGLE

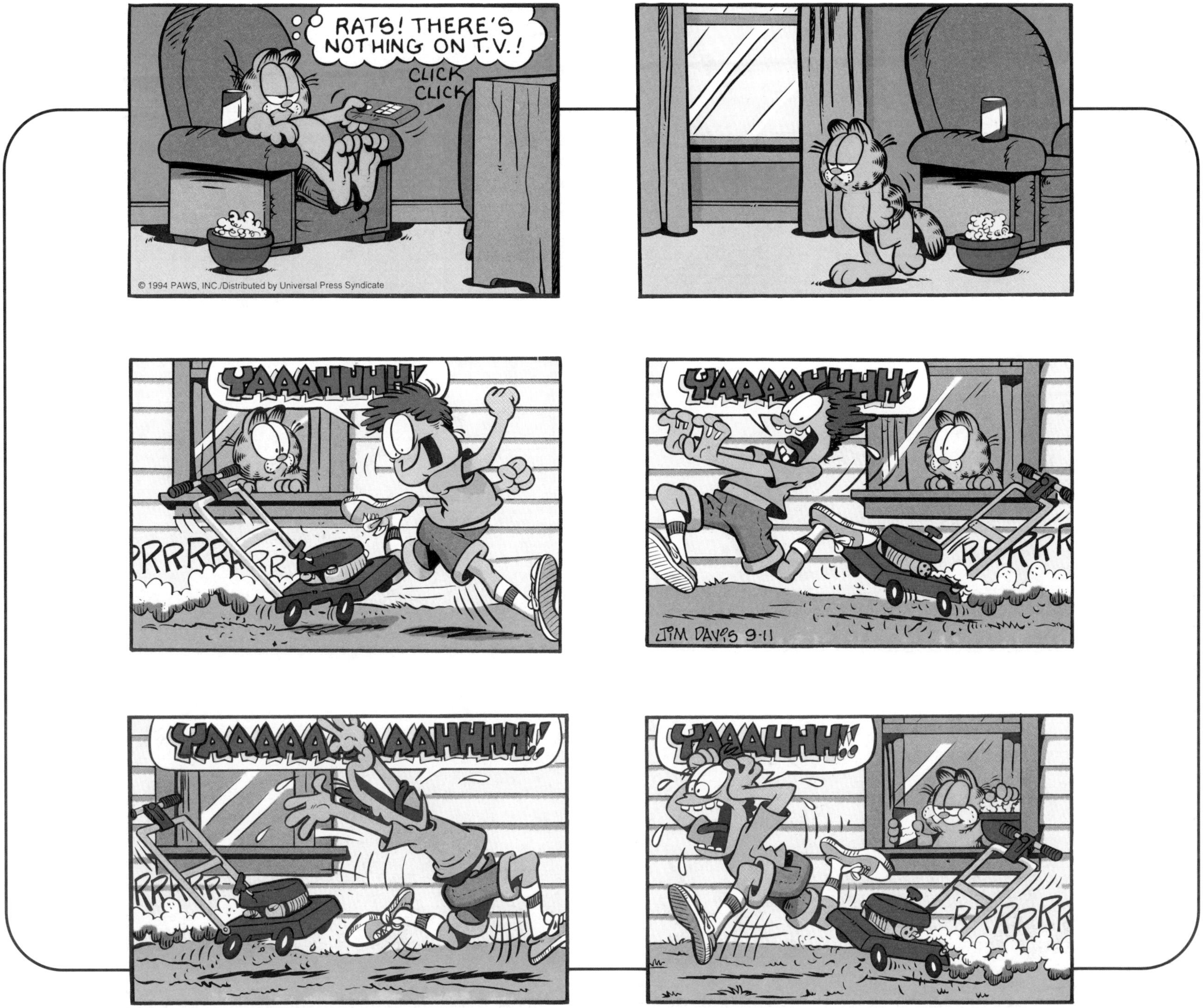

RATS! THERE'S NOTHING ON T.V.!
CLICK CLICK
© 1994 PAWS, INC./Distributed by Universal Press Syndicate
YAAAHHHH!
RRRRRRR
JIM DAVIS 9-11
YAAAHHH!!

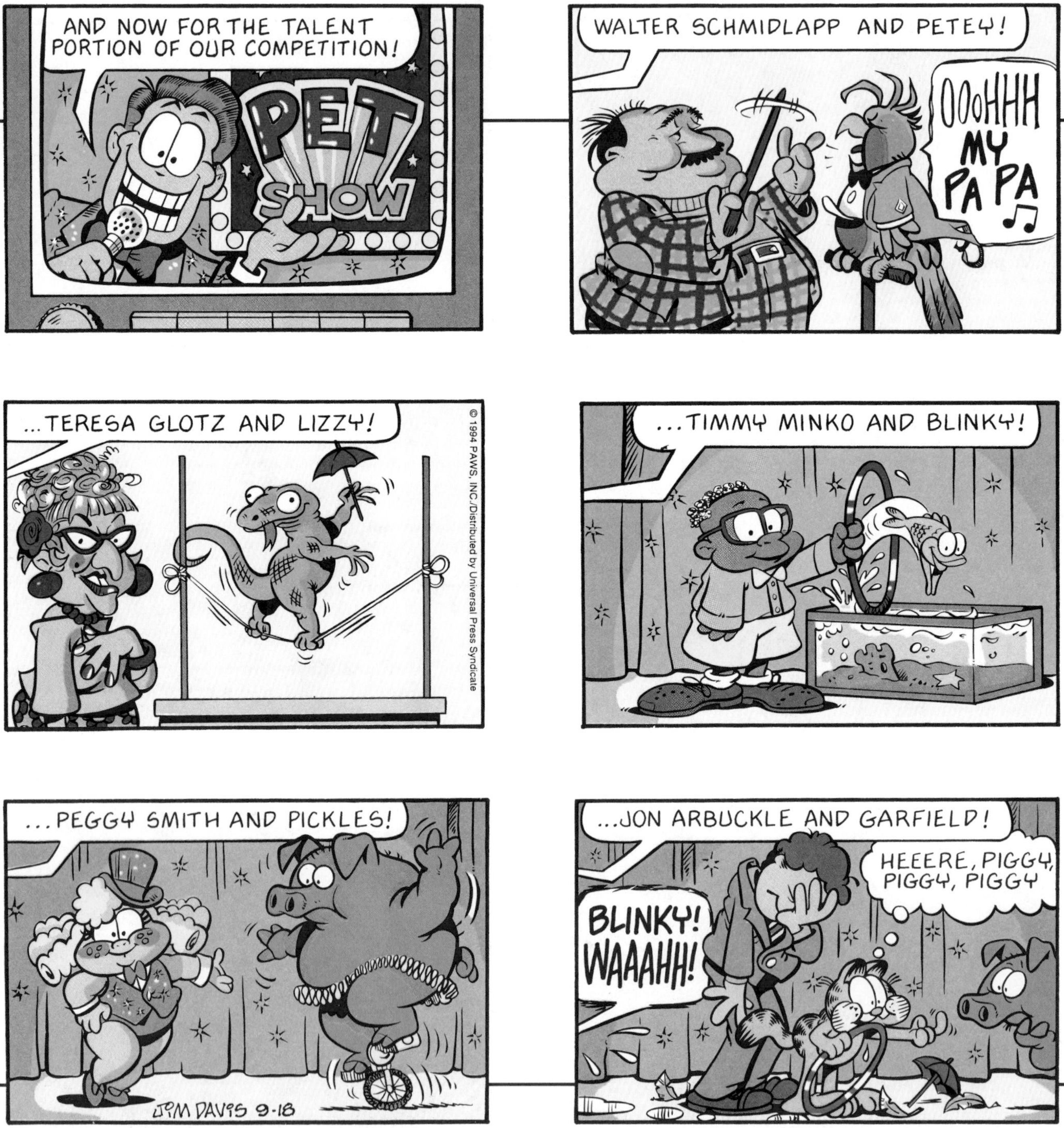
AND NOW FOR THE TALENT PORTION OF OUR COMPETITION!
PET SHOW
WALTER SCHMIDLAPP AND PETEY!
OOoHHH MY PA PA
...TERESA GLOTZ AND LIZZY!
© 1994 PAWS, INC./Distributed by Universal Press Syndicate
...TIMMY MINKO AND BLINKY!
...PEGGY SMITH AND PICKLES!
JIM DAVIS 9-18
...JON ARBUCKLE AND GARFIELD!
HEEERE, PIGGY, PIGGY, PIGGY
BLINKY! WAAAHH!

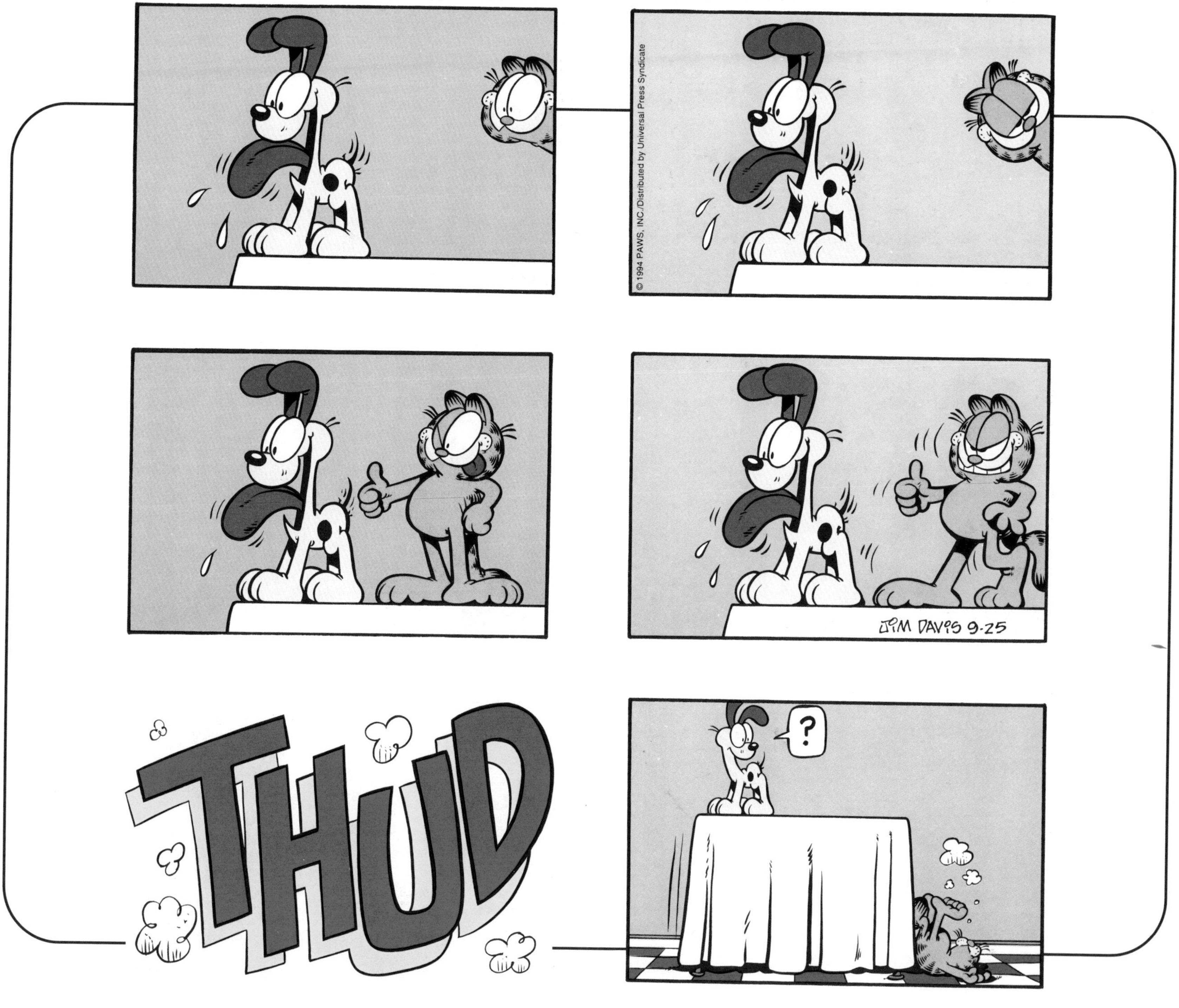
© 1994 PAWS, INC./Distributed by Universal Press Syndicate
JIM DAVIS 9-25
THUD
?

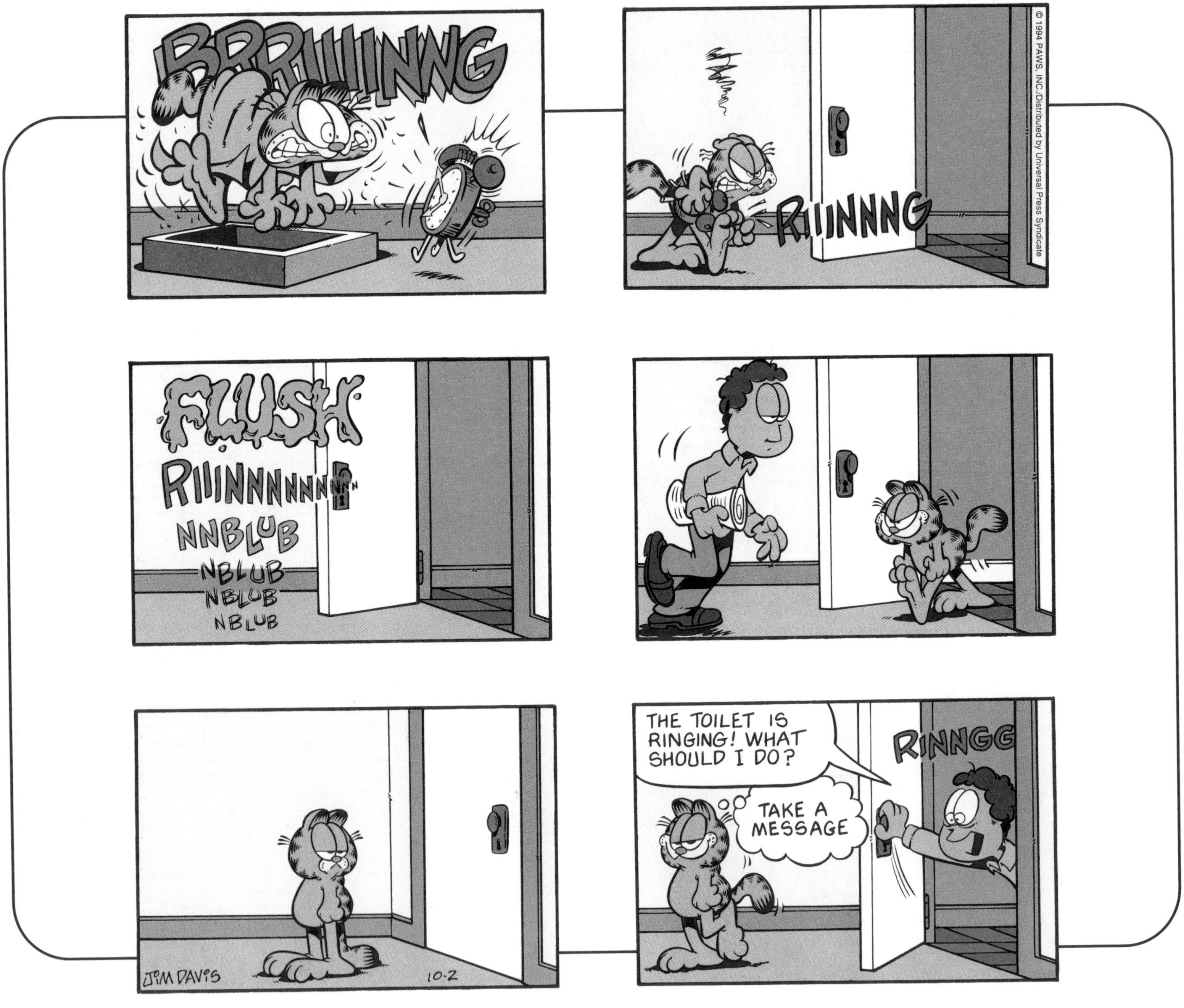

BRRIIIINNG
RIIINNNG
© 1994 PAWS, INC./Distributed by Universal Press Syndicate
FLUSH
RIIINNNNNNN
NNBLUB
NBLUB
NBLUB
NBLUB
THE TOILET IS RINGING! WHAT SHOULD I DO?
TAKE A MESSAGE
RINNGG
JIM DAVIS
10-2

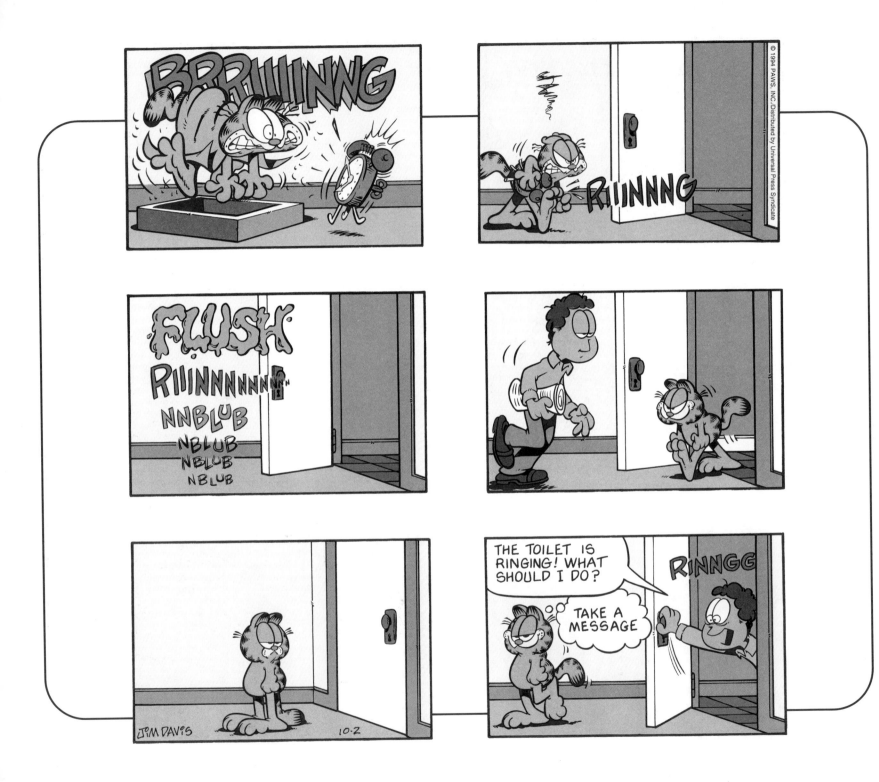

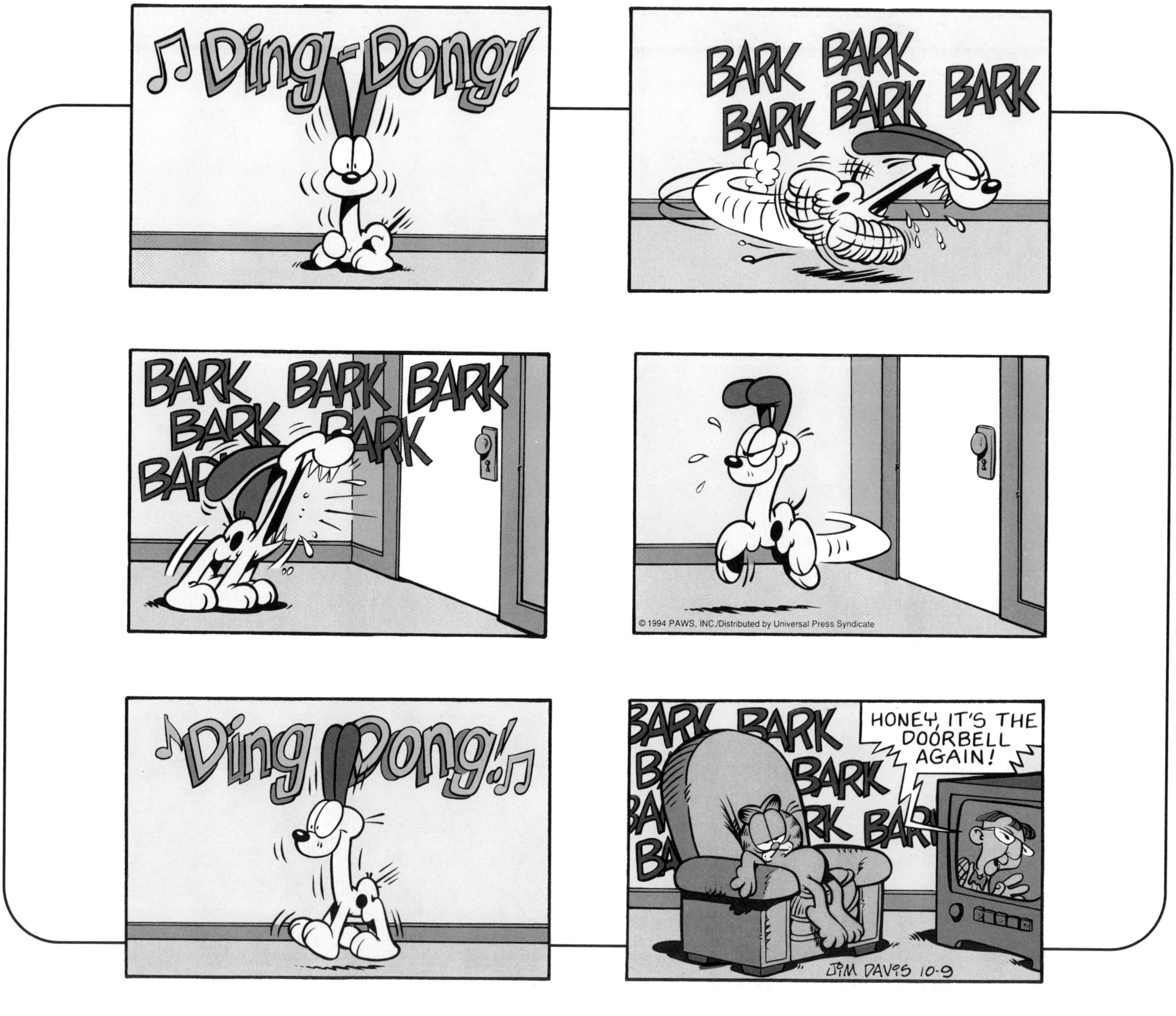
Ding-Dong!
BARK BARK BARK BARK BARK
BARK BARK BARK BARK BARK
© 1994 PAWS, INC./Distributed by Universal Press Syndicate
Ding-Dong!
HONEY, IT'S THE DOORBELL AGAIN!
BARK BARK BARK
JIM DAVIS 10-9

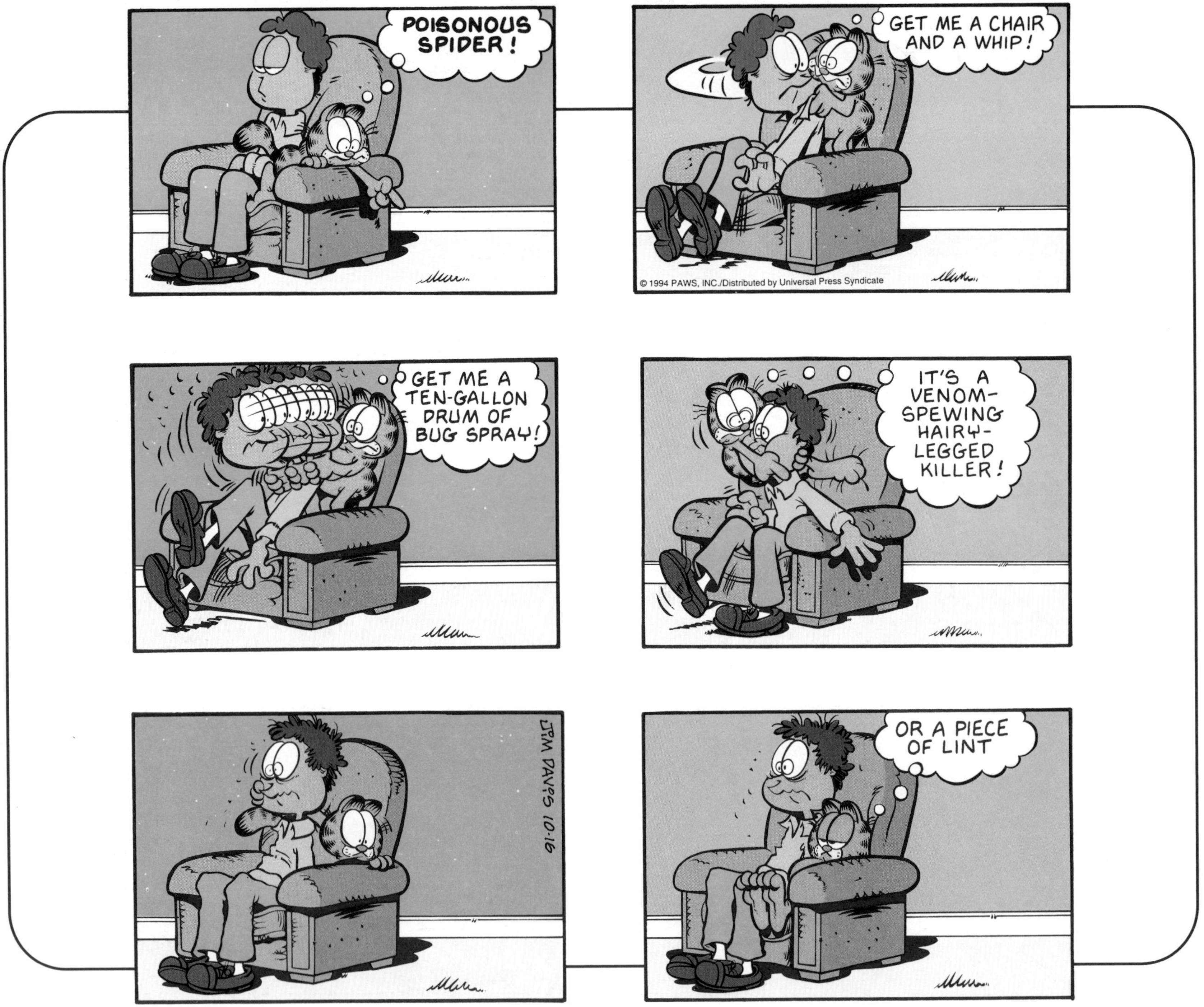
POISONOUS SPIDER!
GET ME A CHAIR AND A WHIP!
© 1994 PAWS, INC./Distributed by Universal Press Syndicate
GET ME A TEN-GALLON DRUM OF BUG SPRAY!
IT'S A VENOM-SPEWING HAIRY-LEGGED KILLER!
JIM DAVIS 10-16
OR A PIECE OF LINT

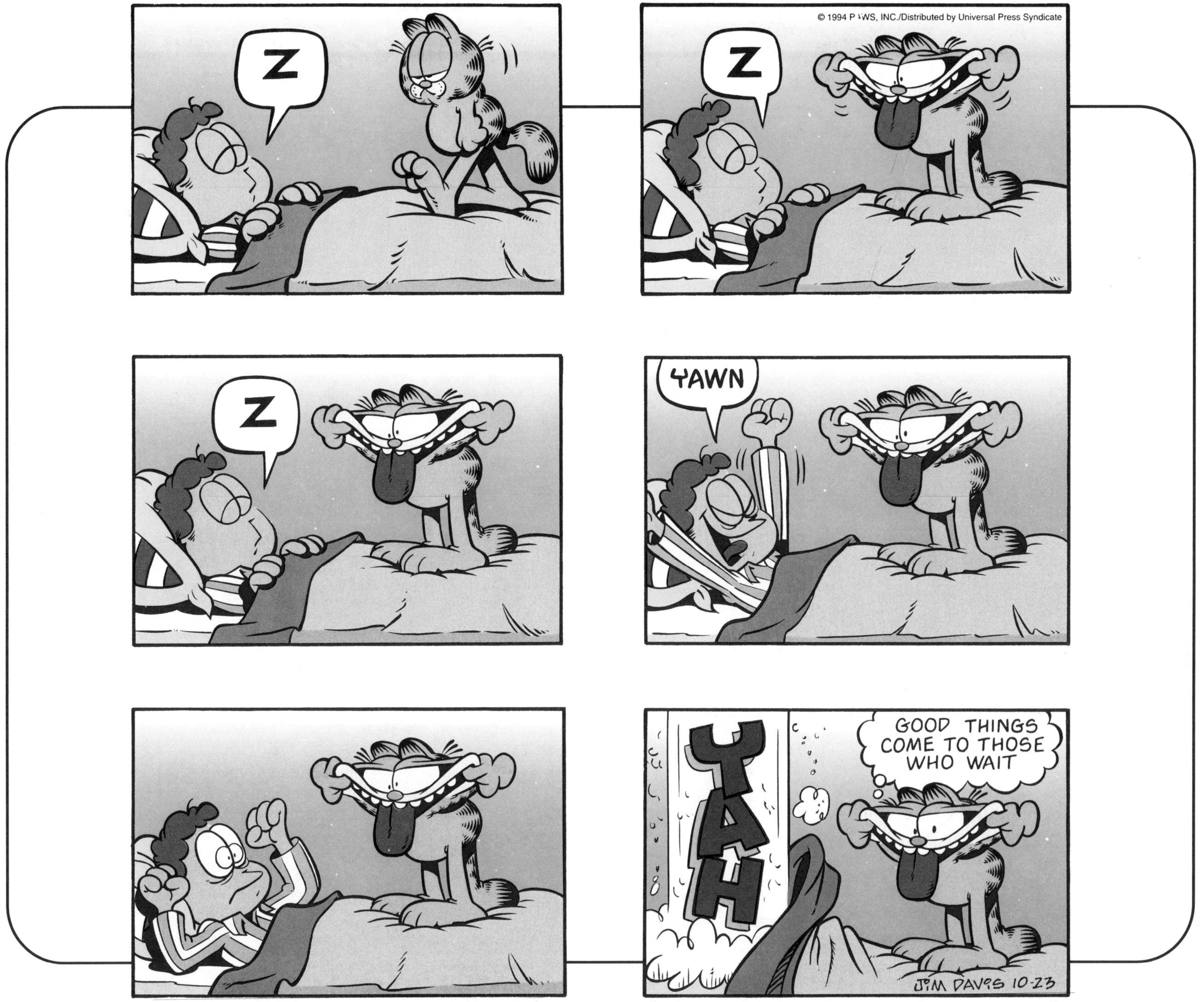

Z
© 1994 PAWS, INC./Distributed by Universal Press Syndicate
Z
Z
YAWN
YAAH
GOOD THINGS COME TO THOSE WHO WAIT
JIM DAVIS 10-23

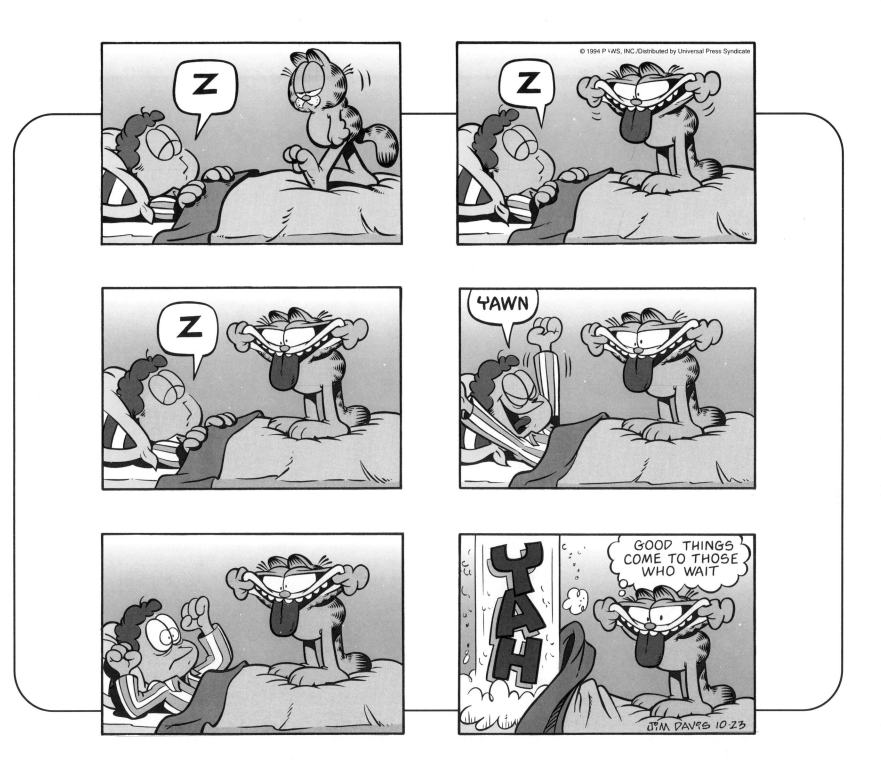

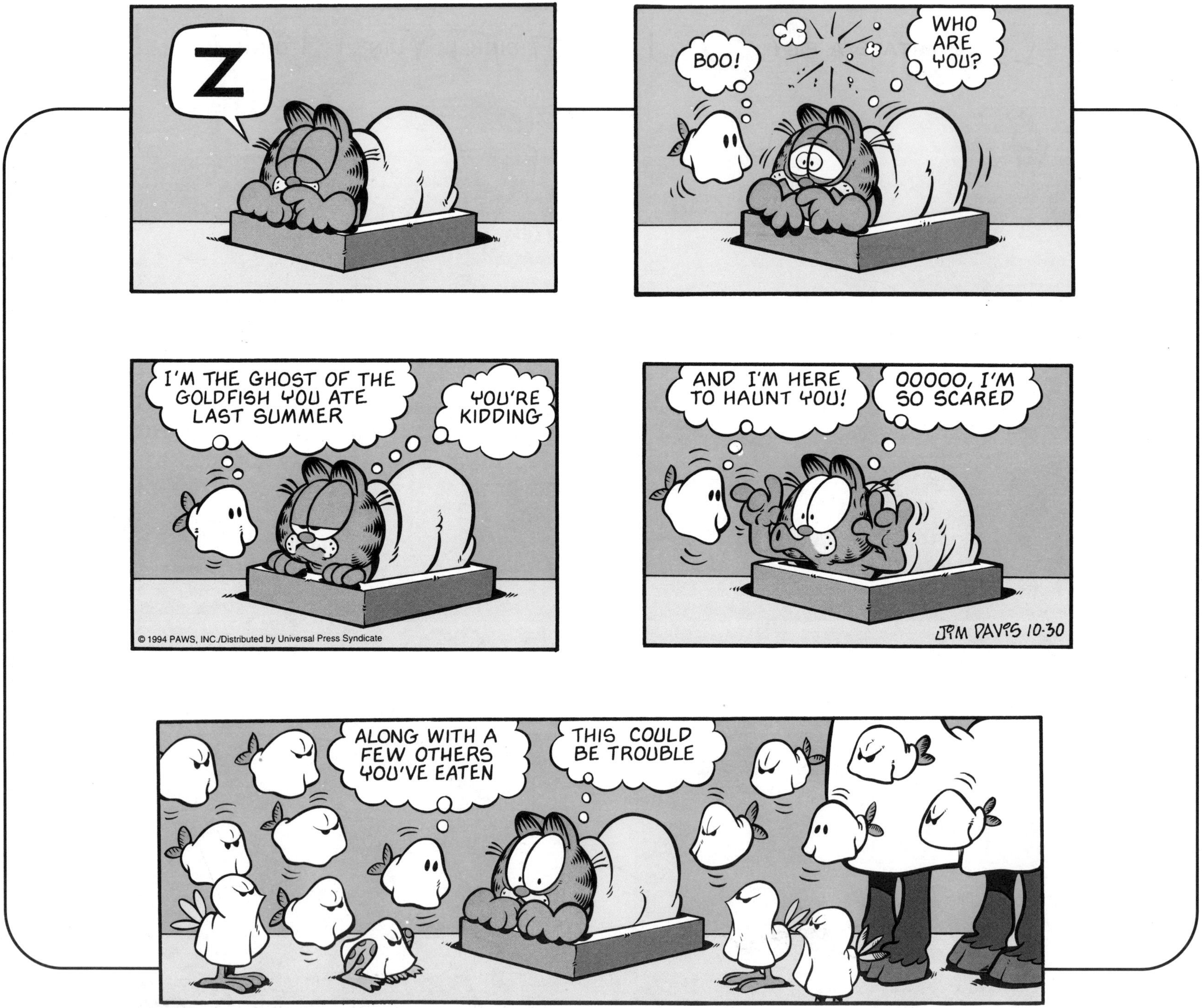

Z
BOO!
WHO ARE YOU?
I'M THE GHOST OF THE GOLDFISH YOU ATE LAST SUMMER
YOU'RE KIDDING
© 1994 PAWS, INC./Distributed by Universal Press Syndicate
AND I'M HERE TO HAUNT YOU!
OOOOO, I'M SO SCARED
JIM DAVIS 10-30
ALONG WITH A FEW OTHERS YOU'VE EATEN
THIS COULD BE TROUBLE

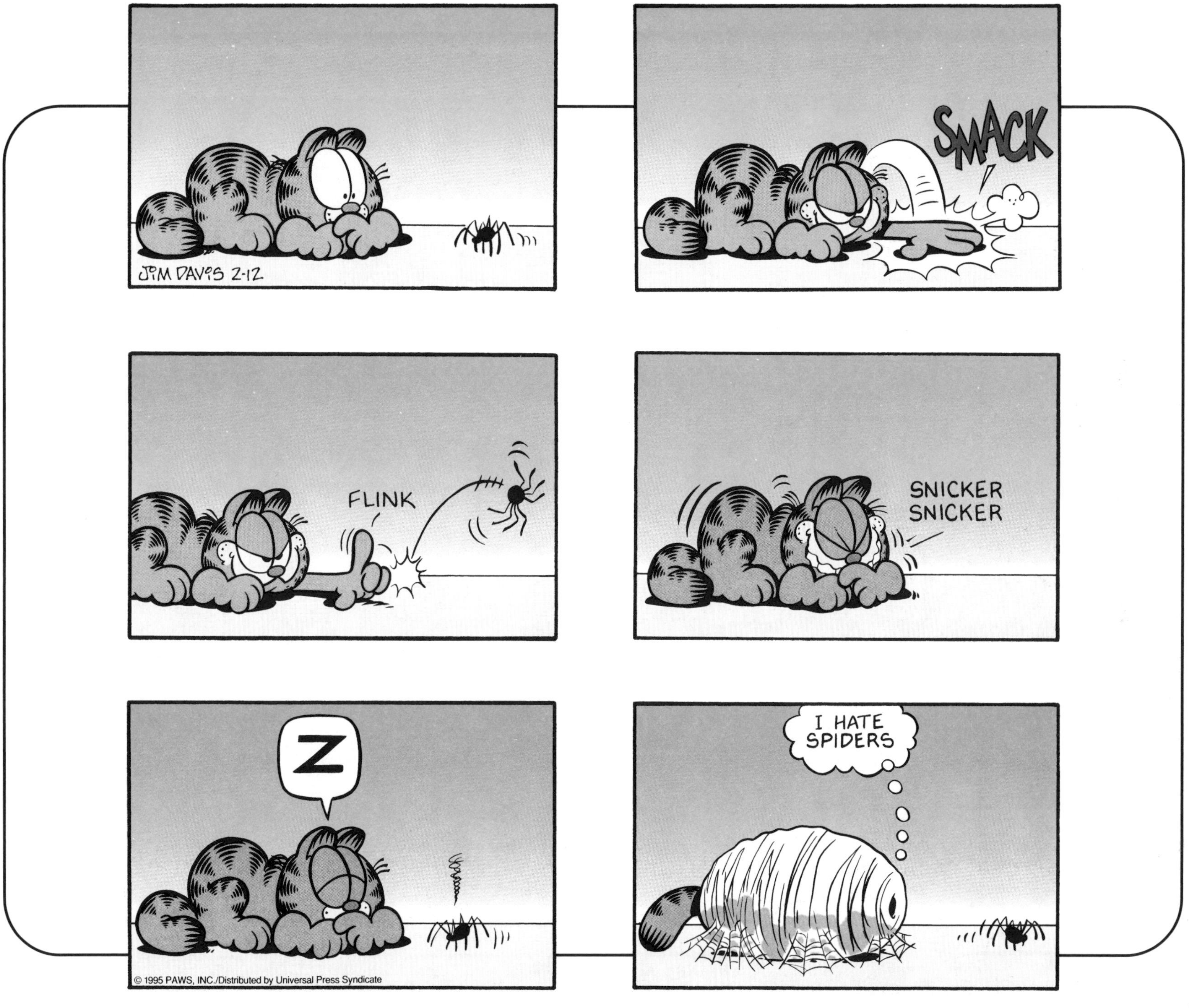
JIM DAVIS 2-12
SMACK
FLINK
SNICKER SNICKER
Z
© 1995 PAWS, INC./Distributed by Universal Press Syndicate
I HATE SPIDERS

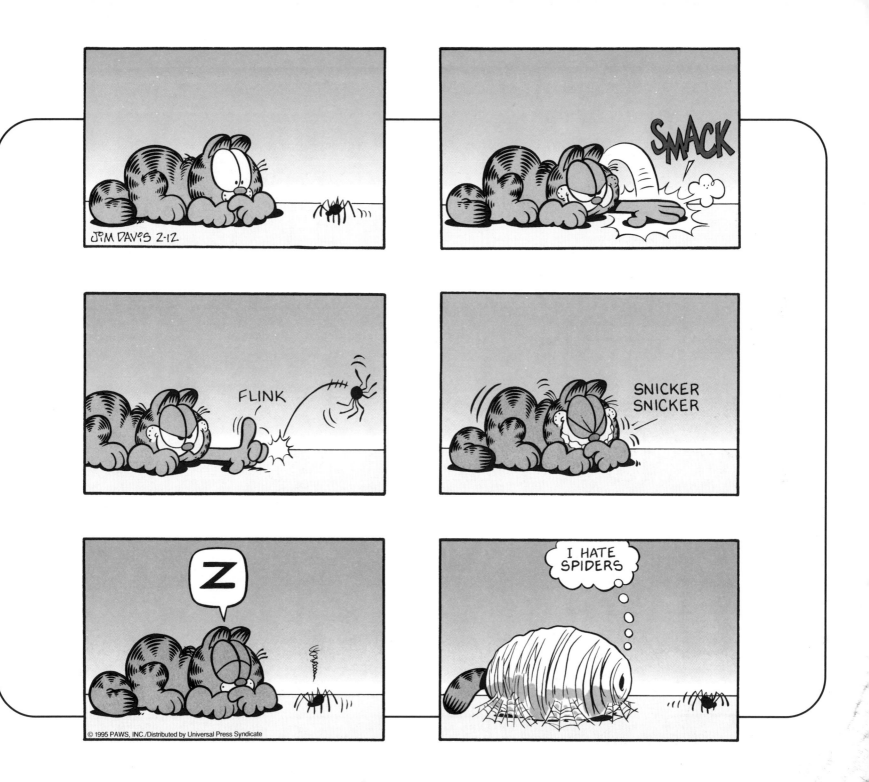

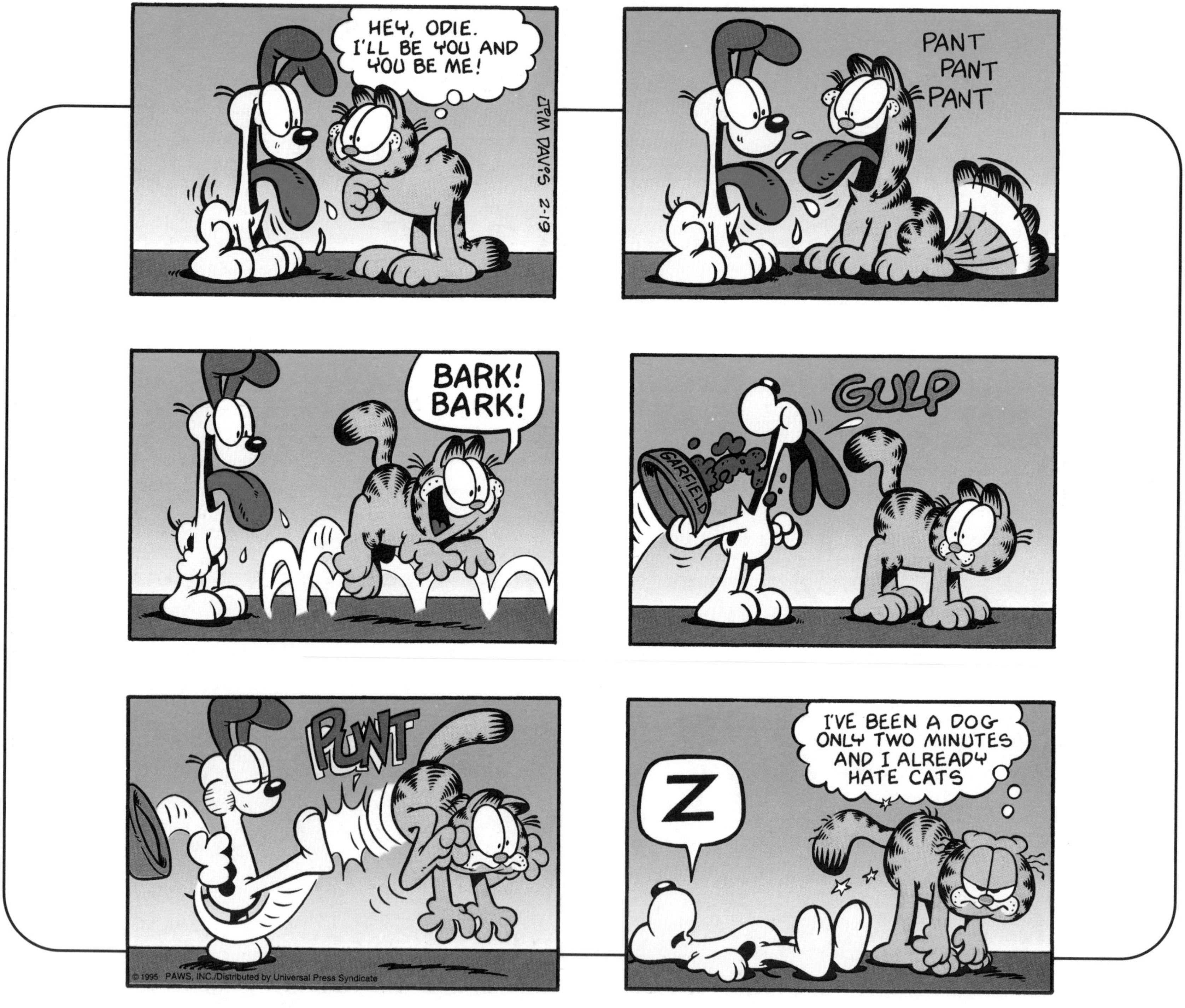
HEY, ODIE. I'LL BE YOU AND YOU BE ME!
JIM DAVIS 2-19
PANT PANT PANT
BARK! BARK!
GULP
GARFIELD
PUNT
Z
I'VE BEEN A DOG ONLY TWO MINUTES AND I ALREADY HATE CATS

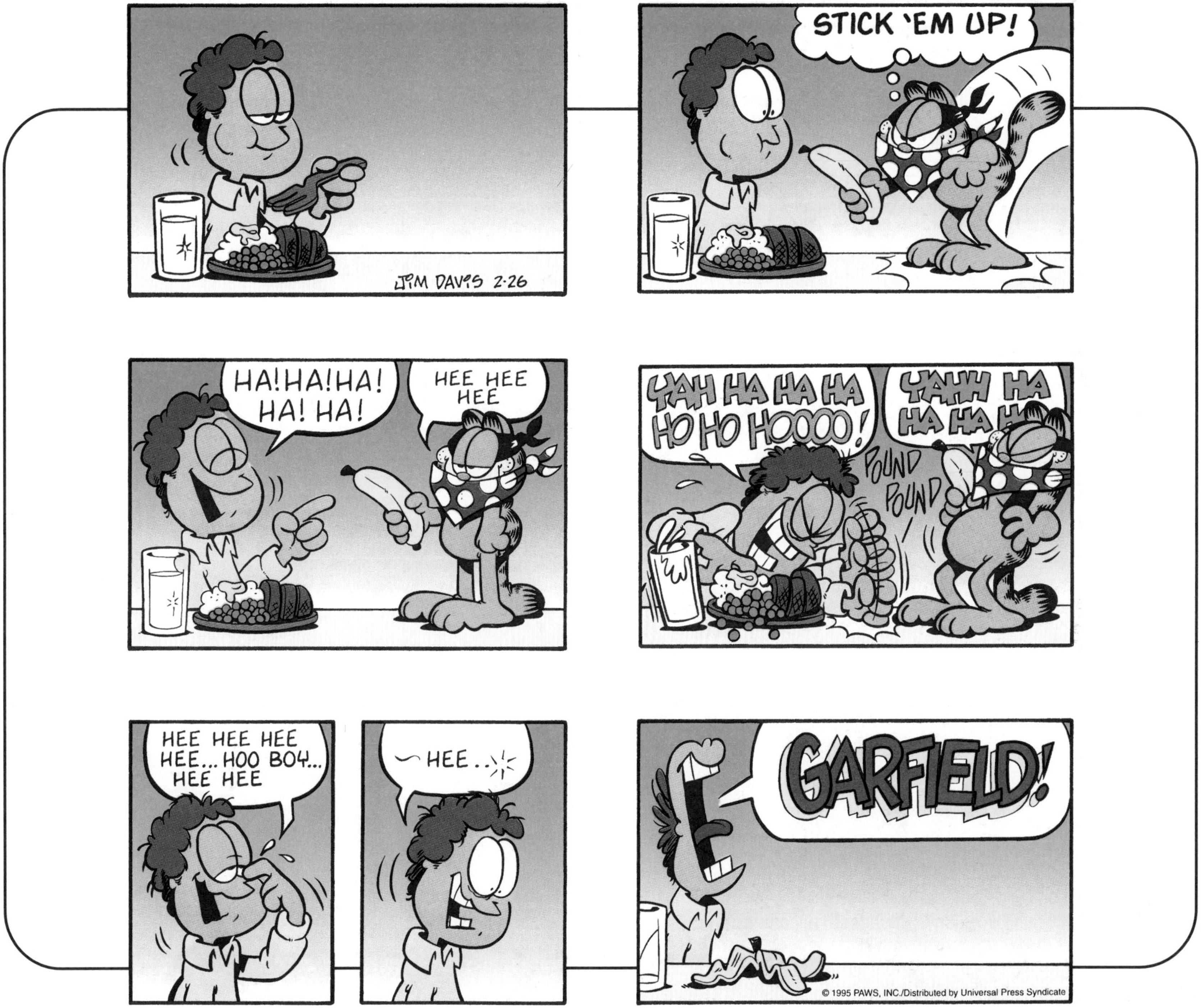
JIM DAVIS 2-26
STICK 'EM UP!
HA! HA! HA! HA! HA!
HEE HEE HEE
YAH HA HA HA HO HO HOOOO!
YAHH HA HA HA
POUND POUND
HEE HEE HEE HEE... HOO BOY... HEE HEE
HEE..
GARFIELD!

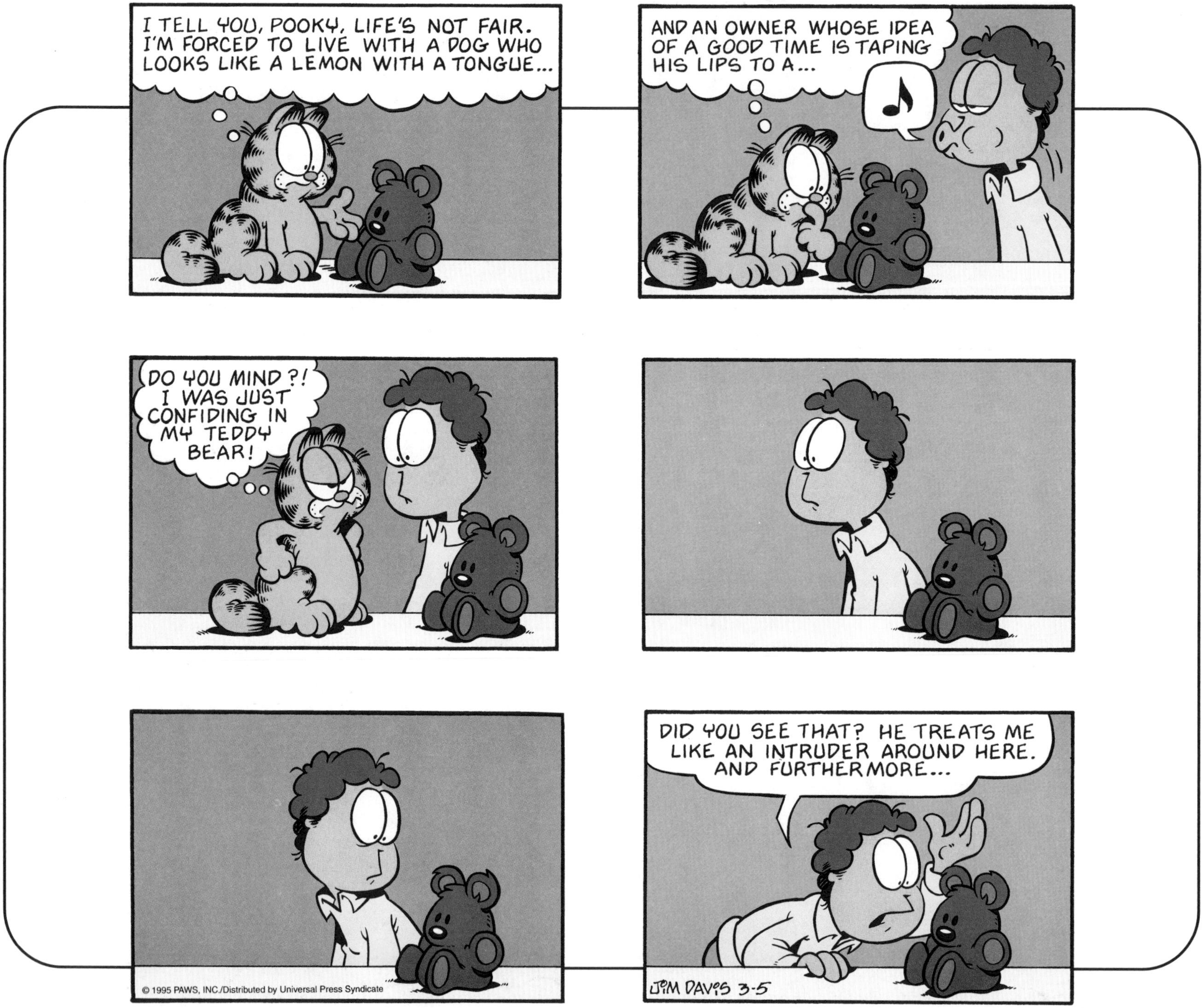
I TELL YOU, POOKY, LIFE'S NOT FAIR. I'M FORCED TO LIVE WITH A DOG WHO LOOKS LIKE A LEMON WITH A TONGUE...
AND AN OWNER WHOSE IDEA OF A GOOD TIME IS TAPING HIS LIPS TO A...
♪
DO YOU MIND?! I WAS JUST CONFIDING IN MY TEDDY BEAR!
DID YOU SEE THAT? HE TREATS ME LIKE AN INTRUDER AROUND HERE. AND FURTHERMORE...
© 1995 PAWS, INC./Distributed by Universal Press Syndicate
JIM DAVIS 3-5

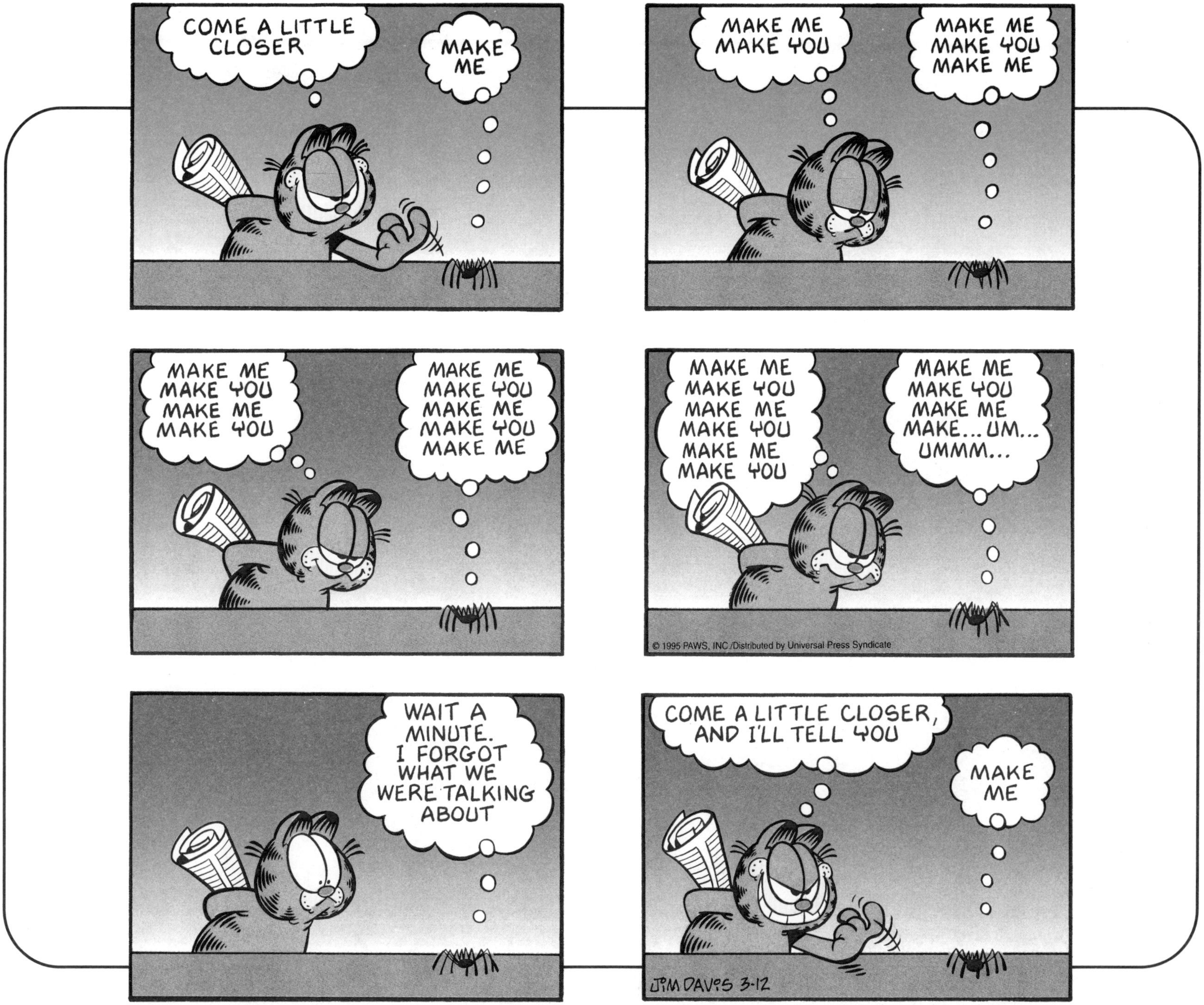
COME A LITTLE CLOSER
MAKE ME
MAKE ME MAKE YOU
MAKE ME MAKE YOU MAKE ME
MAKE ME MAKE YOU MAKE ME MAKE YOU
MAKE ME MAKE YOU MAKE ME MAKE YOU MAKE ME
MAKE ME MAKE YOU MAKE ME MAKE YOU MAKE ME MAKE YOU
MAKE ME MAKE YOU MAKE ME MAKE... UM... UMMM...
WAIT A MINUTE. I FORGOT WHAT WE WERE TALKING ABOUT
COME A LITTLE CLOSER, AND I'LL TELL YOU
MAKE ME
JIM DAVIS 3-12

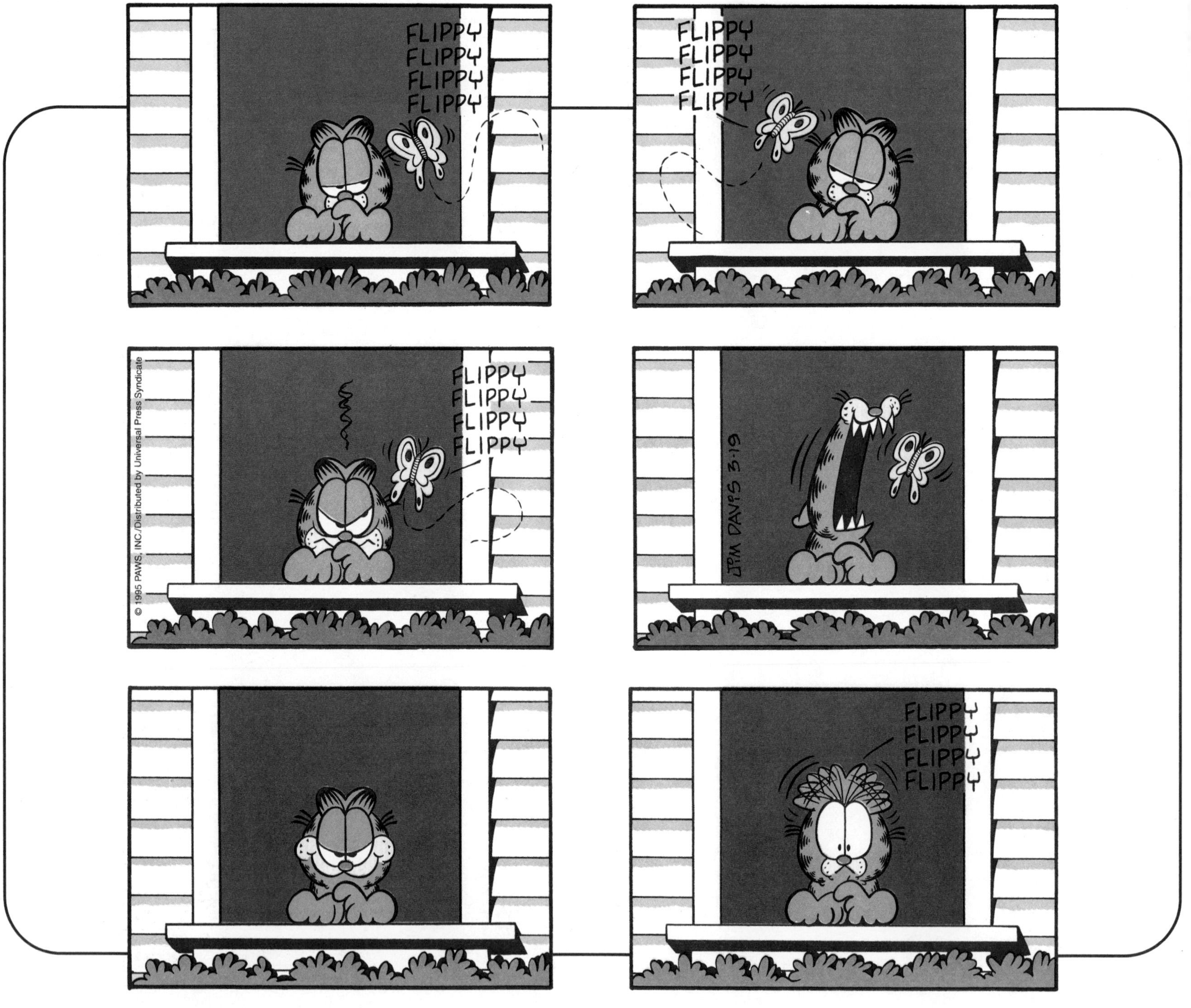
FLIPPY
FLIPPY
FLIPPY
FLIPPY
FLIPPY
FLIPPY
FLIPPY
FLIPPY
© 1995 PAWS, INC./Distributed by Universal Press Syndicate
FLIPPY
FLIPPY
FLIPPY
FLIPPY
JIM DAVIS 3-19
FLIPPY
FLIPPY
FLIPPY
FLIPPY

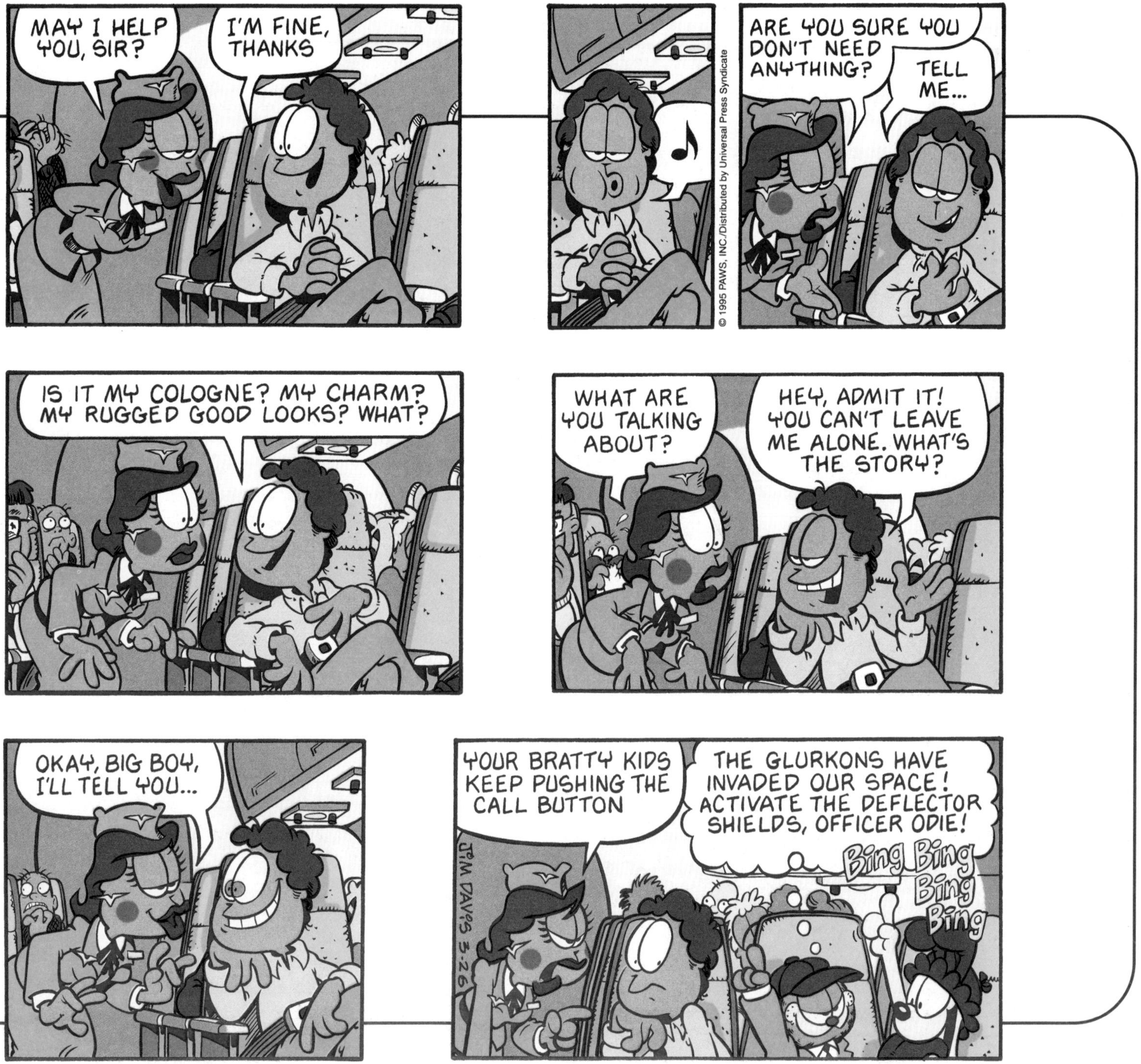
MAY I HELP YOU, SIR?
I'M FINE, THANKS
♪
© 1995 PAWS, INC./Distributed by Universal Press Syndicate
ARE YOU SURE YOU DON'T NEED ANYTHING?
TELL ME...
IS IT MY COLOGNE? MY CHARM? MY RUGGED GOOD LOOKS? WHAT?
WHAT ARE YOU TALKING ABOUT?
HEY, ADMIT IT! YOU CAN'T LEAVE ME ALONE. WHAT'S THE STORY?
OKAY, BIG BOY, I'LL TELL YOU...
JIM DAVIS 3-26
YOUR BRATTY KIDS KEEP PUSHING THE CALL BUTTON
THE GLURKONS HAVE INVADED OUR SPACE! ACTIVATE THE DEFLECTOR SHIELDS, OFFICER ODIE!
Bing Bing Bing Bing

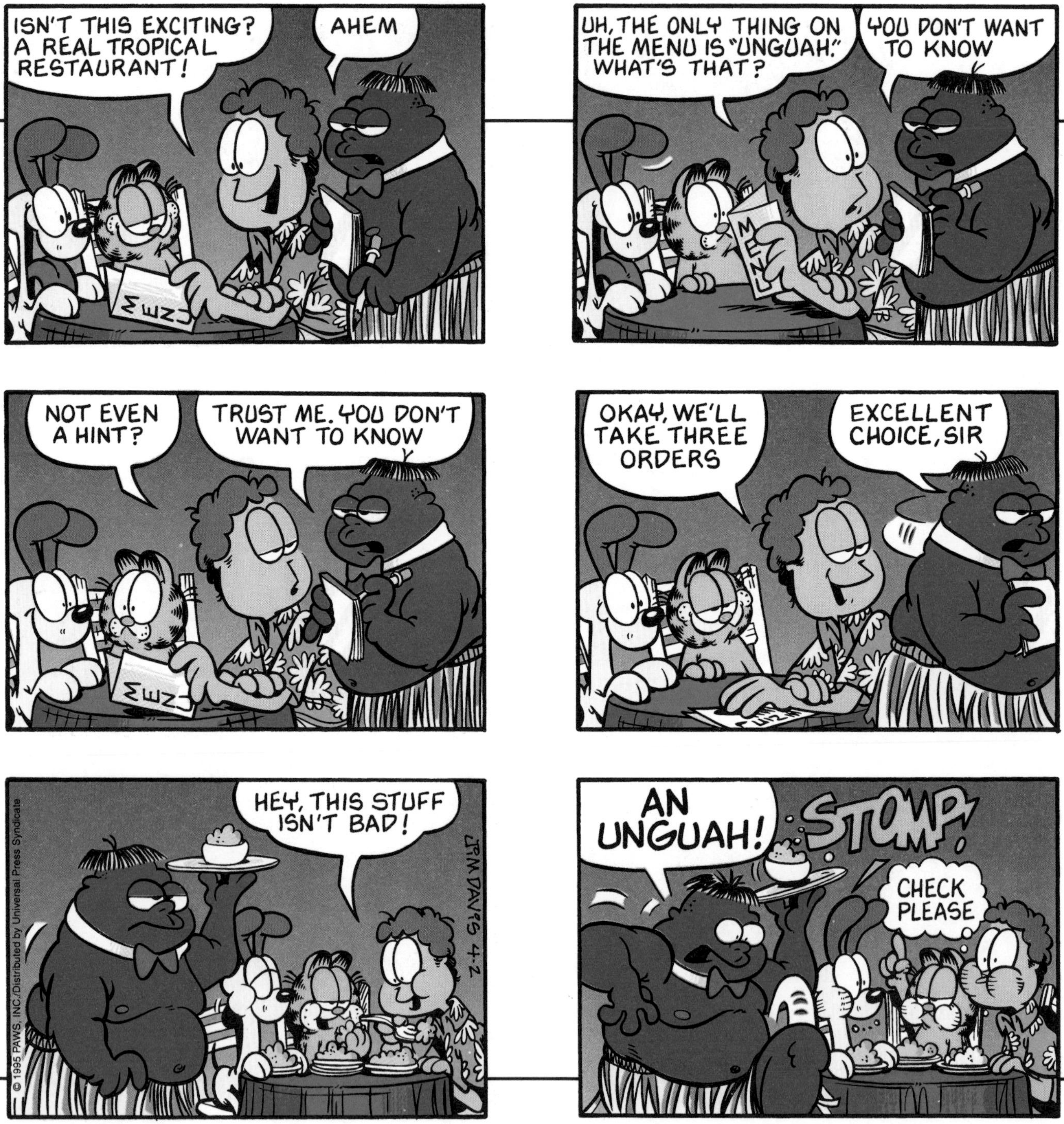
ISN'T THIS EXCITING? A REAL TROPICAL RESTAURANT!
AHEM
UH, THE ONLY THING ON THE MENU IS "UNGUAH." WHAT'S THAT?
YOU DON'T WANT TO KNOW
NOT EVEN A HINT?
TRUST ME. YOU DON'T WANT TO KNOW
OKAY, WE'LL TAKE THREE ORDERS
EXCELLENT CHOICE, SIR
HEY, THIS STUFF ISN'T BAD!
© 1995 PAWS, INC./Distributed by Universal Press Syndicate
JPM DAVIS 4-2
AN UNGUAH!
STOMP!
CHECK PLEASE

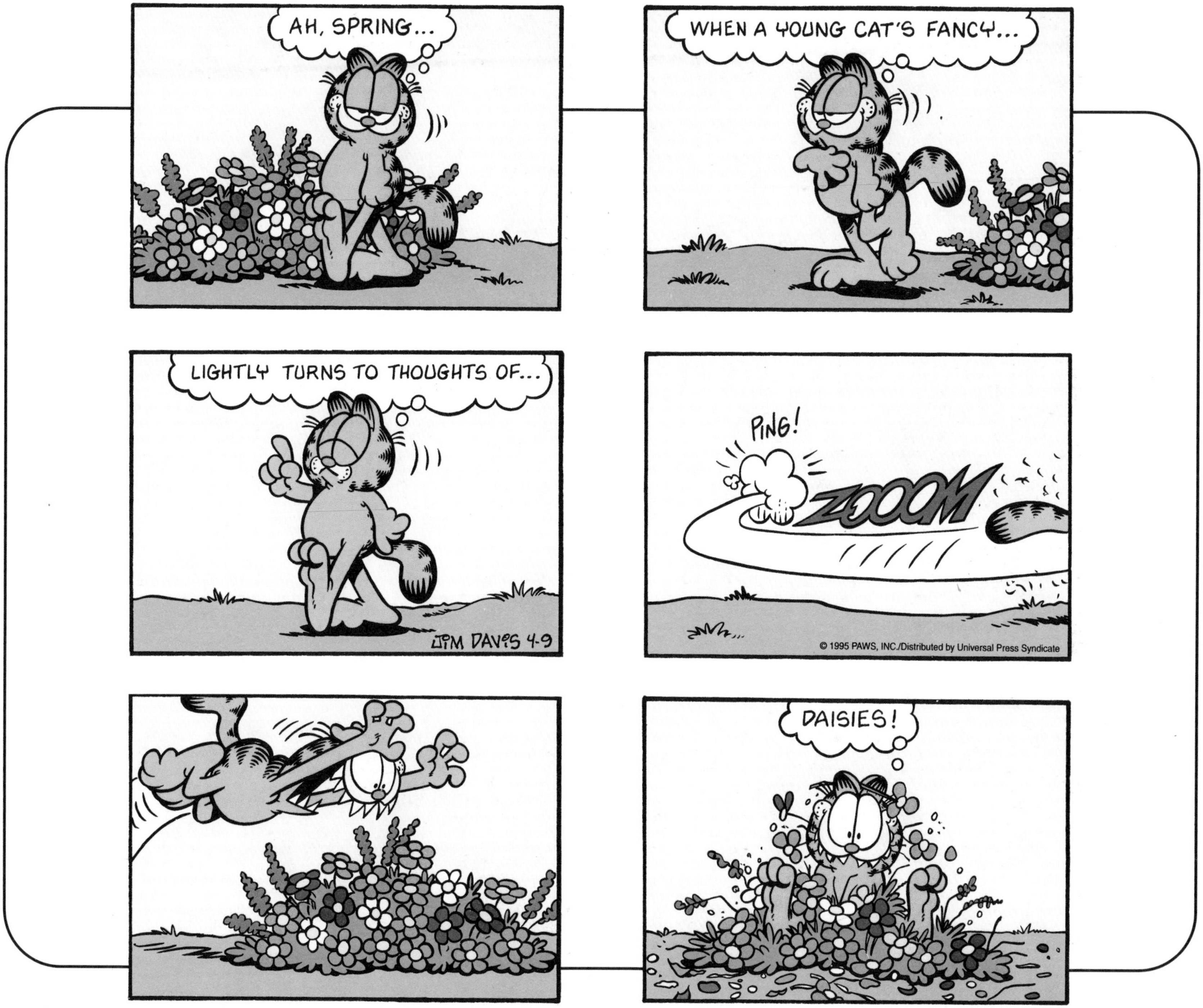
AH, SPRING...
WHEN A YOUNG CAT'S FANCY...
LIGHTLY TURNS TO THOUGHTS OF...
JIM DAVIS 4-9
PING!
ZOOOM
© 1995 PAWS, INC./Distributed by Universal Press Syndicate
DAISIES!

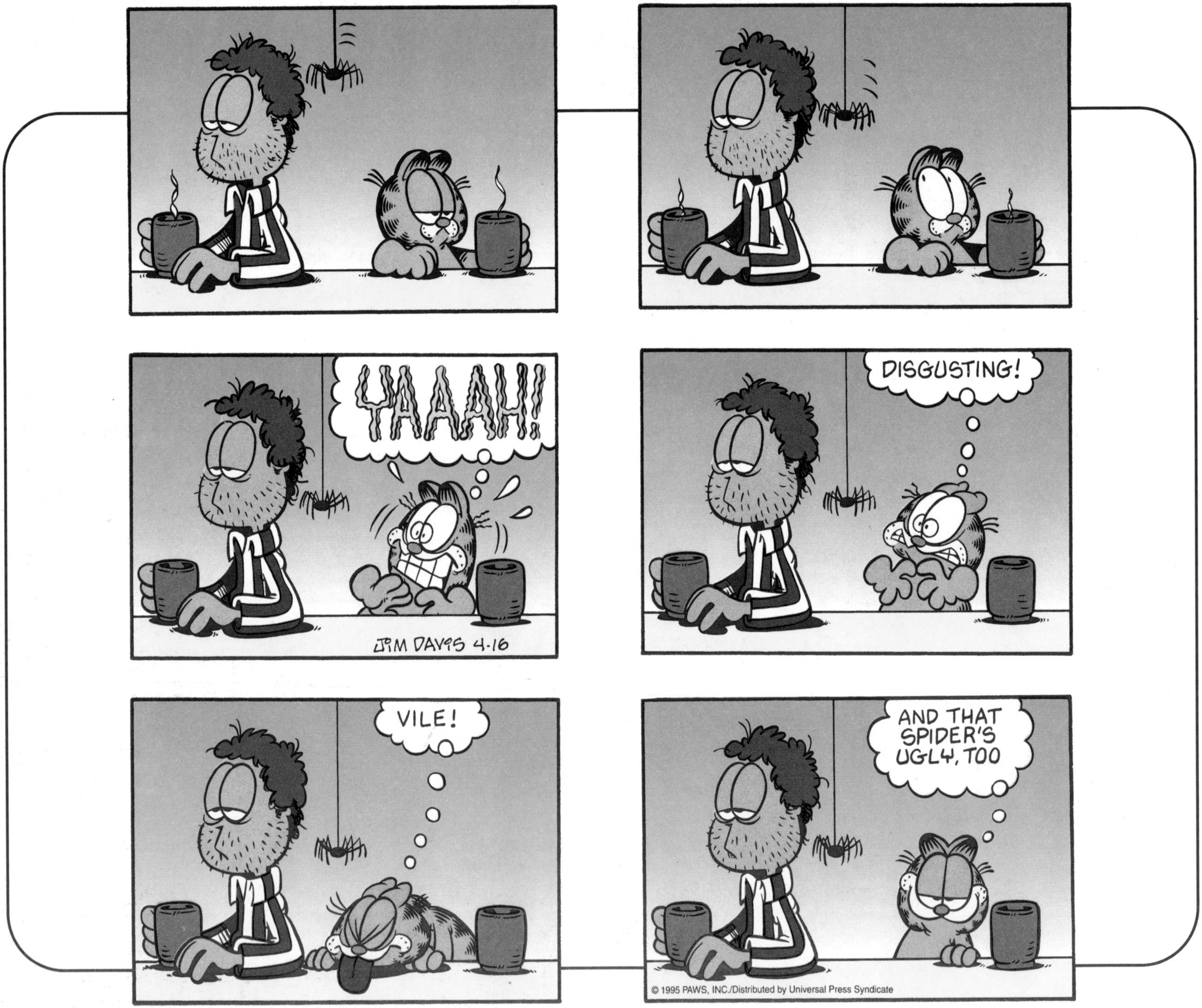
YAAAH!
JIM DAVIS 4-16
DISGUSTING!
VILE!
AND THAT SPIDER'S UGLY, TOO
© 1995 PAWS, INC./Distributed by Universal Press Syndicate

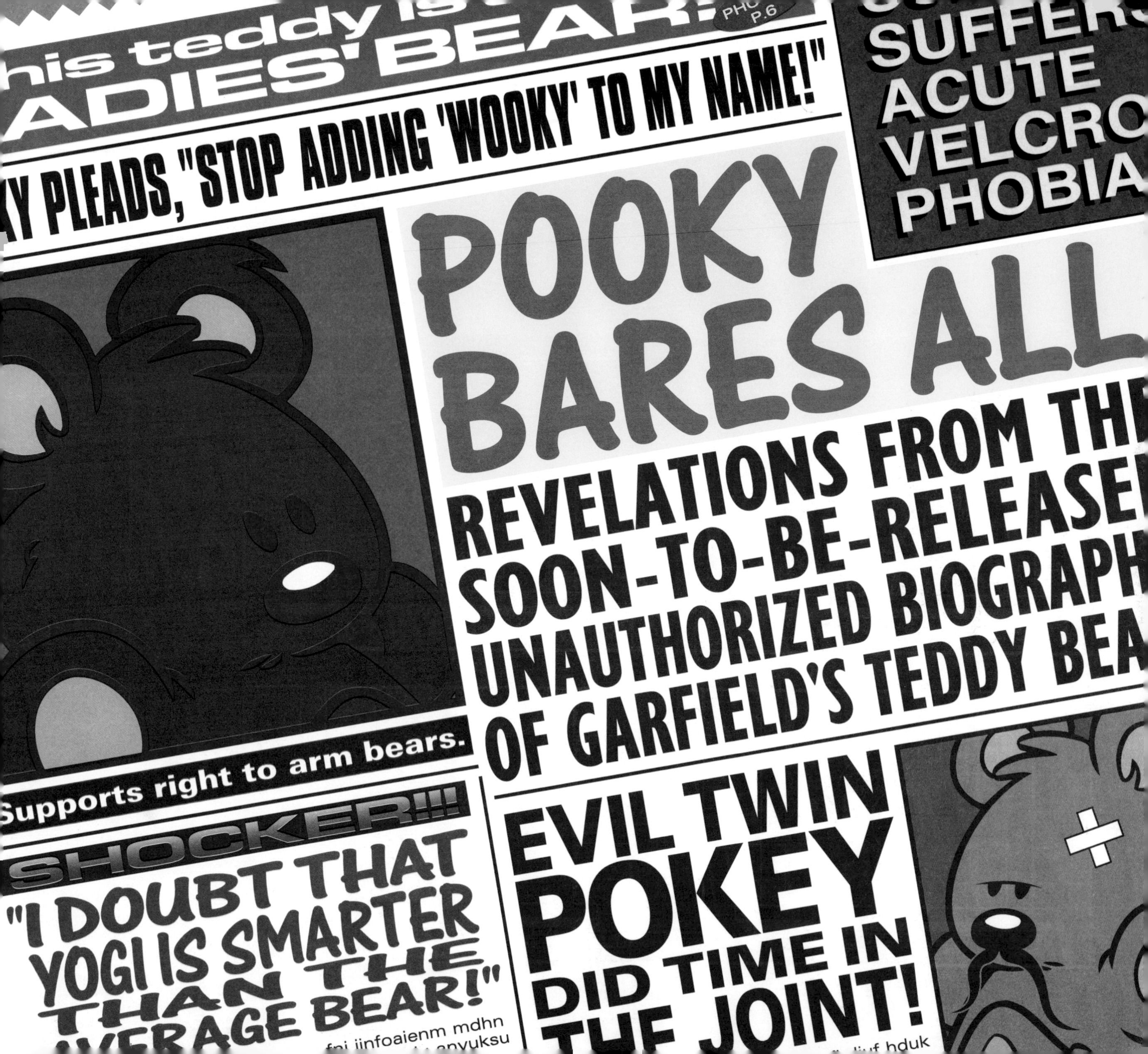

his teddy is
ADIES' BEAR!
PHO P.6
KY PLEADS, "STOP ADDING 'WOOKY' TO MY NAME!"
SUFFERS ACUTE VELCRO PHOBIA
POOKY BARES ALL
REVELATIONS FROM TH
SOON-TO-BE-RELEASE
UNAUTHORIZED BIOGRAPH
OF GARFIELD'S TEDDY BEA
Supports right to arm bears.
SHOCKER!!!
"I DOUBT THAT YOGI IS SMARTER THAN THE VERAGE BEAR!"
EVIL TWIN POKEY DID TIME IN THE JOINT!

STRIPS, SPECIALS, OR BESTSELLING BOOKS . . .
GARFIELD'S ON EVERYONE'S MENU
Don't miss even one episode in the Tubby Tabby's hilarious series!

__GARFIELD AT LARGE (#1) 32013/$6.95
__GARFIELD GAINS WEIGHT (#2) 32008/$6.95
__GARFIELD BIGGER THAN LIFE (#3) 32007/$6.95
__GARFIELD WEIGHS IN (#4) 32010/$6.95
__GARFIELD TAKES THE CAKE (#5) 32009/$6.95
__GARFIELD EATS HIS HEART OUT (#6) 32018/$6.95
__GARFIELD SITS AROUND THE HOUSE (#7) 32011/$6.95
__GARFIELD TIPS THE SCALES (#8) 33580/$6.95
__GARFIELD LOSES HIS FEET (#9) 31805/$6.95
__GARFIELD MAKES IT BIG (#10) 31928/$6.95
__GARFIELD ROLLS ON (#11) 32634/$6.95
__GARFIELD OUT TO LUNCH (#12) 33118/$6.95
__GARFIELD FOOD FOR THOUGHT (#13) 34129/$6.95
__GARFIELD SWALLOWS HIS PRIDE (#14) 34725/$6.95
__GARFIELD WORLDWIDE (#15) 35158/$6.95
__GARFIELD ROUNDS OUT (#16) 35388/$6.95

__GARFIELD CHEWS THE FAT (#17) 35956/$6.95
__GARFIELD GOES TO WAIST (#18) 36430/$6.95
__GARFIELD HANGS OUT (#19) 36835/$6.95
__GARFIELD TAKES UP SPACE (#20) 37029/$6.95
__GARFIELD SAYS A MOUTHFUL (#21) 37368/$6.95
__GARFIELD BY THE POUND (#22) 37579/$6.95
__GARFIELD KEEPS HIS CHINS UP (#23) 37959/$6.95
__GARFIELD TAKES HIS LICKS (#24) 38170/$6.95
__GARFIELD HITS THE BIG TIME (#25) 38332/$6.95
__GARFIELD PULLS HIS WEIGHT (#26) 38666/$6.95
__GARFIELD DISHES IT OUT (#27) 39287/$6.95
__GARFIELD LIFE IN THE FAT LANE (#28) 39776/$6.95

GARFIELD AT HIS SUNDAY BEST!
__GARFIELD TREASURY 32106/$11.95
__THE SECOND GARFIELD TREASURY 33276/$10.95
__THE THIRD GARFIELD TREASURY 32635/$11.00
__THE FOURTH GARFIELD TREASURY 34726/$10.95
__THE FIFTH GARFIELD TREASURY 36268/$12.00
__THE SIXTH GARFIELD TREASURY 37367/$10.95
__THE SEVENTH GARFIELD TREASURY 38427/$10.95
__THE EIGHTH GARFIELD TREASURY 39778/$12.00

Please send me the BALLANTINE BOOKS I have checked above. I am enclosing $_____. (Please add $2.00 for the first book and $.50 for each additional book for postage and handling and include the appropriate state sales tax.) Send check or money order (no cash or C.O.D.'s) to Ballantine Mail Sales Dept. TA, 400 Hahn Road, Westminster, MD 21157.

To order by phone, call 1-800-733-3000 and use your major credit card.

Prices and numbers are subject to change without notice. Valid in the U.S. only. All orders are subject to availability.

Name_____

Address_____

City_____ State_____ Zip_____

30   Allow at least 4 weeks for delivery   7/93

BIRTHDAYS, HOLIDAYS, OR ANY DAY . . .

Keep GARFIELD on your calendar all year 'round!

GARFIELD TV SPECIALS
__BABES & BULLETS 36339/$5.95
__GARFIELD GOES HOLLYWOOD 34580/$6.95
__GARFIELD'S HALLOWEEN ADVENTURE 33045/$6.95
  (formerly GARFIELD IN DISGUISE)
__GARFIELD'S FELINE FANTASY 36902/$6.95
__GARFIELD IN PARADISE 33796/$6.95
__GARFIELD IN THE ROUGH 32242/$6.95
__GARFIELD ON THE TOWN 31542/$6.95
__GARFIELD'S THANKSGIVING 35650/$6.95
__HERE COMES GARFIELD 32021/$6.95
__GARFIELD GETS A LIFE 37375/$6.95
__A GARFIELD CHRISTMAS 35368/$5.95

Please send me the BALLANTINE BOOKS I have checked above. I am enclosing $_____. (Please add $2.00 for the first book and $.50 for each additional book for postage and handling and include the appropriate state sales tax.) Send check or money order (no cash or C.O.D.'s) to Ballantine Mail Sales Dept. TA, 400 Hahn Road, Westminster, MD 21157.

To order by phone, call 1-800-733-3000 and use your major credit card.

Prices and numbers are subject to change without notice. Valid in the U.S. only. All orders are subject to availability.

GREETINGS FROM GARFIELD!
GARFIELD POSTCARD BOOKS FOR ALL OCCASIONS.
__GARFIELD THINKING OF YOU 36516/$6.95
__GARFIELD WORDS TO LIVE BY 36679/$6.95
__GARFIELD BIRTHDAY GREETINGS 36771/$7.95
__GARFIELD BE MY VALENTINE 37121/$7.95
__GARFIELD SEASON'S GREETINGS 37435/$8.95
__GARFIELD VACATION GREETINGS 37774/$10.00
__GARFIELD'S THANK YOU POSTCARD BOOK 37893/$10.00

ALSO FROM GARFIELD:
__GARFIELD: HIS NINE LIVES 32061/$9.95
__THE GARFIELD BOOK OF CAT NAMES 35082/$5.95
__THE GARFIELD TRIVIA BOOK 33771/$6.95
__THE UNABRIDGED UNCENSORED
  UNBELIEVABLE GARFIELD 33772/$5.95
__GARFIELD: THE ME BOOK 36545/$7.95
__GARFIELD'S JUDGMENT DAY 36755/$6.95
__THE TRUTH ABOUT CATS 37226/$6.95

Name_____

Address_____

City_____ State_____ Zip_____

30   Allow at least 4 weeks for delivery   7/93 TA-267